THEN & NOW

ASBURY PARK AND NEPTUNE

OPPOSITE: Vacationers make their way to the boardwalk in 1904. (Library of Congress, SZ62-120493.)

THEN & NOW

ASBURY PARK AND NEPTUNE

Robert Gilinsky

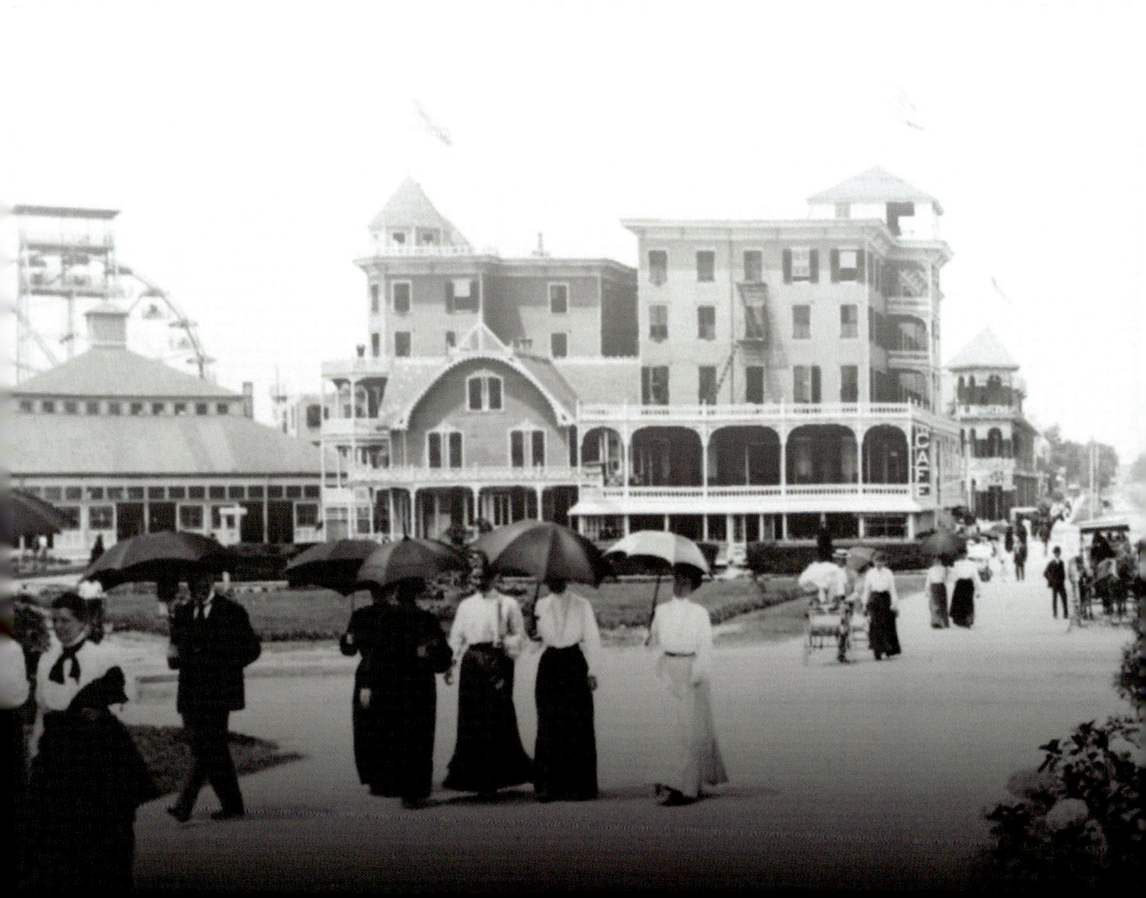

For my little princesses. Daddy loves you with all of his heart.

ISBN 978-0-7385-7536-0

Library of Congress Control Number: 2010941252

Published by Arcadia Publishing
Charleston, South Carolina

Printed in the United States of America

For all general information, please contact Arcadia Publishing:
Telephone 843-853-2070
Fax 843-853-0044
E-mail sales@arcadiapublishing.com
For customer service and orders:
Toll-Free 1-888-313-2665

Visit us on the Internet at www.arcadiapublishing.com

On the Front and Back Covers: Wesley Lake is pictured in turn-of-the-century views on both the front and back covers. Boating was a favorite pastime of the early vacationers, as contemporary accounts document up to 200 boats on the lake at one time. There were a series of small islands existing in Wesley Lake that were removed when the lake was dredged during the last two decades of the 19th century. (Library of Congress B2-2770-13 front, D4-13701 back.)

Contents

Acknowledgments

Unless otherwise noted, all modern photographs were taken by the author. A good number of the vintage photographs are from the author's extensive collection. Many, however, are included via the courtesy of several organizations and individuals, which are likewise noted in the corresponding captions. Much gratitude is owed to the following and those erroneously omitted, without whom the completion of this volume would not have been possible.

First and foremost, all-out appreciation is extended to Thomas W. Appleby Sr. The third generation of Applebys to run the T. Frank Appleby Agency, Tom graciously permitted the author to draw from his extensive collection of area negatives. He gave generously of his time and provided valuable details regarding many of the photographs featured. Sadly, Tom passed away before the completion of the book. Gratitude is also extended to his lovely wife of 51 years, Joan.

Also, my sincere thanks to my buddy, "the first beat from E Street," Vini "Mad Dog" Lopez, an invaluable source of information on the rock revival scene in Asbury Park. Vini is also the guardian of priceless scrapbooks kept by his late father, Vincent "the Big Dog" Lopez Sr., which provide many photographs, dates, and articles documenting the shore area. Anybody who has yet to catch one of Mad Dog's Steel Mill Retro shows is strongly urged to do so. He is still one of the greatest, most ferocious drummers of all time.

Also, thanks to Don Lewis, who, with veteran area historian Shirley Ayres, has organized a wonderful museum display of the archives of the Bradley Beach Historical Society; Scott Pilling, who granted access to the massive photo archive of Park Steel and Iron; my close friend Raul Rodriguez for the use of his computer equipment; Rich Yorkowitz, savior of the granddaddy of the Asbury rock scene, the Upstage Club; Carrie Potter; Caroline from the Stone Pony; library director Robert Stewart and the ever-helpful Malakia Oglesby and Marta Otero from the Asbury Park Library; the fantastic Chris Ellwood, archives manager at Monmouth University Library; the great Don Stine of the Asbury Park Historical Society; Asbury Park fire chief Kevin Keddy; Emmett Francois; Marian "the librarian" Bauman, director of the Neptune Public Library; James and Catherine Gilligan for the view at Skytop; my fellow local historian and friend of many years, Michael Corio; Chris Adams of the S.S. Adams Company; Jere Ryder of the Morris Museum; the Draughting Table for the "Lindy" scoop; the fellas at Ferguson; renown postcard collector Jane Gannon; Richard Simonsen of the McNeely Agency; Kevin Kelly Sr. of Kelly's Tavern; and of course, Arcadia editor Erin Rocha, whose belief in this project made everything possible.

I would also like to acknowledge my parents, who have always encouraged me in my pursuit of knowledge and research, my beautiful daughters, my brother Michael, and my loving family. And for my Rosalita, wherever you are . . .

Introduction

Change can be good, but it is often nice to feel that some things never change. The roads of home beckon so many fond memories. Childhood acquaintances, times of adolescent rebellion, and lessons of adult responsibility all have a backdrop that, when revisited, can revive these precious moments.

Asbury Park and Neptune will always remain intertwined to those who live nearby. Longtime scholastic rivalries aside, so many shared reminiscences exist. Contained within this small geographic space are city streets, country roads, factories, hotels, religious retreats, woods, golf courses, miles of beaches, and millions of irreplaceable experiences.

New York brush manufacturer James Adam Bradley had converted to Methodism in the late 1860s and visited the new Methodist retreat of Ocean Grove shortly after it was founded in 1869. The popular area resort of the day was Long Branch, which had garnered a reputation as a bit of a hedonistic celebrity stomping ground. Ocean Grove offered an alternative environment, where religion and sobriety were core principals of the vacation experience.

Bradley took to the idea and, having the financial resources in 1871, purchased the land in Ocean Township between Wesley and Deal Lakes. Asbury Park Borough was incorporated in 1874 (and would reorganize as a city in 1897). Bradley personally involved himself in virtually every aspect as he laid out his plans. He built the boardwalk, for which he enacted tight restrictions. He established the post office and served as the postmaster. He set up the first newspaper and was the editor. He donated money and land for schools, libraries, hotels, homes, businesses, parks, and factories. He set up the sewer, gas, and water service. Bradley served as both a councilman and mayor and also represented the district in the New Jersey Senate. To this very day, many businesses in the area still operate under perpetual clauses that Bradley stipulated in the original land agreements and deeds.

Neptune was also carved out of Ocean Township and incorporated as an independent township in 1879. At this time, Neptune constituted all of the portions of Asbury Park west of the railroad tracks, Ocean Grove, Bradley Beach, Neptune City, and Avon-by-the-Sea. The western tracts were mostly woods and farmlands, while the beachfront regions of Ocean Grove, Ocean Park (Bradley Beach), and Key East (Avon) styled themselves into resort destinations. During the last decade of the 19th century, many of the residents of these communities felt that they were unfairly taxed and broke away from Neptune. Ocean Grove attempted to do so in 1920, but the state ruled that action unconstitutional, and the governance was returned to Neptune Township the next year, although the Camp Meeting Association maintained a municipal organization until 1981.

Neptune City seceded from Neptune in 1881. Formerly known as New Branch, Neptune City originally included the southern portion of Bradley Beach and all of Avon. Many of the same types of problems that existed with the previous affiliation with Neptune Township arose again as the people and businesses situated in the beachfront areas felt that they were unfairly taxed.

In 1871, the same year he purchased the area that would become the eastern section of Asbury Park, James Bradley also invested in 54 acres stretching south from Fletcher Lake. His partners in this venture, William Bradner and Henry Winsor, appealed to the citizens to break away and form their own municipality. With help from Bradley, they seceded and formed the borough of Bradley Beach in 1893. In 1907, Bradley Beach annexed the Neptune City beachfront area (from Brinley Avenue to Sylvan Lake).

Edward Batchelor was for Avon what James Bradley was for Asbury Park. Batchelor was a wealthy cigar magnate from Philadelphia who took a fishing trip to Ocean Grove in 1879. Passing through the undeveloped area on his way to Shark River, he fell in love with the land and bought all 300 acres the very next day. He initially wanted to set up a massive tobacco processing facility there and named his community Key East (at the time, Key West was the cigar capital of the world). Batchelor was convinced by his partners to follow the example set by Bradley and develop the land as a resort. When the borough won its independence from Neptune City in 1900, it was officially renamed Avon-by-the-Sea, after the Avon Inn, which was the prime attraction of the young retreat.

The years passed, and the communities blossomed. Asbury Park became one of the most famous resorts in the world. Ocean Grove maintained its appeal as a Methodist retreat. Houses and shops sprang up, filling out the landscape. Farms gave way to shopping centers. Racial tensions within Asbury Park were building, and riots ensued in the summer of 1970. It seemed as though Asbury's peak had passed.

In the late 1960s, three members of the class of 1967 from Neptune High School had been spending a lot of time in Asbury Park making music. Initially, Tom and Margaret Potter ran a beauty shop at 710 Cookman Avenue. In 1968, they opened a coffee house and rock club in the upper floors of the Thom McAn store down the block. Because the original deed for the land excluded the sale of alcohol on the premises, as dictated by Bradley, the Potters' venture catered to local teenagers. Neptune alums Vini Lopez, "Southside" Johnny Lyon (from Ocean Grove), and Garry Tallent (Neptune City) could be found at the Upstage Club on any given night. In early 1969, Vini Lopez was with his friend Danny Federici at the Upstage when the guitar prowess of the young man on stage caught his attention. His parents having moved to California, 19-year-old Freehold native Bruce Springsteen had arrived in Asbury Park to try his had at fame and fortune. Within a few weeks, these three individuals were sharing that same stage in a group called Child. The wheels of history had been set in motion.

Many other clubs sprang up or retooled themselves to cater to the growing rock scene in the area: the Hullabaloo (which would undergo expansion in 1970 and reopen as the Sunshine In), the Student Prince, the Wonder Bar, and the Captain's Garter to name a few. As the kids matured, the clubs matured as well. The Stone Pony and the Fastlane both opened in 1974. The Pony took up residence in the former restaurant portion of Mrs. Jay's (the adjoining *biergarten* had become a home to area bikers and would continue to operate as such until 1988). Mainstream rock music had split into many different factions by the mid-1970s. It was the 1975 release of Springsteen's *Born to Run* that renewed an interest in rock and roll with both the record-buying public and critics alike.

This book is not meant to be a complete history of Asbury Park and Neptune. It is intended to be a visual trip down memory lane with the hope that the spirit of preservation within these communities and the rich history they contain is not only appreciated but also maintained and continued forevermore. Each chapter title page is dedicated to an area landmark that sadly no longer exists. Enjoy the ride.

CHAPTER 1

Asbury Park

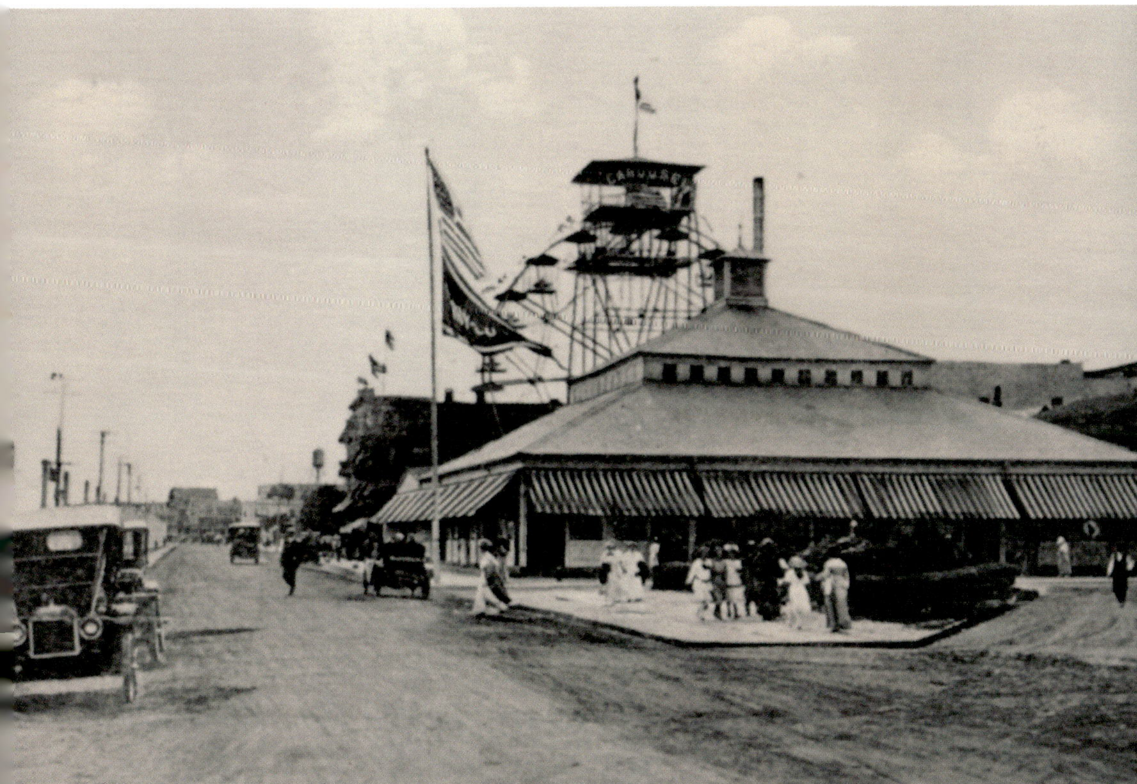

Ernest Schnitzler built a carousel house in 1888 at the corner of Lake Avenue and Kingsley Street that he named Palace Amusements, pictured here in 1910. In 1895, he added a Ferris wheel, for which he filed a patent. In 1956, then-owners Edward Lange and Zimel Resnick built a substantial addition along Kingsley Street to Cookman Avenue. The building was demolished in 2004.

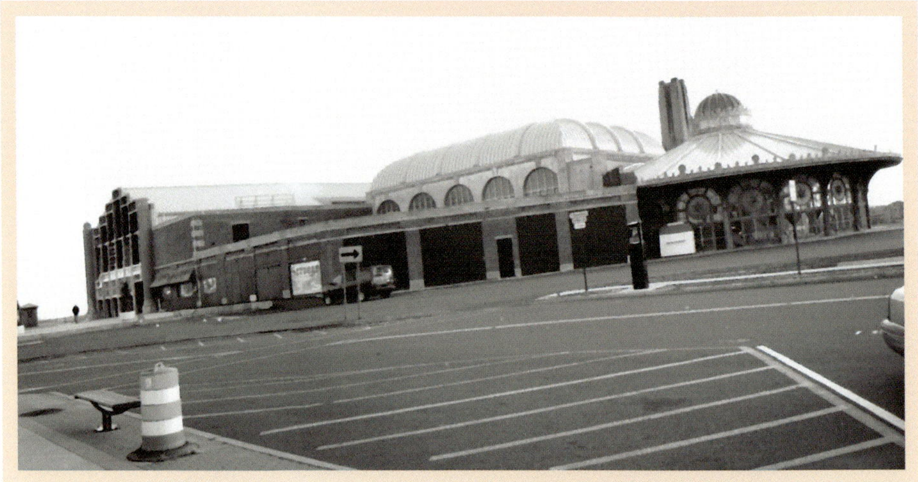

The Asbury Casino, pictured shortly after its completion, was built during 1929 and 1930. The site had previously been host to two different pavilions; the first was replaced in 1903 and was in turn destroyed by fire in 1928. Whitney Warren, senior partner of Warren and Wetmore of New York City, designed the casino and the adjoining art nouveau heating plant. The auditorium portion fell into disrepair and was demolished in December 2006. (Asbury Park Historical Society.)

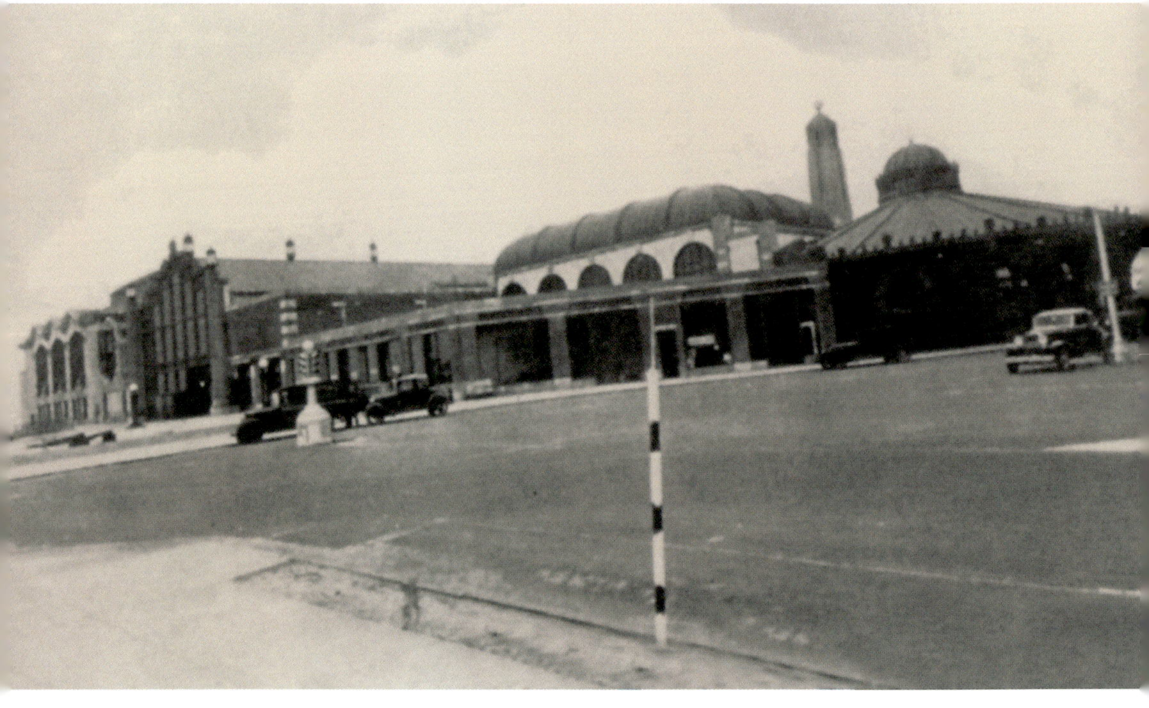

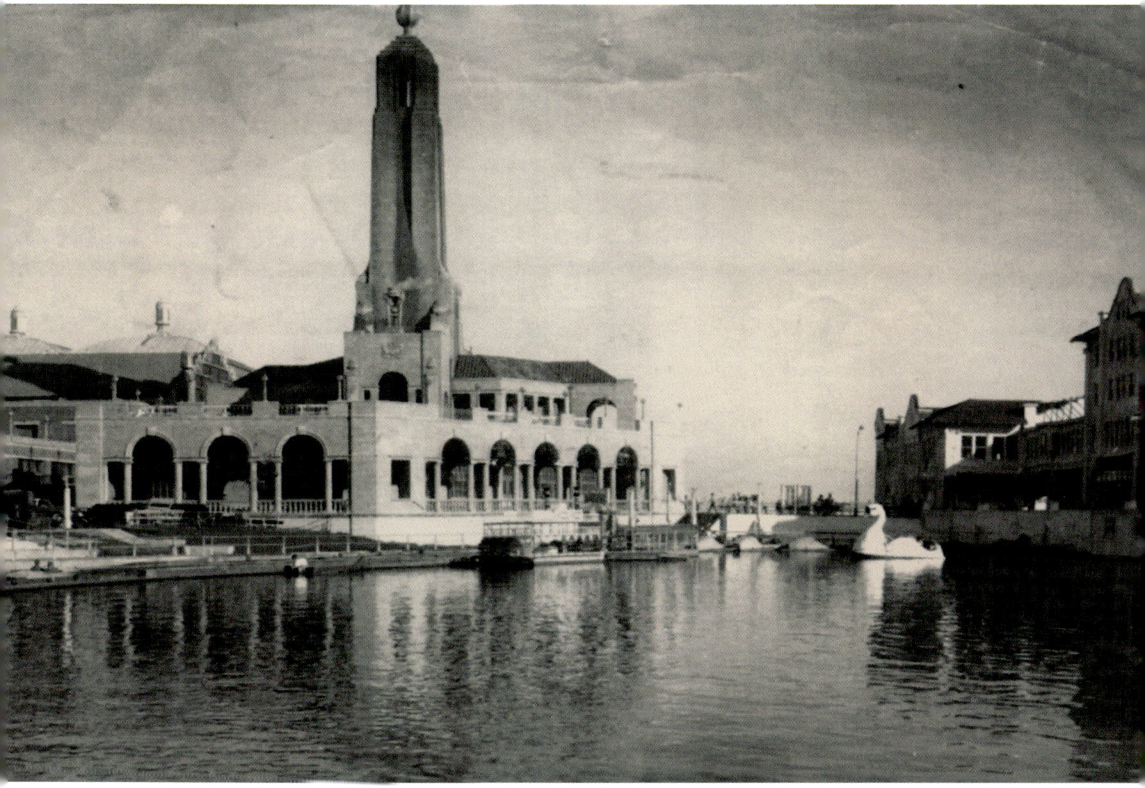

One of the famous swan boats can be seen in Wesley Lake in this 1960s view of the central steam-heating plant. At one time, the plant provided heat to all of the buildings on the boardwalk. Built concurrently with the casino, its topmost flourish was removed during the early 1970s. The structure is under consideration for possible future use as an art gallery. (Courtesy Vini "Mad Dog" Lopez.)

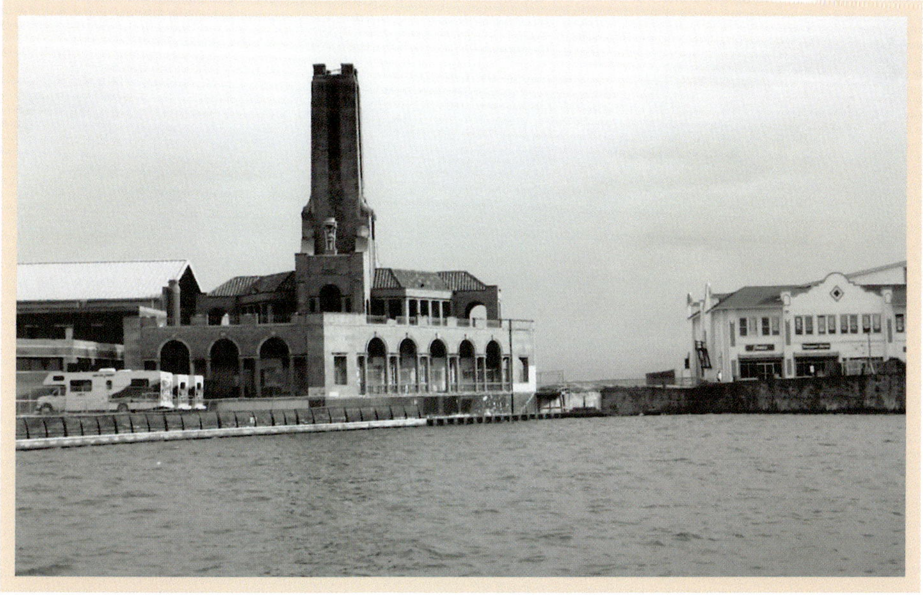

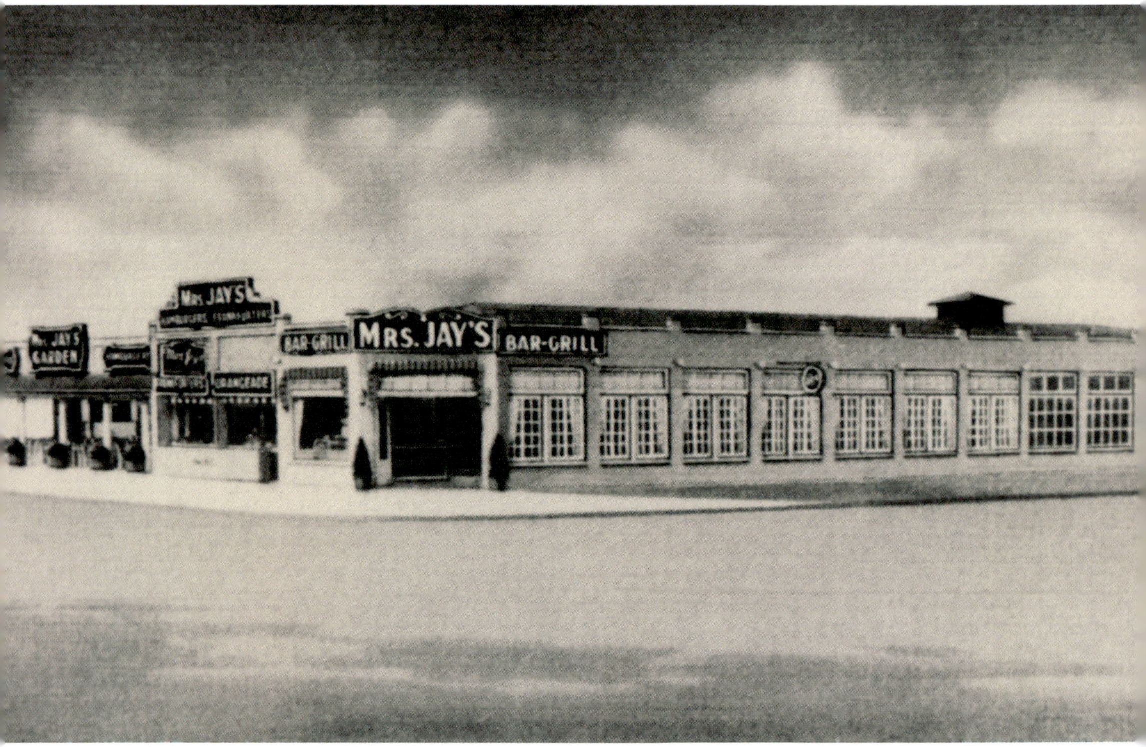

Mrs. Jay's Bar and Grill is shown in this early 1940s postcard. Roland Hines had built a small restaurant in 1917 on the former site of the Pierrepont Hotel at Ocean and Second Avenues. John and Ida Jacobs bought the property in 1922 and renamed it Mrs. Jay's. After Prohibition, the Jacobses built an addition that housed a bar along Second Avenue. John Roig and Robert Pielka purchased the club in 1974 and reopened it as the Stone Pony.

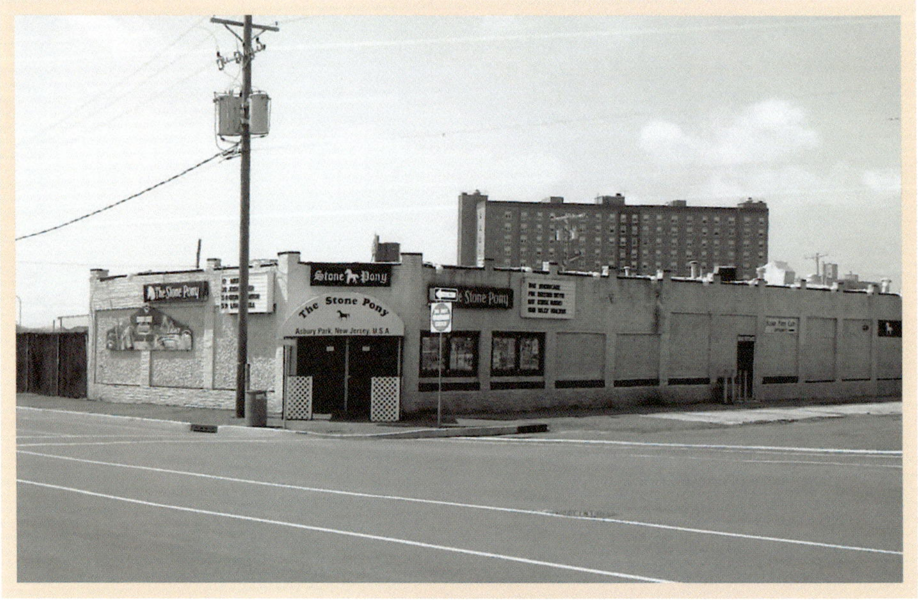

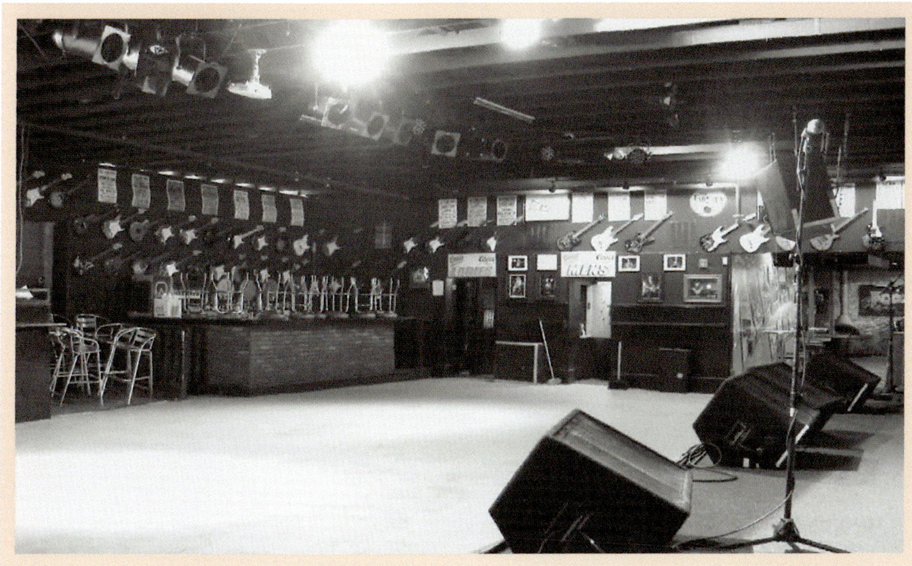

This mid-1950s interior view of Mrs. Jay's was taken from what is now extreme stage left at the famous Stone Pony. The roof support beams have been removed from the dance floor area, although there is still one original support located at the front of club. "Southside" Johnny Lyon (Neptune High, class of 1967) led the Pony's first house band. Bruce Springsteen has consistently made surprise cameo appearances at the venue since its opening.

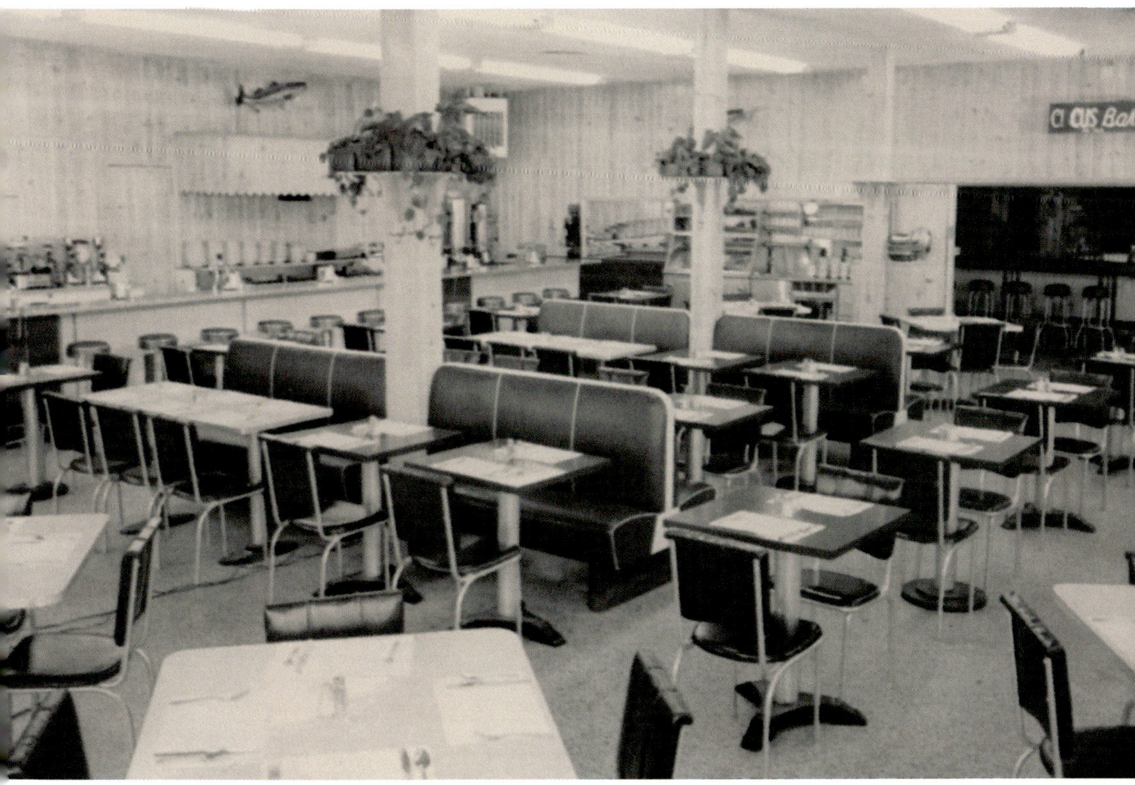

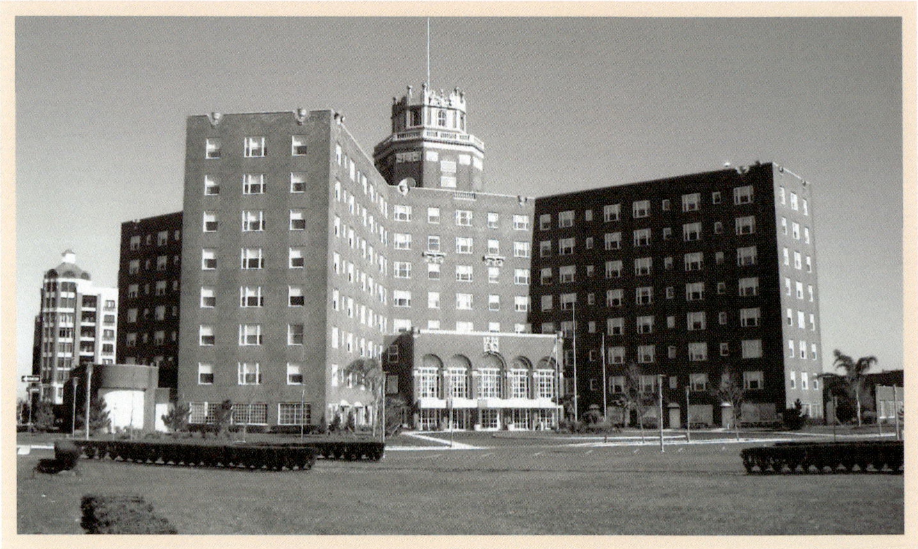

Pictured in the 1940s, the Berkeley-Carteret Hotel was built in 1924 by Arthur Steinbach. The architect was the New York City firm of Warren and Wetmore, one of the firms that designed Grand Central Terminal. The Vaccaro brothers, along with singer Johnny Cash, attempted to restore the building in the 1980s. Maharishi Mahesh Yogi purchased the hotel in 1994 with the intention of converting it into a mediation center. In 2007, it was purchased by the Chetrit Group and renamed the Berkeley. (Appleby Collection.)

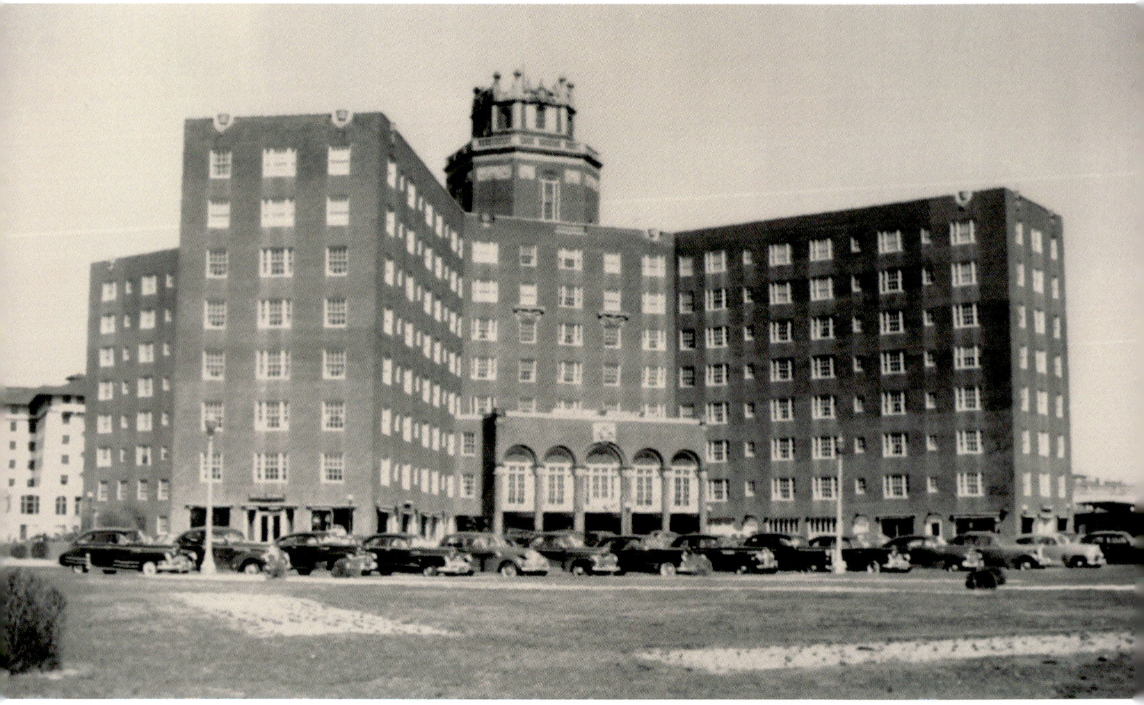

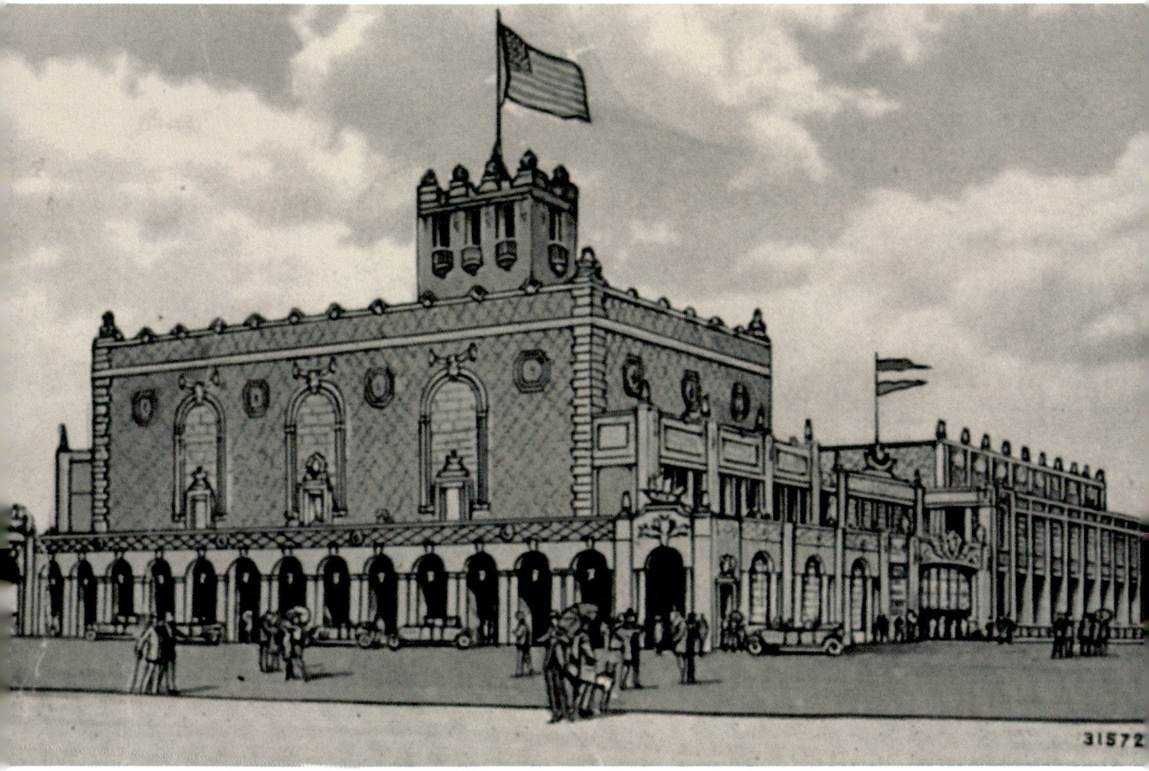

This 1929 postcard view of the Paramount Theatre and Convention Hall was made using an architectural rendering, as the building was not completed until late that year. When compared to an image of the completed building, it is apparent how closely the plans were followed. Also of note is how remarkable the condition is for an oceanfront building, considering the many storms that have left the boardwalk in ruins at least once per decade since it was constructed.

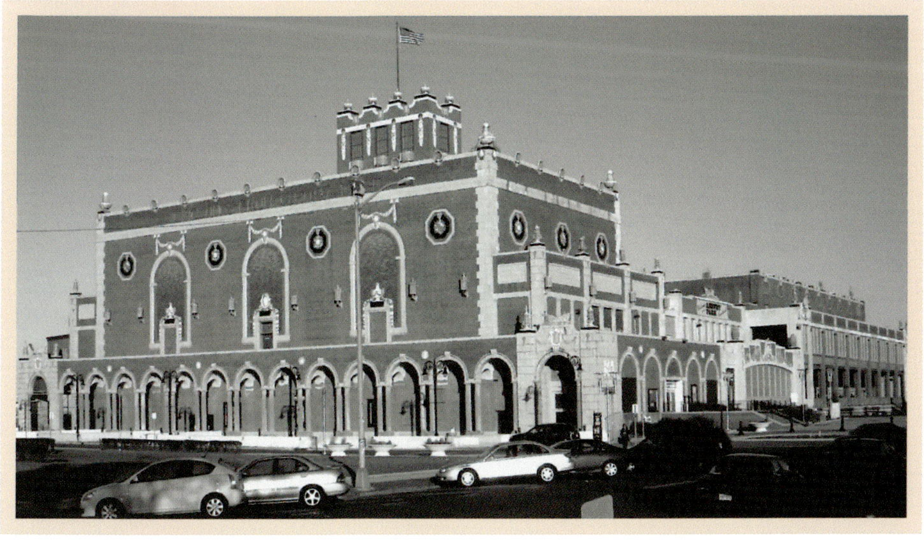

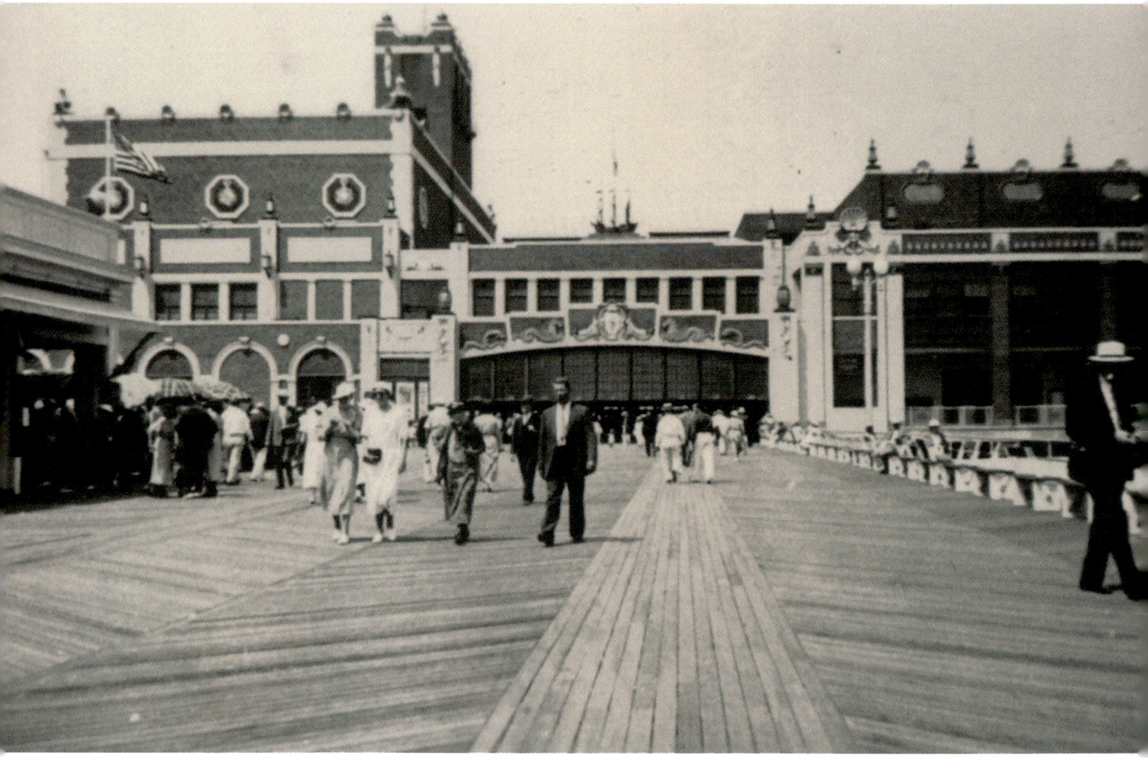

This boardwalk photograph was taken during the summer of 1930, shortly after the Convention Hall complex opened. Another interesting comparison is of the actual boardwalk itself. Even though the boards have been replaced several times, the placement pattern has not changed. The former Howard Johnson restaurant on the left is now a successful supper club run by Tim McLoone.

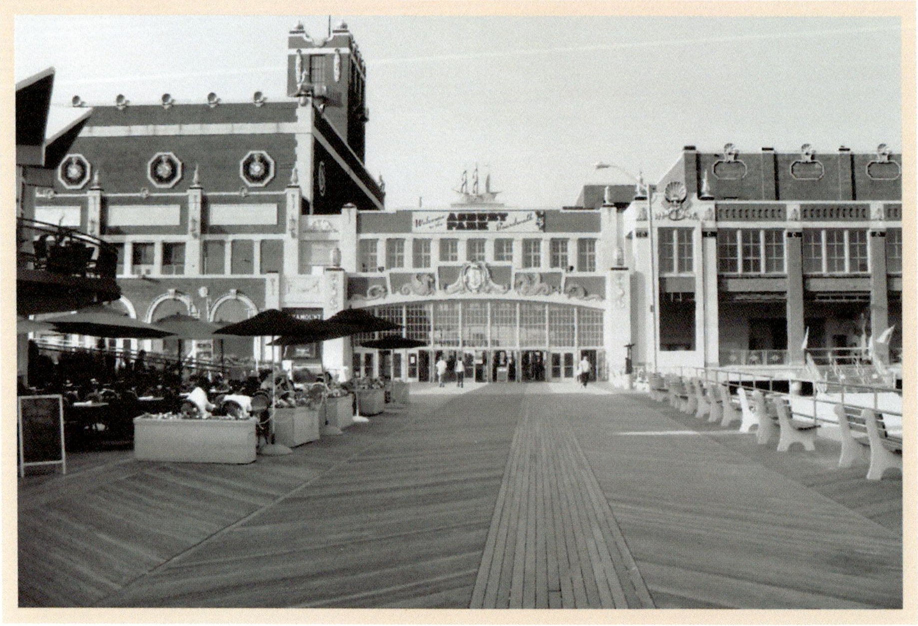

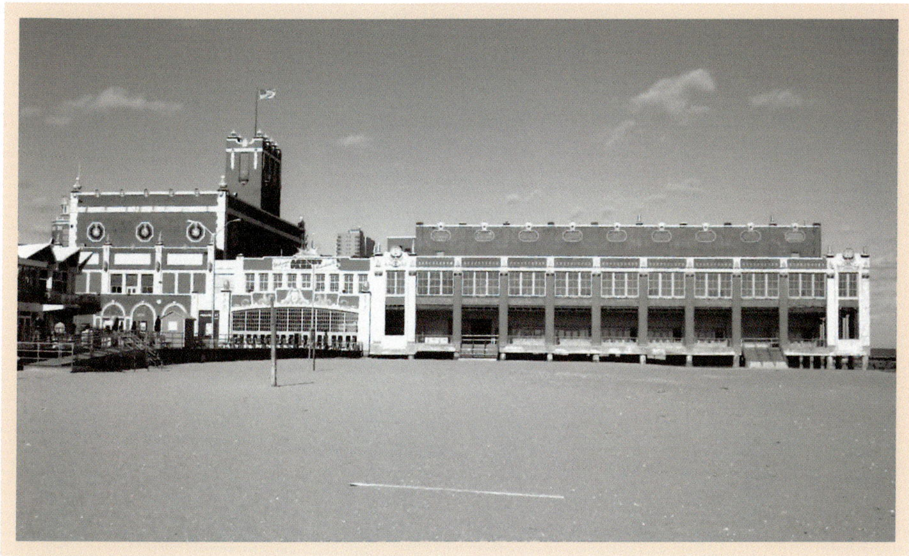

This late-1930s view of Convention Hall from the beach further demonstrates the remarkable condition of the building and its proximity to the ocean. Unlike in neighboring towns that have pushed their boardwalks back because of shrinking beaches, Asbury's beach has actually gained considerable space due to jetty design and various sand-pumping efforts led by the Army Corps of Engineers. (Appleby Collection.)

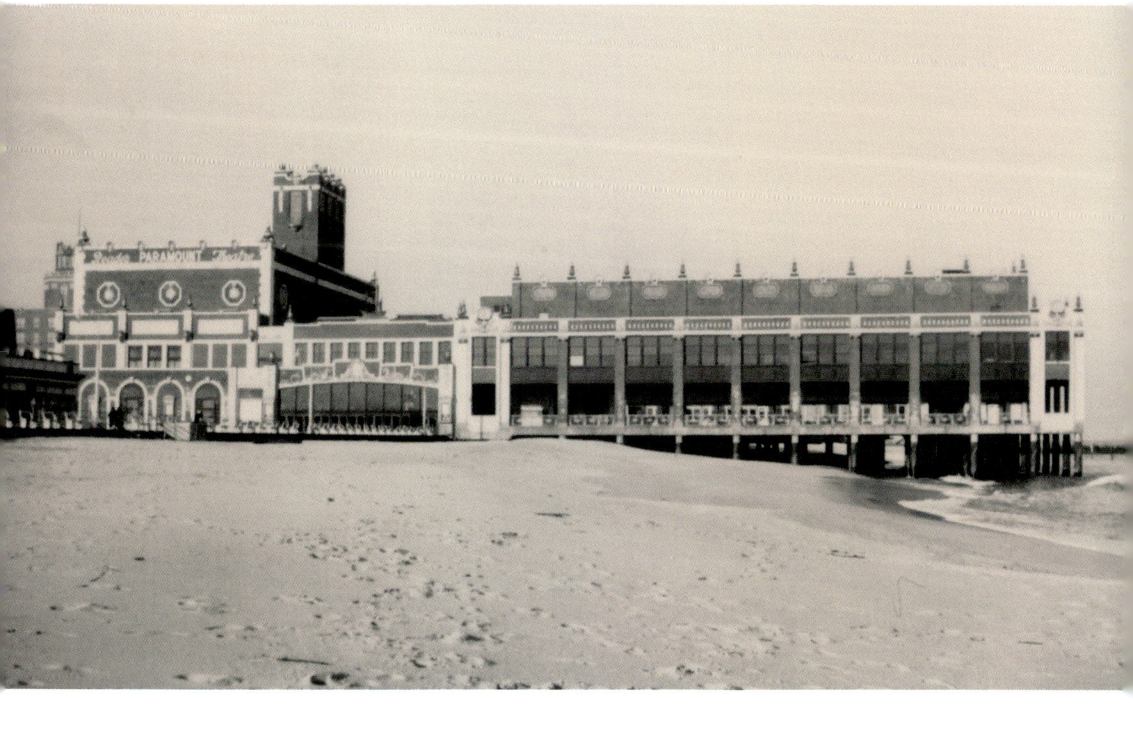

Asbury Tower is pictured shortly after its completion in 1974. For many years, this plot of land was the site of the Monte Carlo pool. Although controversy exists over the claim, the Monte Carlo billed itself as "the world's largest saltwater pool." The Asbury Tower complex is a senior apartment complex that offers magnificent views of the entire shore area. The building's exterior was resurfaced in 2008.

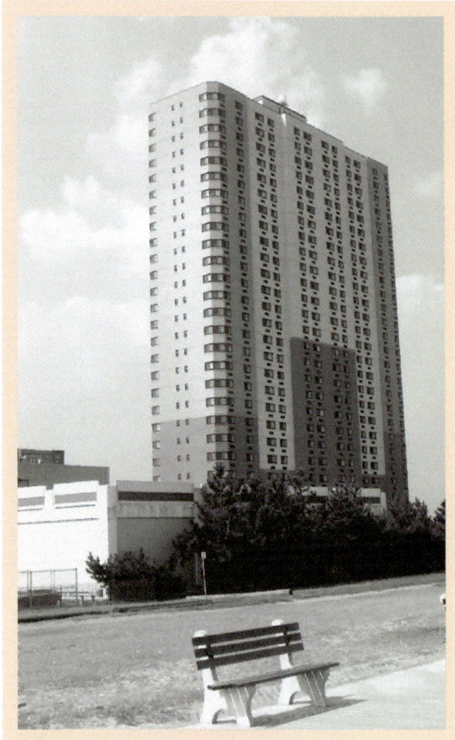

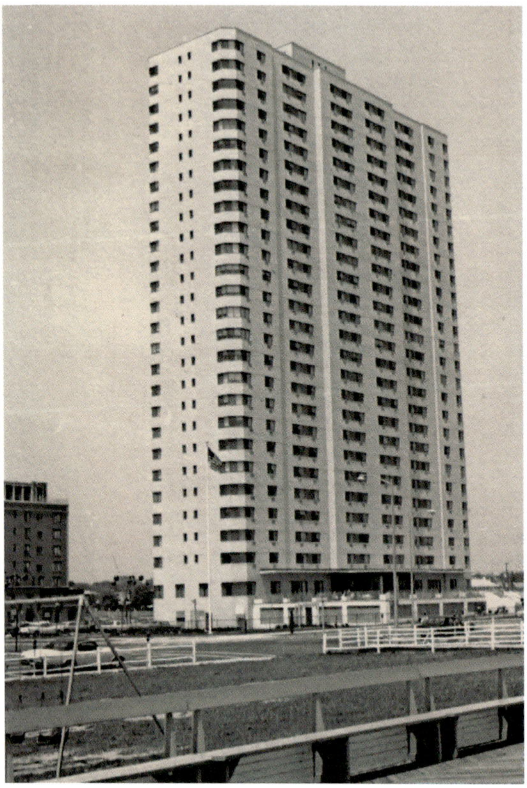

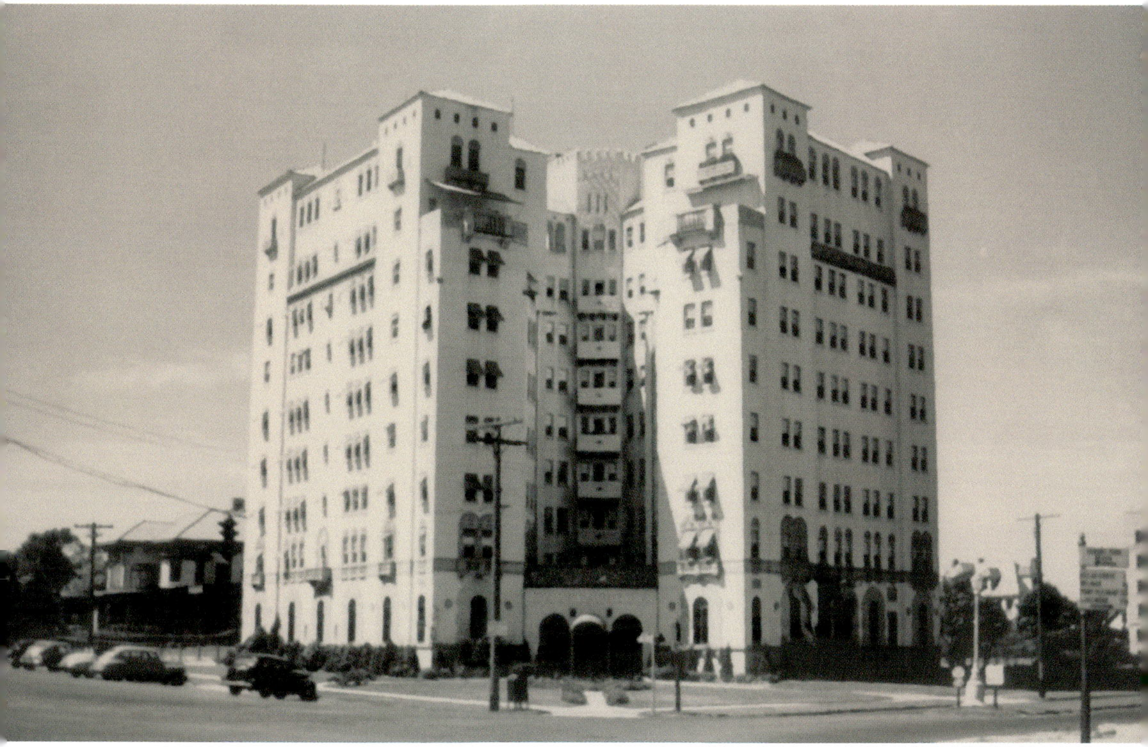

The Santander Apartments were built as a luxury residential hotel in 1928 by Richard Stout. The building style was influenced by the architecture Stout had encountered while on a trip to Santander, the regional capital of Cantabria, on the northern coast of Spain. Pictured in the late 1930s, the building's unique design features fountains, courtyards, gargoyles, and elaborate tile work. The ground floor boasted a well-known exclusive tearoom and restaurant. (Appleby Collection.)

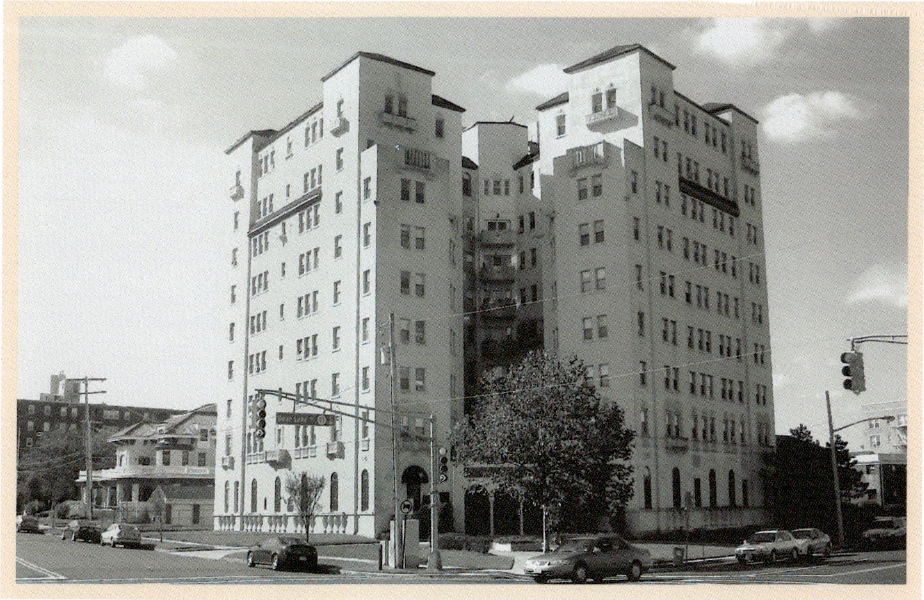

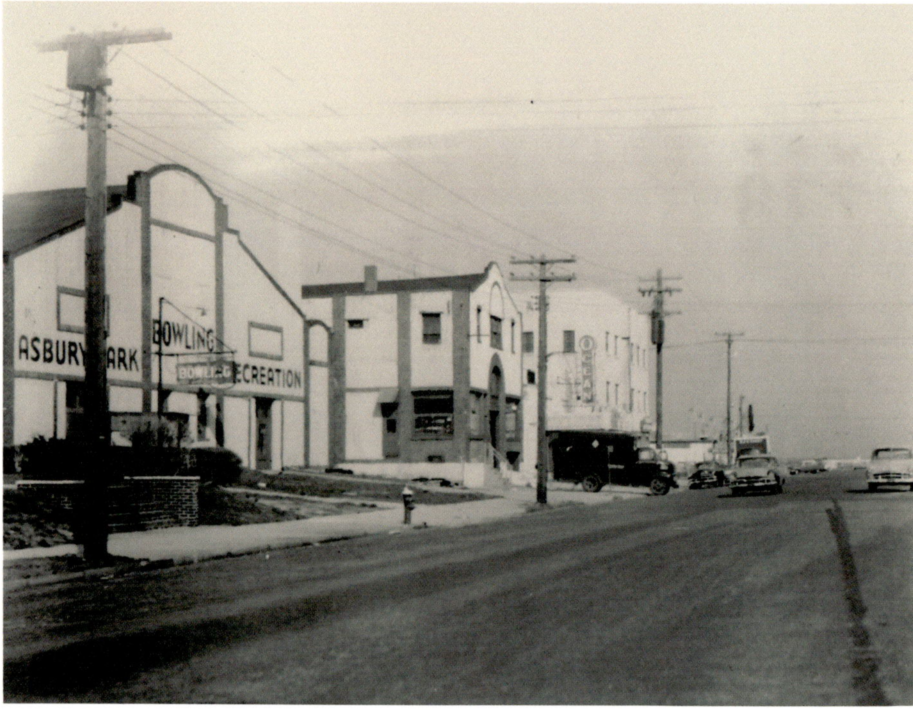

The north side of the 200 block of Fourth Avenue is shown in this photograph from 1962. Asbury Lanes, still a popular bowling and music attraction, opened in 1961. The building was constructed in 1927 as an expansion of Samuel Ehrlich's Garage and Autoworks next door, which had been built six years earlier. Minus the second story, it became the Fastlane, as documented on the next page. The Baronet was still named the Ocean Theatre in 1962. (Appleby Collection.)

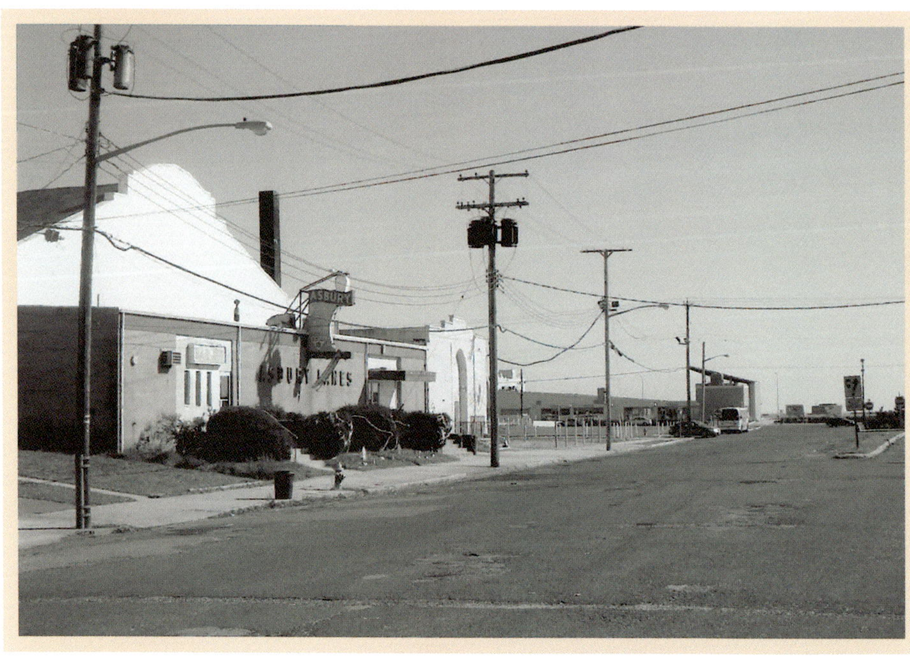

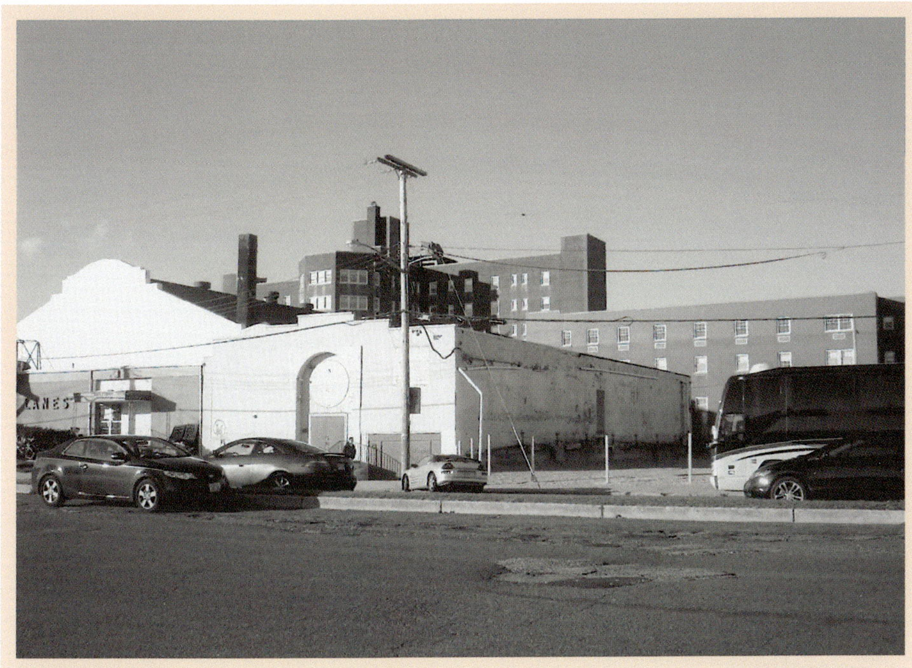

This mid-1990s view of the same block is taken from Fourth Avenue. Originally built by Ehrlich in 1921, the Fastlane club opened in 1974. Bon Jovi gained much exposure as the club headliner starting in 1979. The Ocean Theatre was built in 1913. Walter Reade Jr. purchased the building in 1953 and renamed it the Baronet sometime later, in part because of a sign he salvaged from another theatre he had once owned. The Baronet was razed in September 2010.

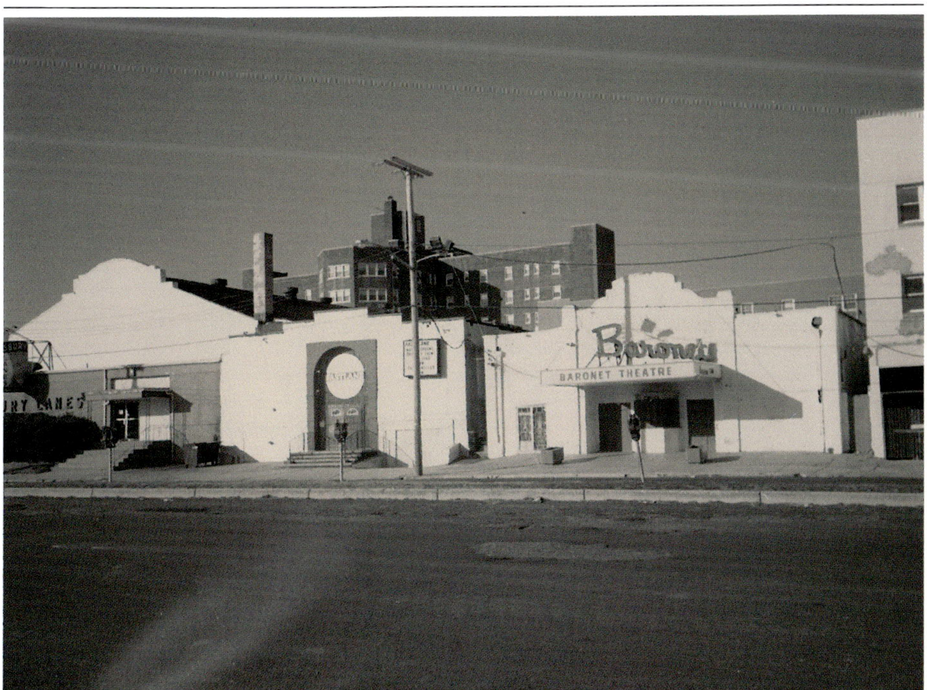

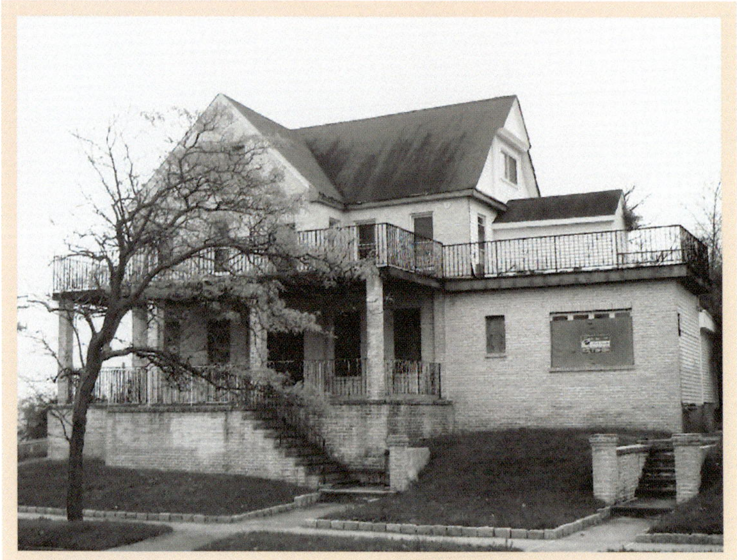

During its heyday, Asbury Park was renowned for its grand hotels. However, to accommodate the overwhelming number of tourists, many larger homes were converted into small hotels or boardinghouses. This was the case for the Wherwood, pictured here on an advertising postcard from the 1940s. The house was built in the early 1900s, and despite the many improvements and alterations, it has been abandoned and has fallen into neglect.

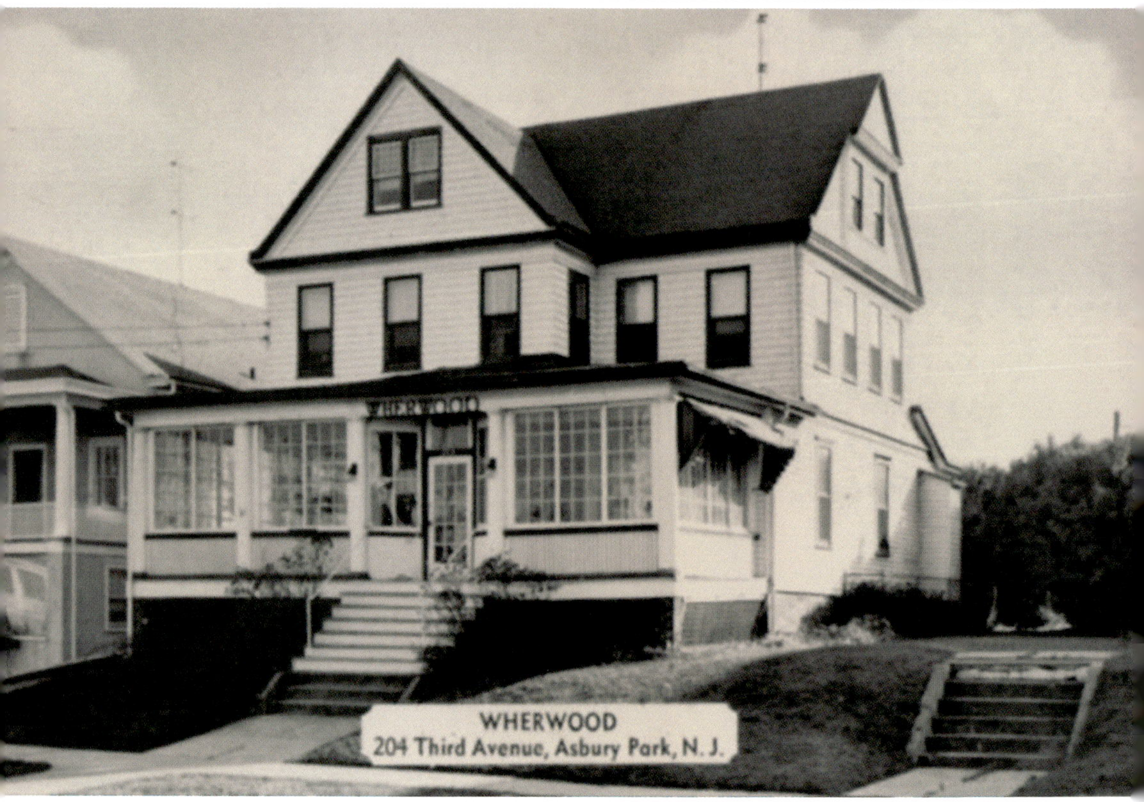

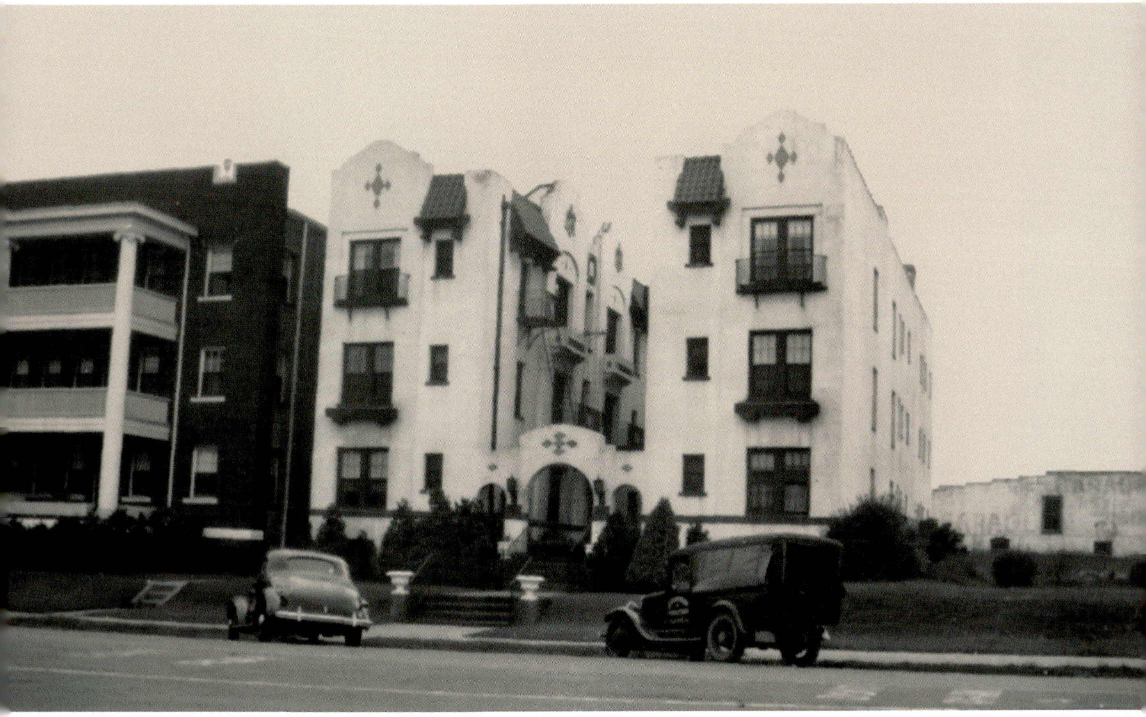

The Jersey Apartments were constructed on Second Avenue in 1922. This image was taken in the early 1930s. They were sandwiched between the Virginia Apartments on the east (also built in 1922) and the Willis Apartments (built in 1923) on the west. Arguably the most picturesque of the three, the Jersey Apartments are, sadly, the only ones that have been abandoned as of early 2011. (Appleby Collection.)

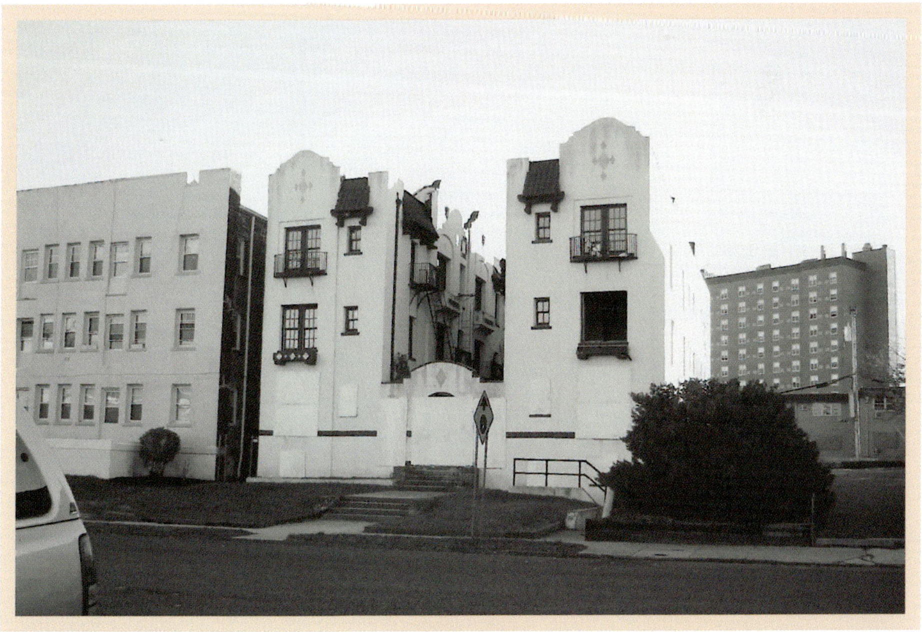

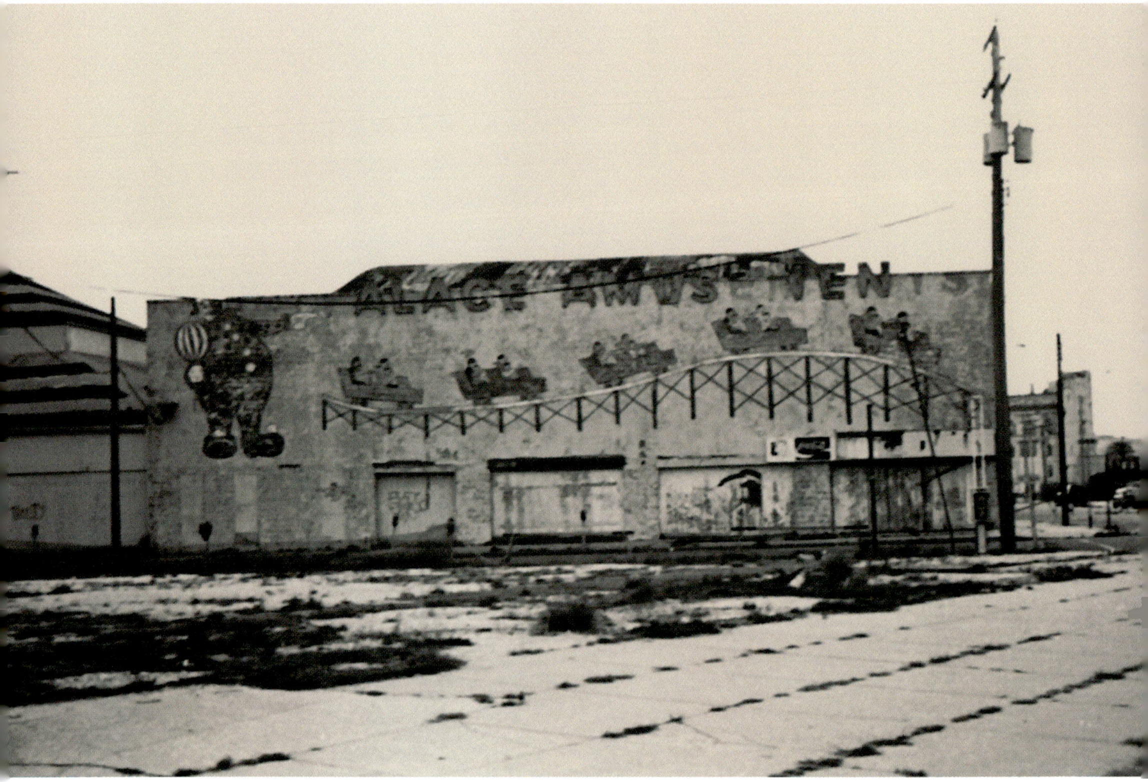

By the late 1990s, the Palace, the Casino, the Stone Pony, the Fastlane, and the Empress Motel were all closed. Springsteen penned his anthem *My City of Ruins* as a reflection of the sad state of affairs. The beachfront area was revitalized during the 2000s. This 1998 view would be almost impossible to locate if not for the utility poles that still stand after the 2004 demolition of Palace Amusements. (Compare these images to the 1904 title-page photograph.)

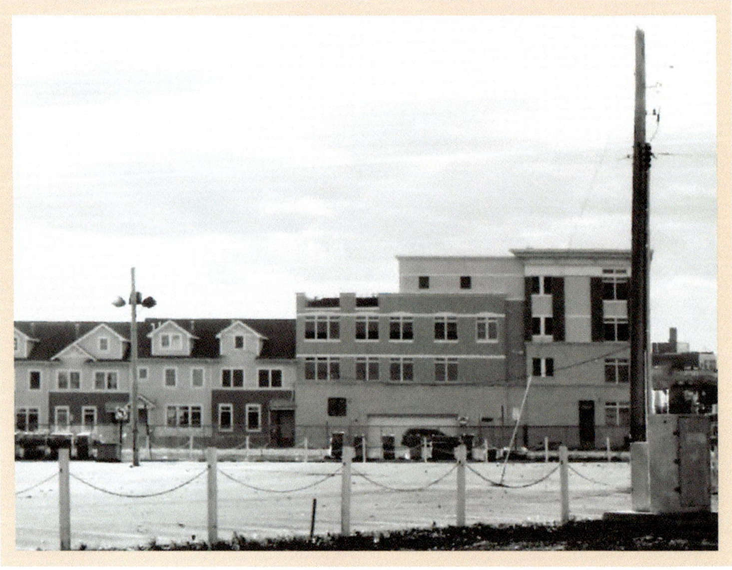

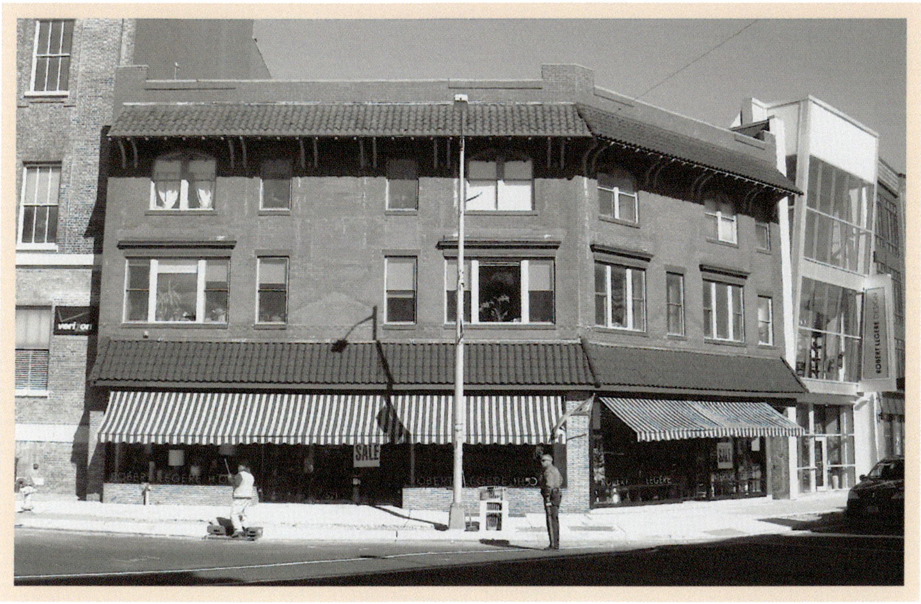

The 1890s building at the northeastern intersection of Cookman and Bangs Avenues has played host to many businesses in the heart of the Asbury Park shopping district. This 1940s view shows the building shortly after the Anna Maude Beauty Shoppe had vacated the premises. To the left, the women's petite shop Dainty Apparel can be seen. An upscale interior design firm currently occupies the building. (Appleby Collection.)

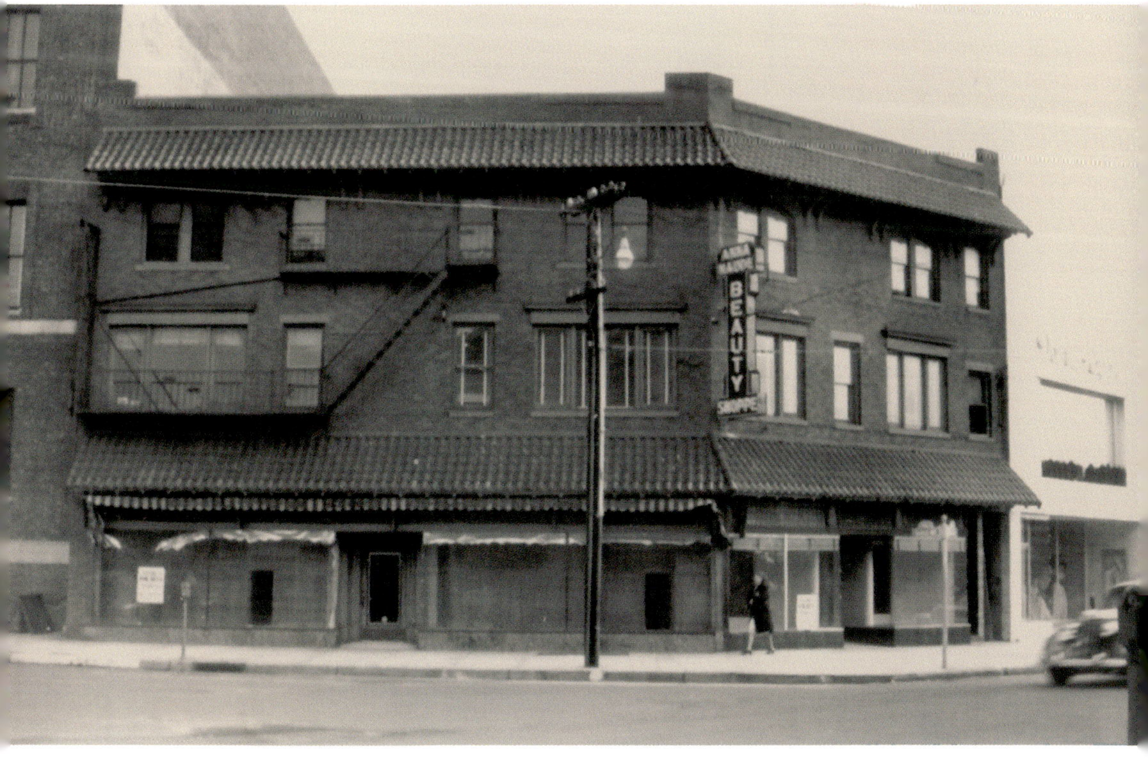

In 1896, John Steinbach purchased the Commercial Hotel on Emory Street. He sold the building and furniture to Henry C. Winsor, who had it moved to Fourth Avenue. In October 1896, construction of the mammoth Steinbach store commenced on the site, pictured here in 1907. In 1910, Steinbach expanded the structure into the familiar block-sized edifice that exists today. After the store closed in 1979, the building stood vacant for over 25 years but was successfully converted into residential and retail space in 2007.

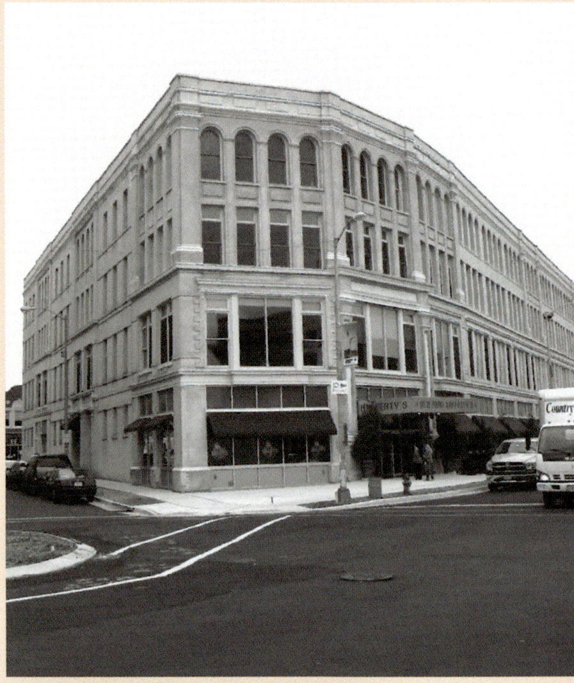

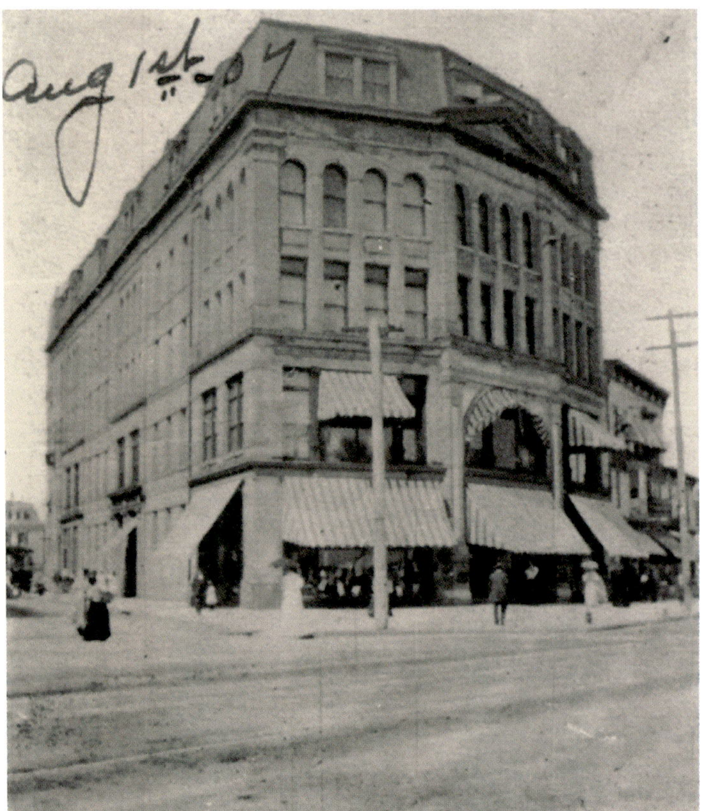

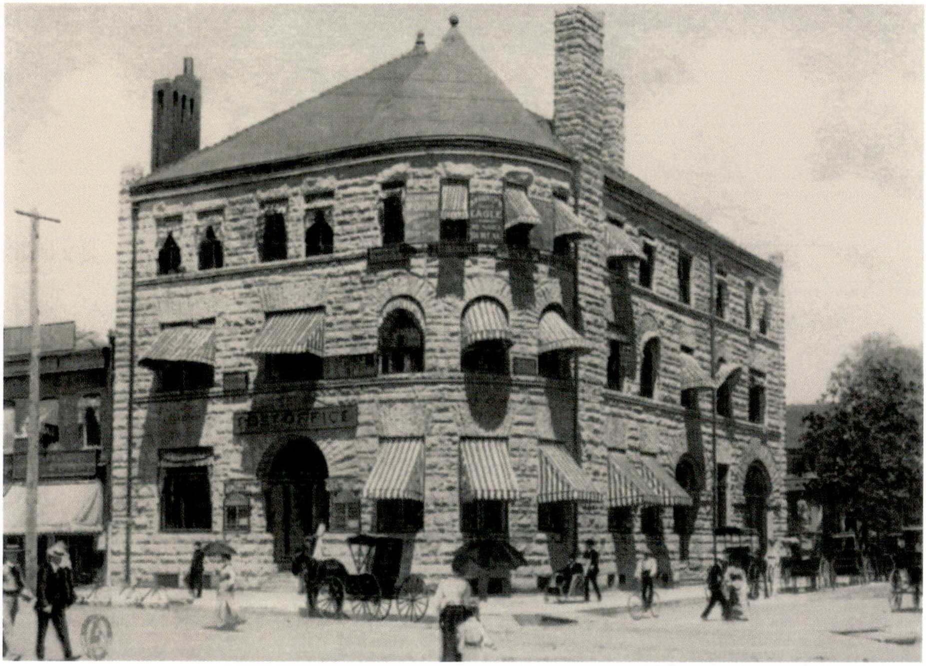

The Byram Bank and Office Building was constructed in 1881 on the northwest corner of Mattison Avenue and Emory Street. Pictured here in 1905, the Asbury Park Post Office occupied the building from 1895 to 1909. Woodrow Wilson used it as headquarters for his 1916 presidential campaign. A 1916 fire gutted the interior, and it was refurbished with two more stories. The Asbury Park Trust Company occupied this handsome landmark for many years. In 2008, the structure was remodeled into retail and residential units and rechristened The Post Building.

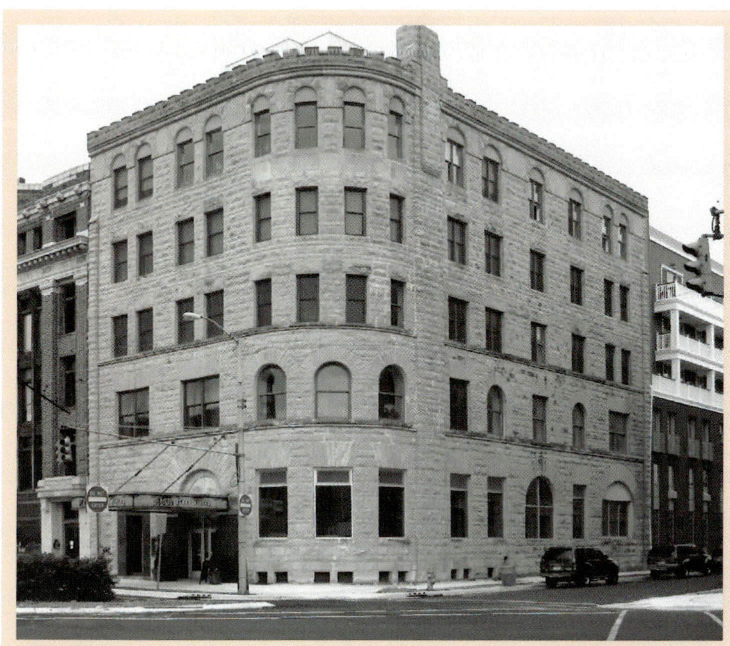

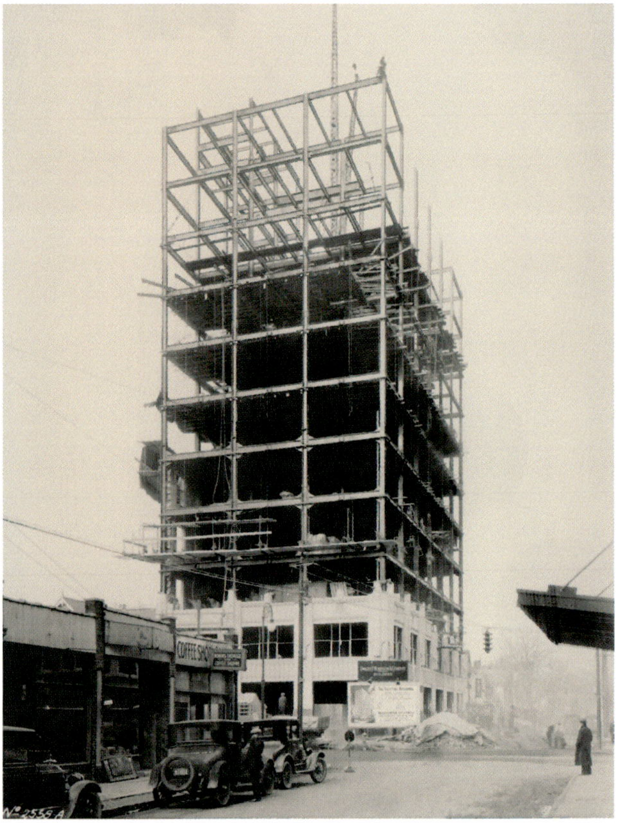

Pictured at right is the electric company building under construction on December 14, 1926. Park Steel and Iron of Neptune City did the fabrication work. The building was designed by the noted Chicago industrial architect Frank David Chase. At the time of its completion, it was the tallest in central New Jersey. The building continues as an important commercial center, housing many different offices and business ventures. (Park Steel and Iron.)

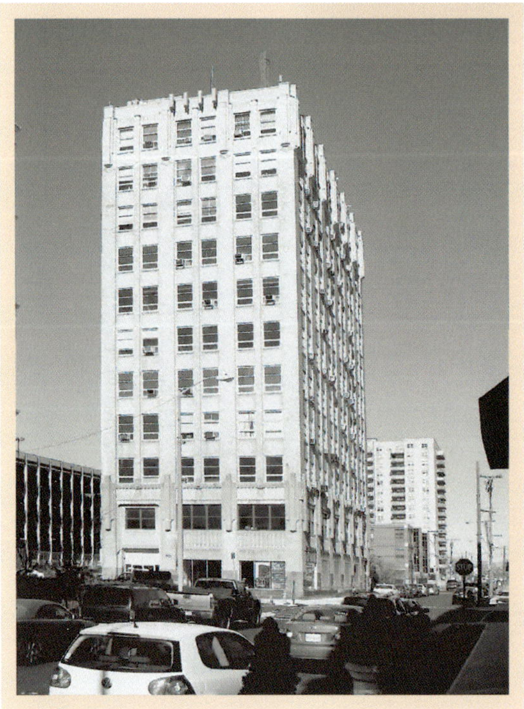

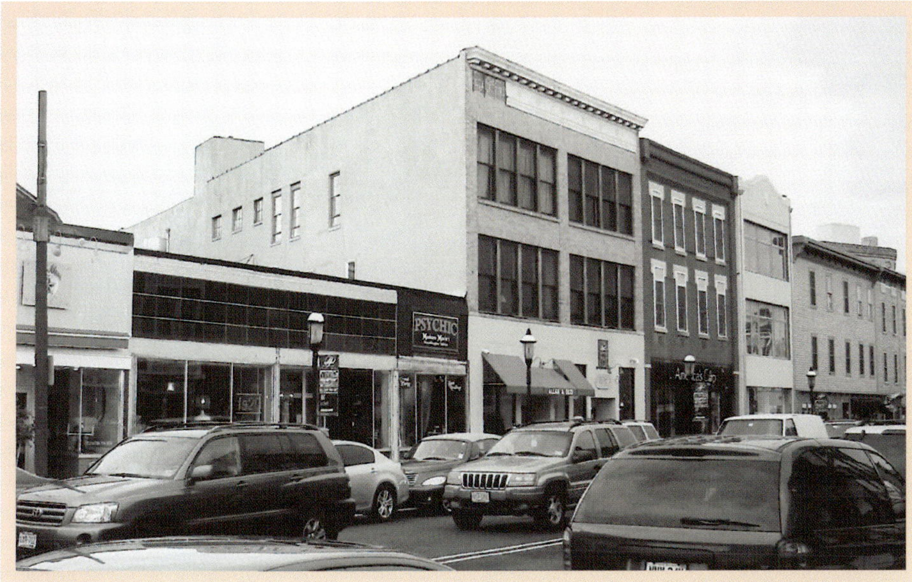

The classic downtown shoe district is shown in wonderful detail in this late 1940s view: Philadelphia pharmacy chain Sun Ray Drugs' Asbury location, the Smartwear shop (which has lost its upper two floors), Walter's Fabrics, Miller Shoes (which had recently suffered a fire), Berkeley's Shoes, and Eidelsberg's Shoes. At the time, there were four shoe stores on the same block. (Appleby Collection.)

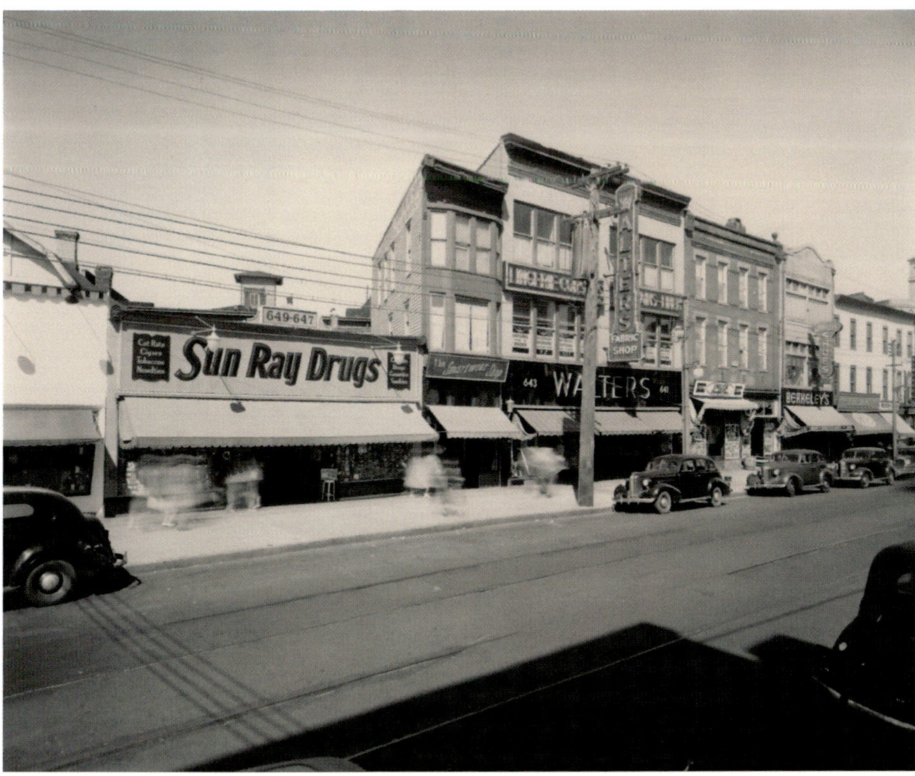

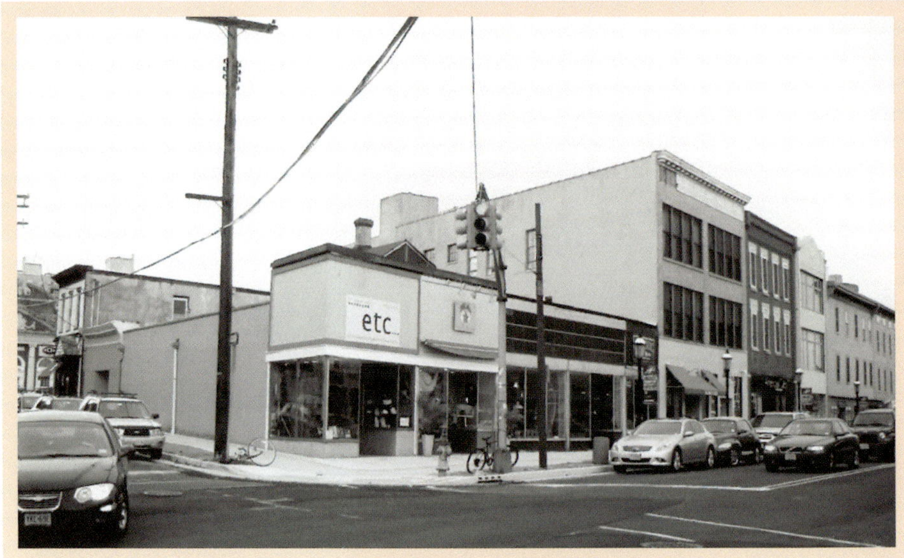

The northeast corner of Bond Street and Cookman Avenue is pictured in the early 1940s. Blanche Lewis opened the Bond Street Bar and Grill shortly after the repeal of Prohibition. The Thom McAn shoe store is seen here in its original location. In the early 1960s, it would move to the first floor of the tall three-story building (built in 1921) diagonally across Cookman Avenue. (Appleby Collection.)

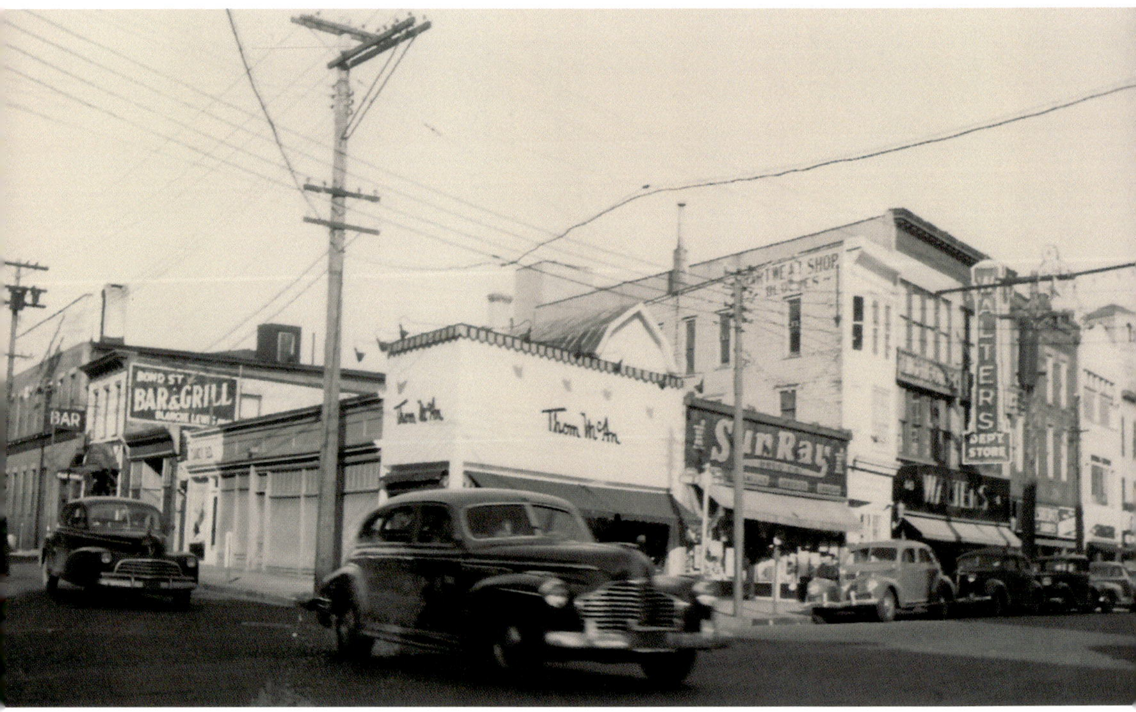

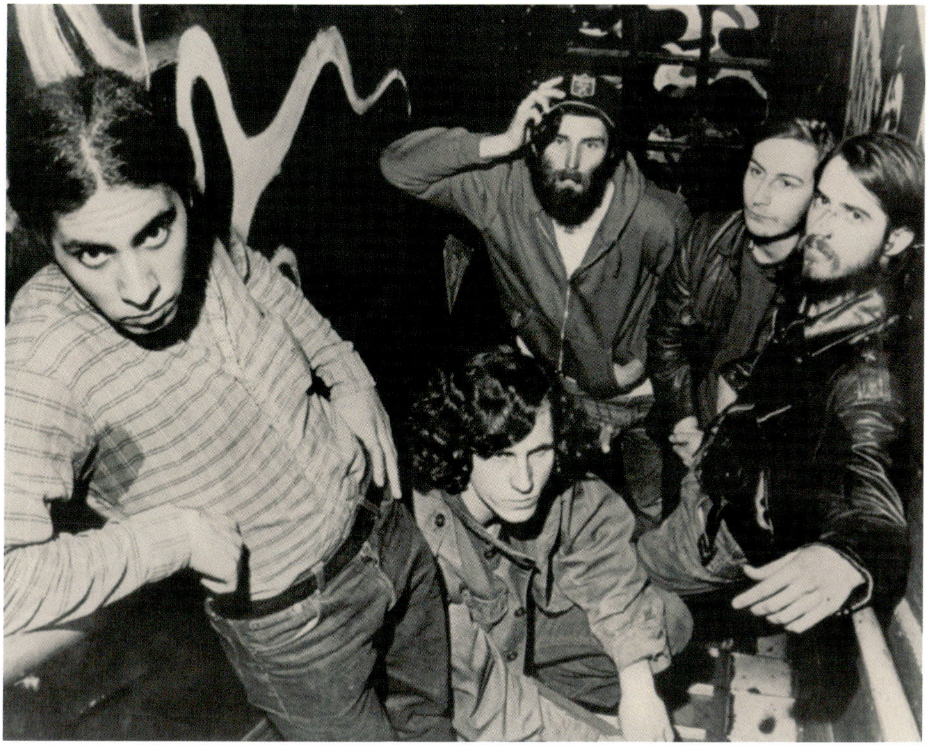

From 1968 to 1971, free-spirited hairstylist Thomas Potter ran the epicenter of the local rock scene at the shore, the Upstage Club, on the top floor of the Thom McAn building. The Sundance Blues Band is pictured here in the club stairwell in April 1971. From left to right are Steve Van Zandt, Joe Hagstrom, Vini Lopez, "Southside" Johnny Lyon, and Garry Tallent. Hagstrom would be replaced the following month by a young guitarist named Bruce Springsteen. (Courtesy Vini "Mad Dog" Lopez.)

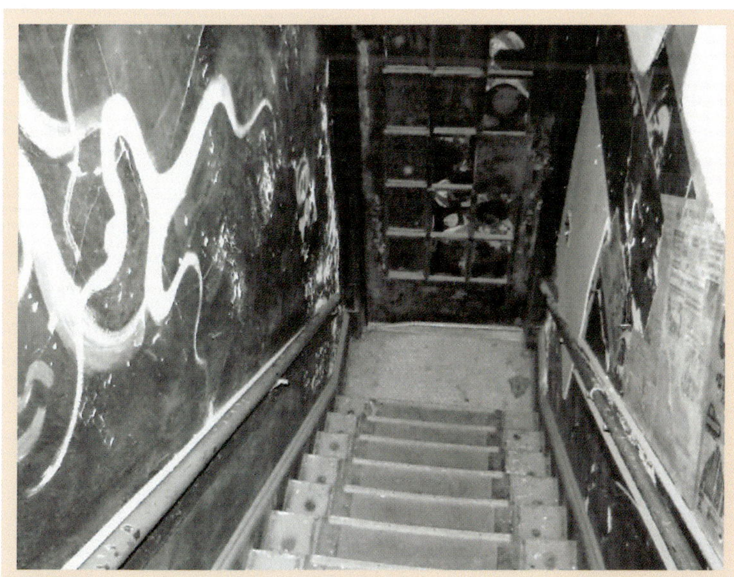

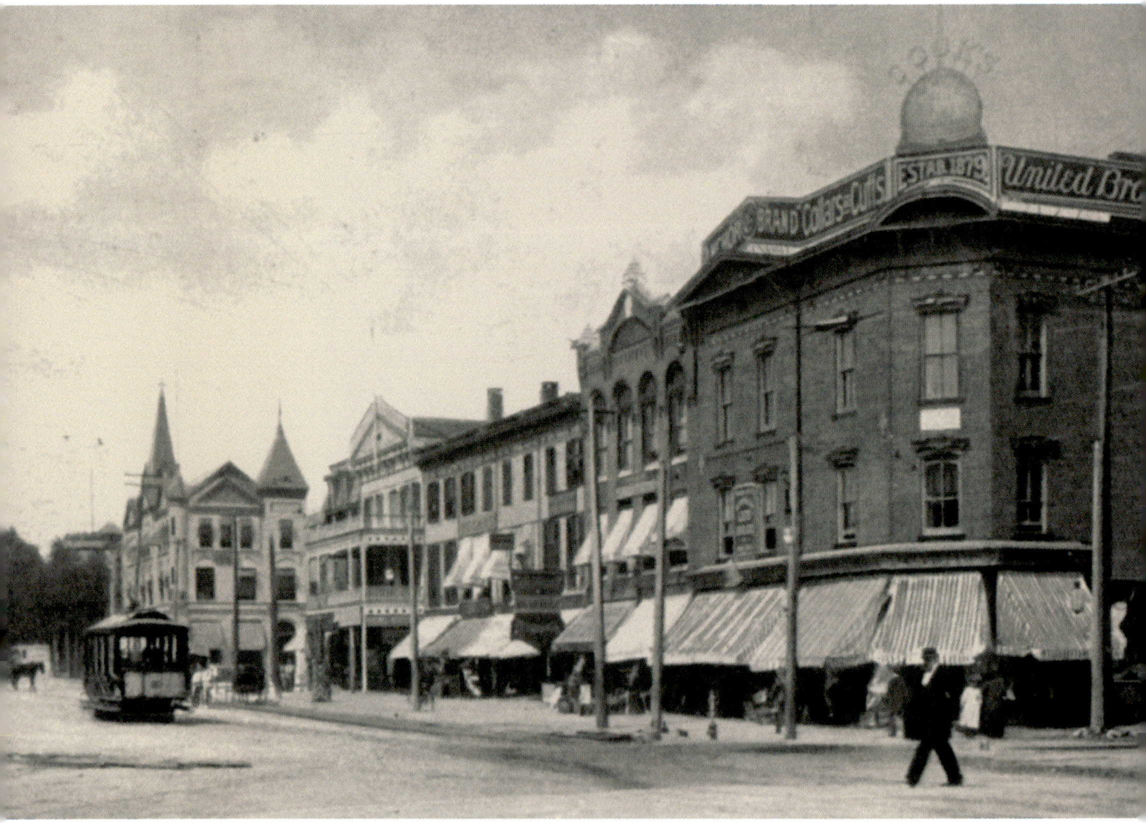

Entrepreneur John Cook came from Philadelphia in 1881. He opened a shop in a rented room on the east end of Cookman Avenue, and by the late 1880s, he had built the "Beehive" adjoining the Milan Ross Insurance building (built in 1886) on the northern corner of Cookman Avenue and Main Street. Pictured above in 1905, the building's first floor now houses a real estate office, while the upper floors are home to the Hot Dog House, comprised of private rehearsal studios for local bands. (Asbury Park Library.)

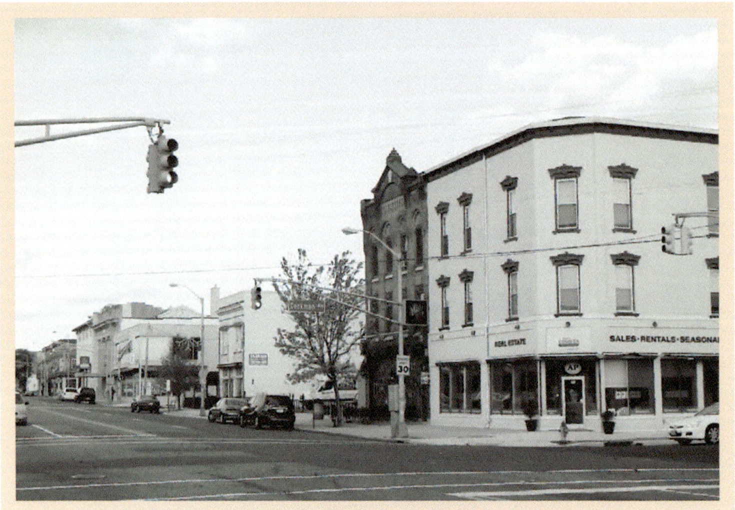

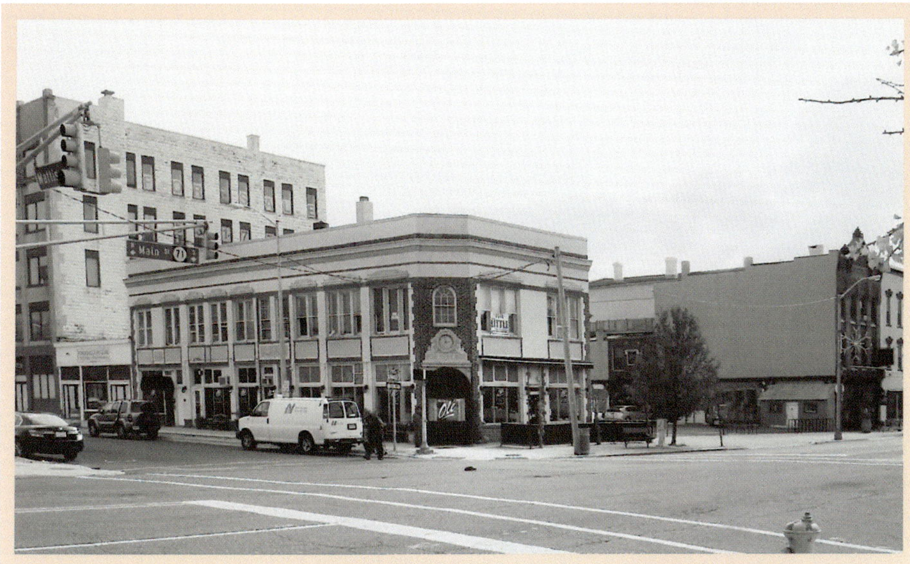

The T. Frank Appleby Agency was founded in 1885. Its headquarters were located at the southeastern corner of Mattison Avenue and Main Street. Appleby specialized in all aspects of real estate and insurance. The original three-story building was replaced in 1922 with this distinctive brick building (pictured here in 1945). Today, a bistro occupies this site. Erected in 1931, the Kinmouth Building, which housed the Savoy Theatre, stands tall at right. (Appleby Collection.)

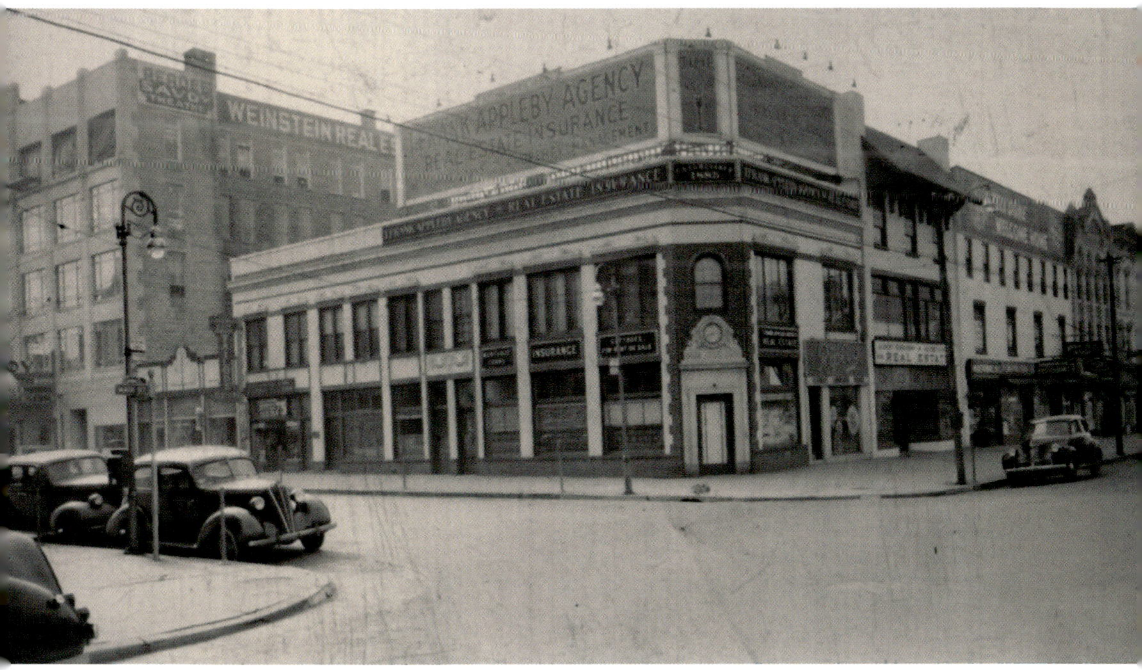

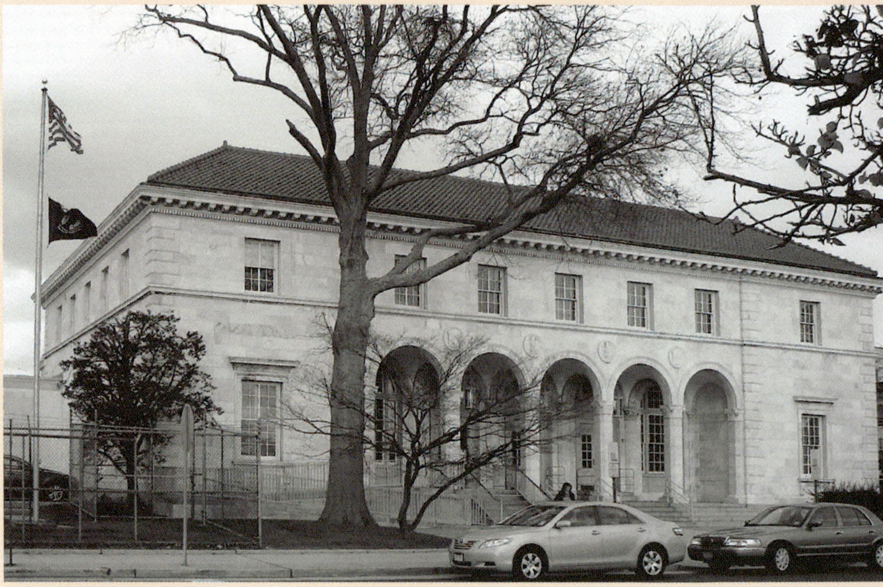

The Asbury Park Post Office moved in 1909 to the current location on Bangs Avenue. James Bradley owned a private park on the site, for which he was paid $30,000 to vacate. The need for a larger post office nearer to the rail line was essential for the rapidly growing city. This image is from a postcard that was postmarked in 1913. Expansions were made to the processing area throughout the next few decades.

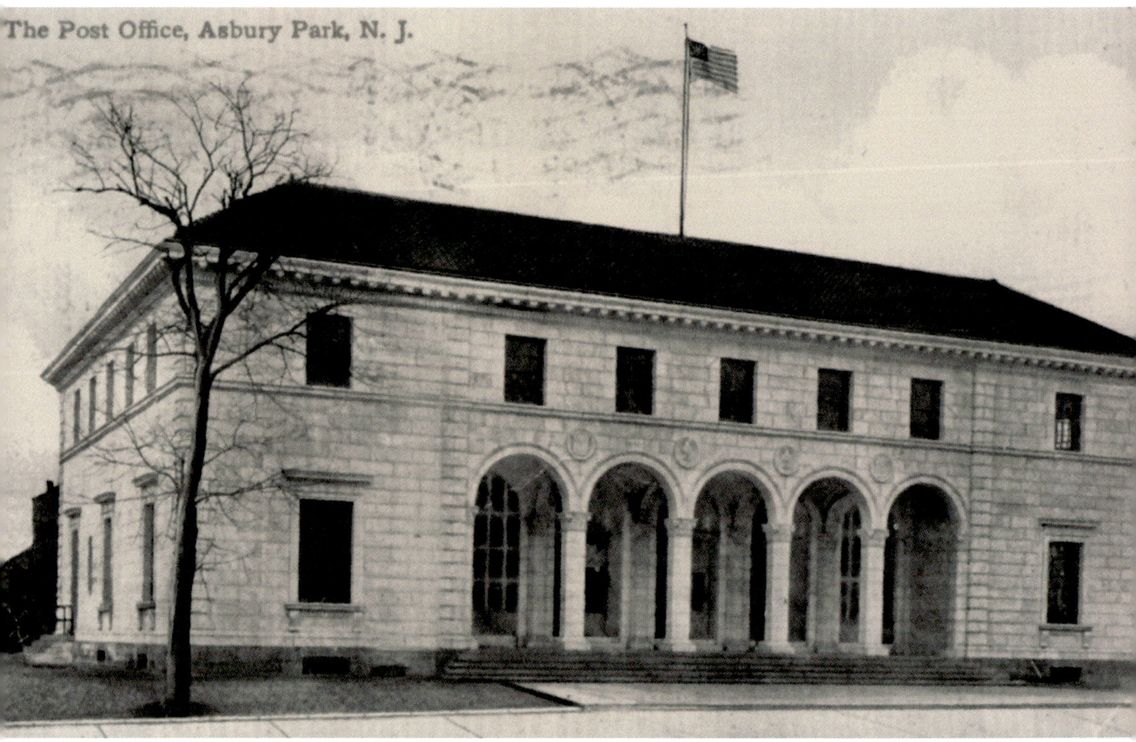

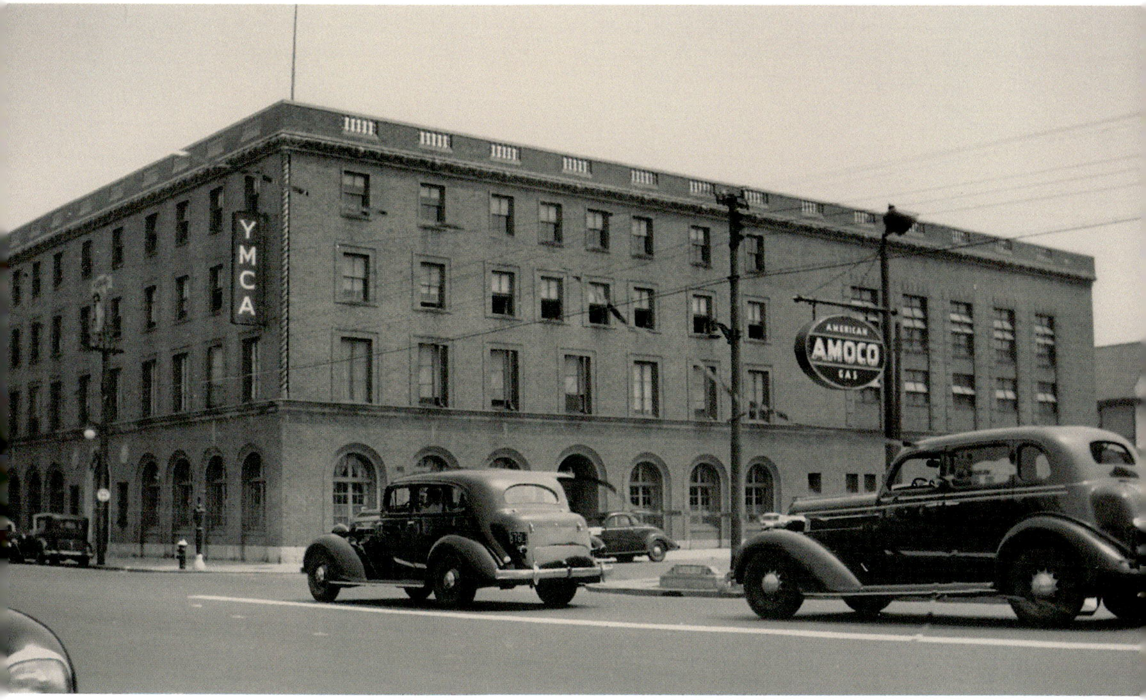

The Asbury Park YMCA was built in 1927, and its steel framework was fabricated by Park Steel and Iron. It is pictured here in the early 1930s. A full-size indoor basketball court and large swimming pool attracted many city residents and vacationers alike. Low-rent rooms were available on the upper floors. The building currently houses a health care career training service, a medical clinic, and an adult day-care facility. (Appleby Collection.)

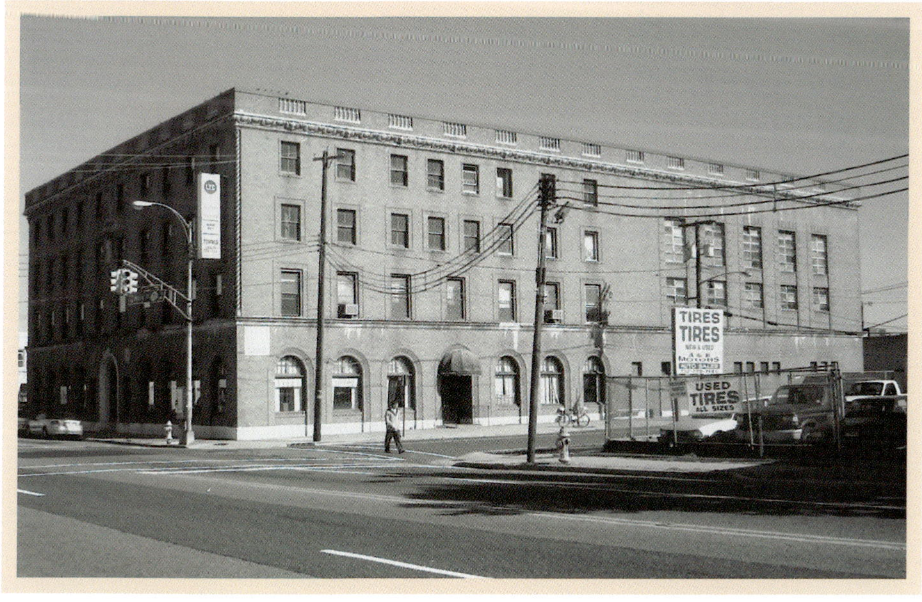

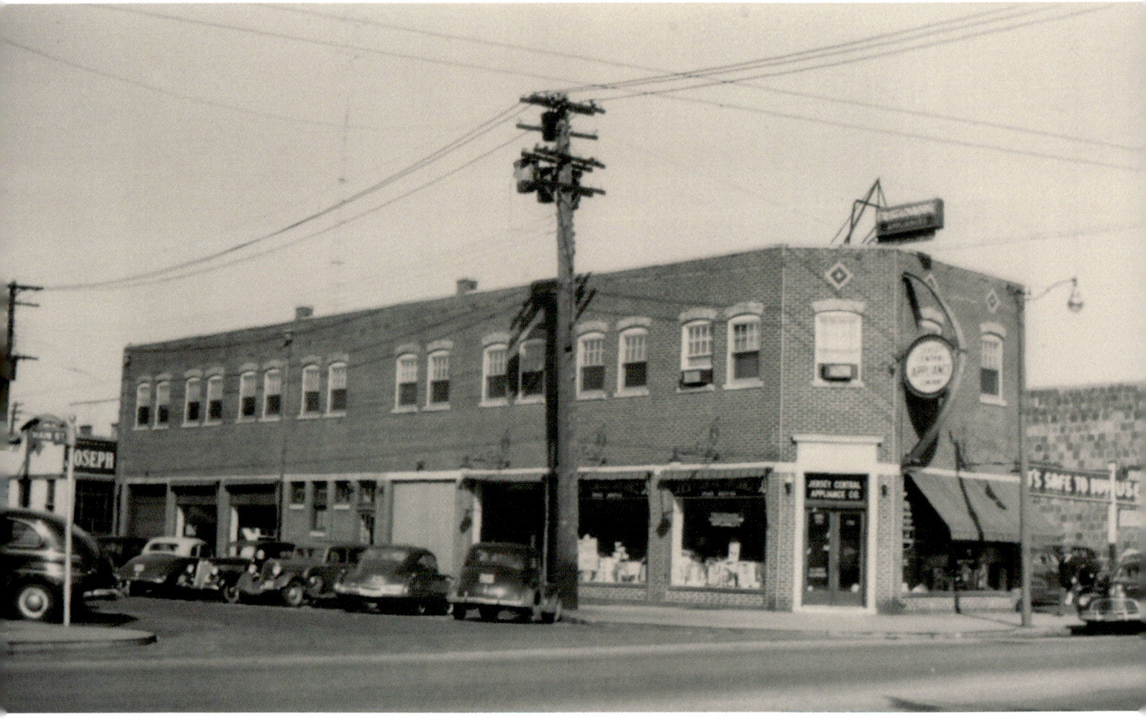

Originally built in 1922 by Henry Zobel, this building housed a Packard dealership. In this late 1930s incarnation, the main structure has been taken over by the Jersey Central Appliance Company. Stein's used car dealership occupied the former Packard lot. In the late 1960s, a building was constructed on the car lot, solidifying a storefront on the western 700 block. Today, the block is home to the Plaza Tapatia, a pillar of the local Mexican community. (Appleby Collection.)

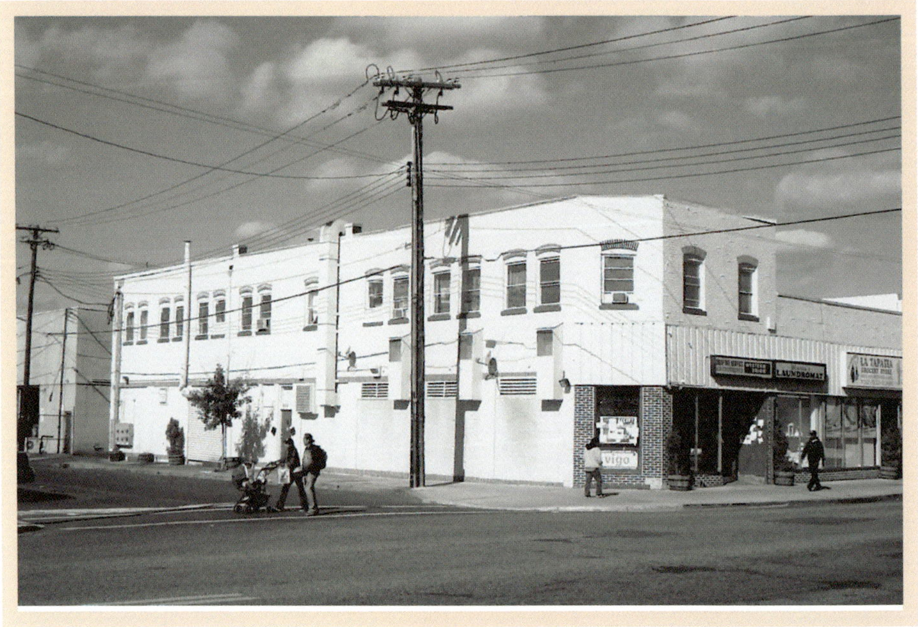

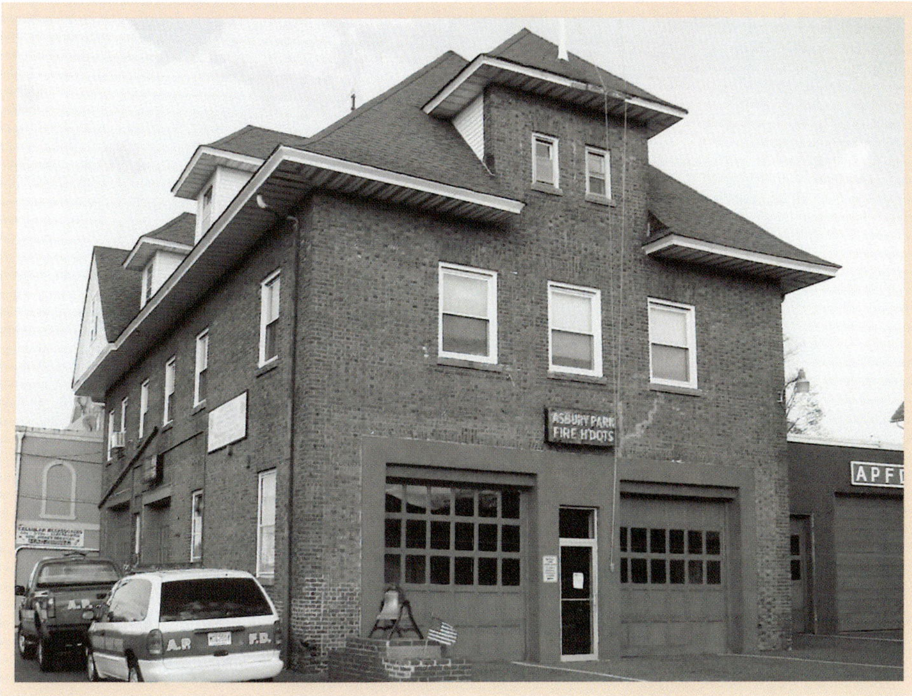

The Asbury Park Fire Department headquarters was built on the northeast corner of Asbury Avenue and Main Street in the mid-1880s. The Neptune Steam Fire Engine Company originally occupied this building. When the fire companies of Asbury Park were unified, this location was chosen as headquarters. The photograph below was taken in 1931. Interior structural repairs were conducted in 2006. (Asbury Park Historical Society.)

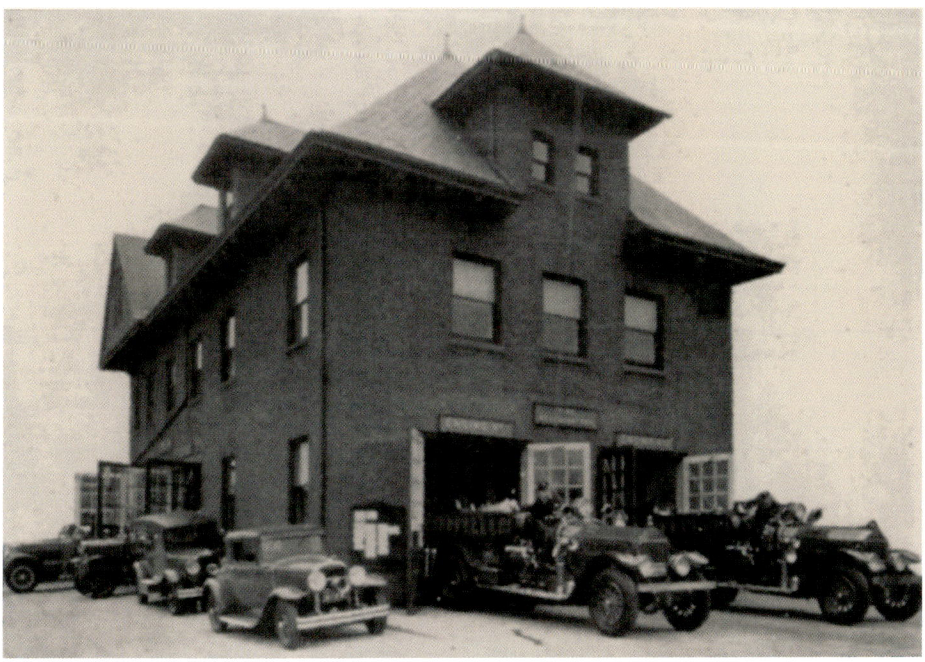

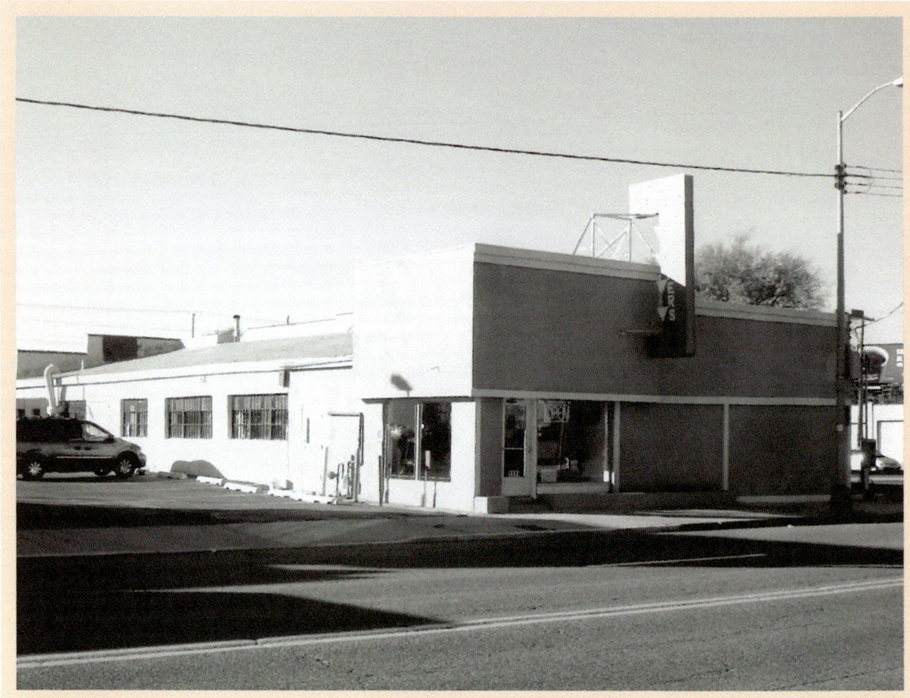

Le Parisien Cleaners and Dyers on Main Street is pictured in the 1940s, shortly after the building was refaced and expanded. During the 1930s, Le Parisien had a fleet of nearly a dozen service trucks. Still operating today, Le Parisien has been at the same location since opening for business in 1929. The firm is well known as a specialist in the cleaning and storage of furs. (Appleby Collection.)

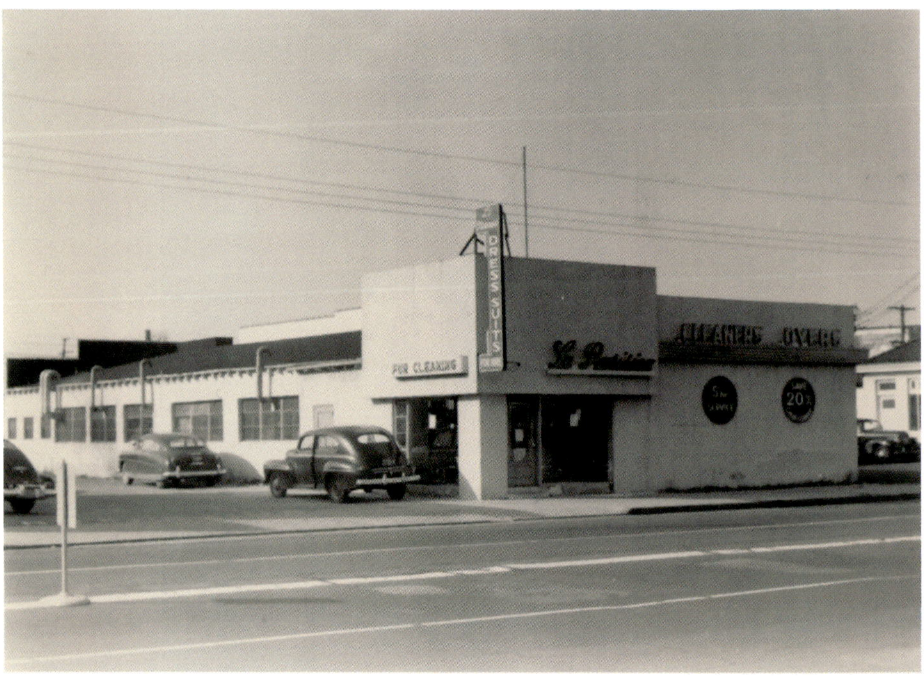

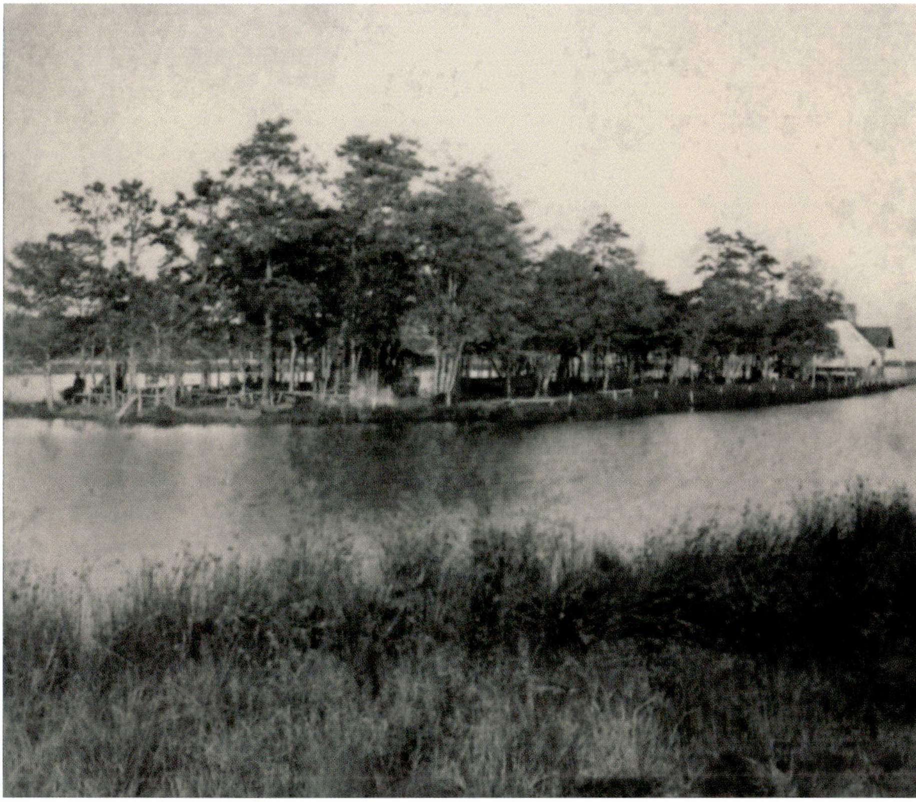

This photograph of St. John's Island in Sunset Lake was taken by the Pach brothers in the early 1870s. Gustavus, Gotthelf, and Morris Pach came from Germany to New York City, where they set up a photography shop in the Bowery in 1865. By 1868, they had opened up a location in Long Branch and, shortly afterward, in Ocean Grove. They catered to the tourist industry. Many of their area images show early boating activity on Wesley and Sunset Lakes.

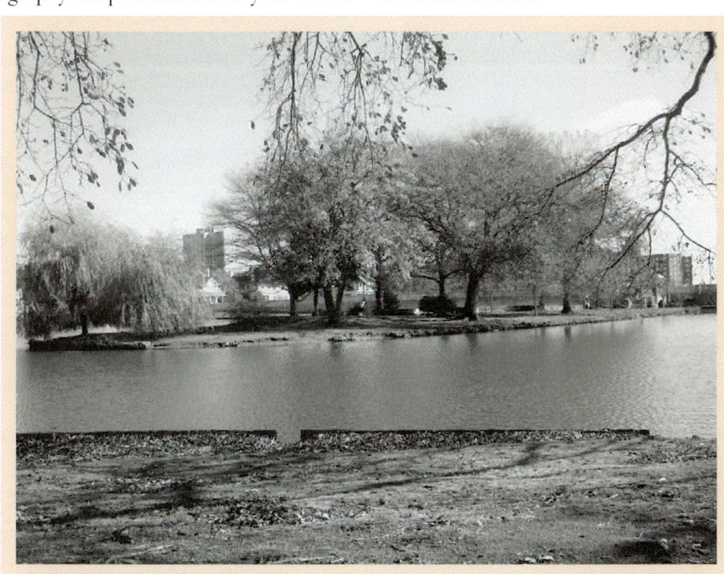

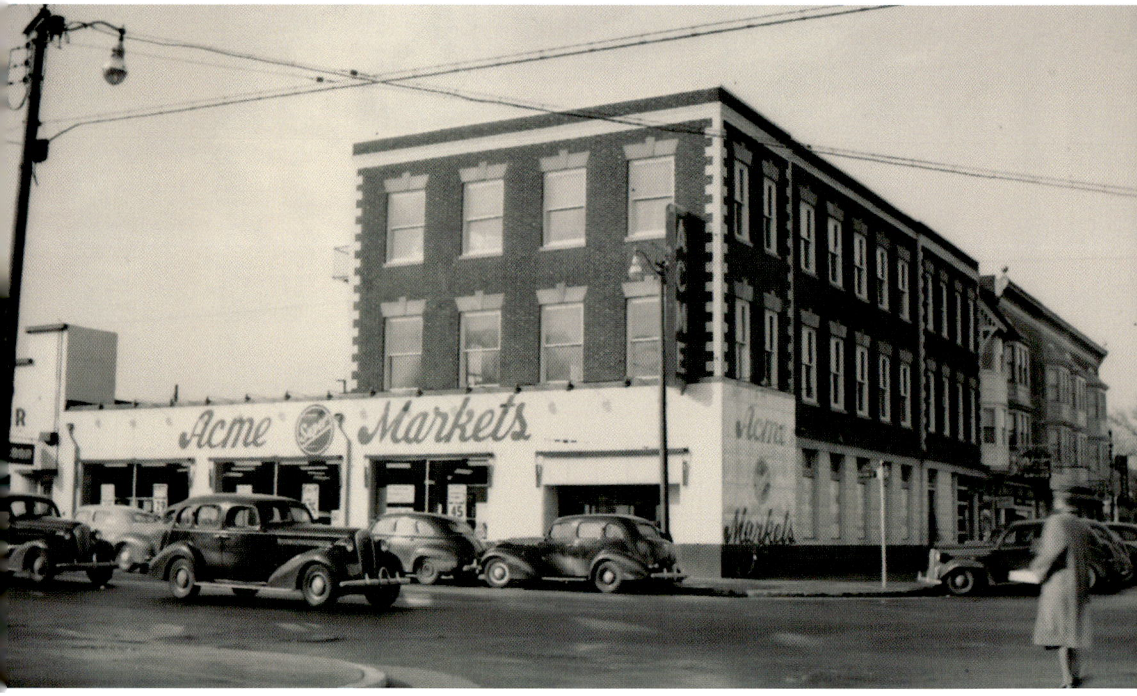

This 1940s view of the Acme market on the 1200 block of Main Street also features the Cameo Bar, which remains visually unchanged. The supermarket building itself had been constructed in the early part of the 20th century. Philadelphia-based Acme Supermarkets opened a location there in the 1920s. Originally home to various manufacturing outfits, the upper floors have been converted to apartments. (Appleby Collection.)

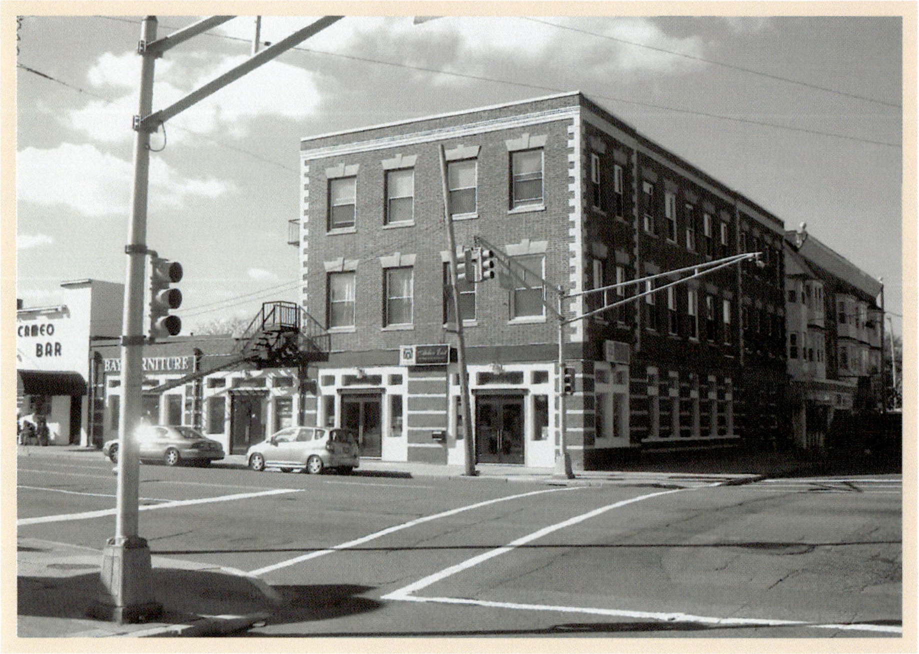

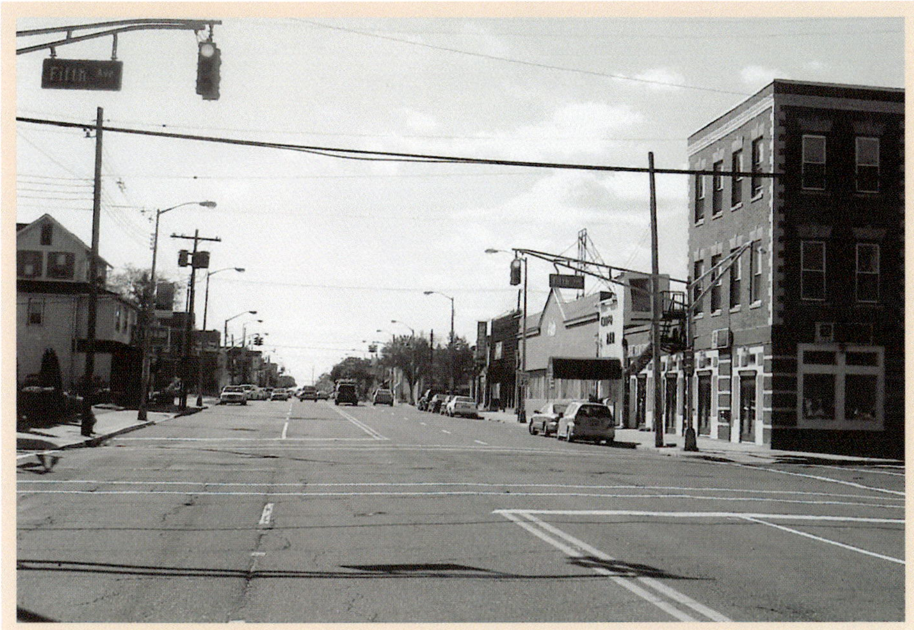

Acme was given stiff competition when A&P purchased the former Nash dealership and set up shop on the opposite side of the Cameo Bar in the late 1930s. By the time this photograph was taken in September 1962, Acme had relocated to Ocean Township, and Olden Paint had moved into the former Acme building. It is currently home to an interior design studio and a discount furniture showroom. (Appleby Collection.)

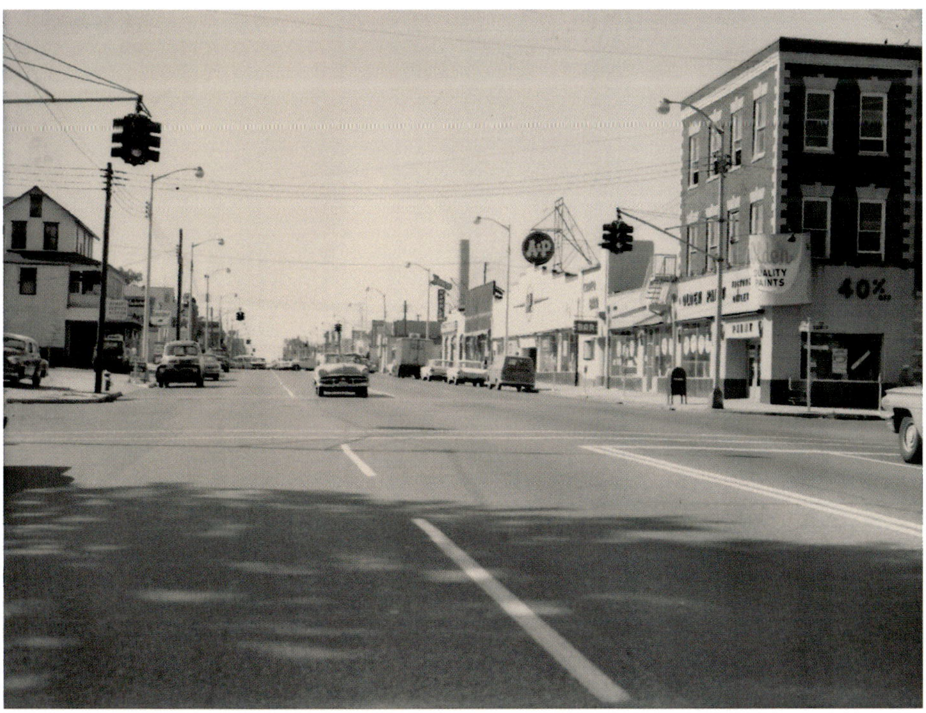

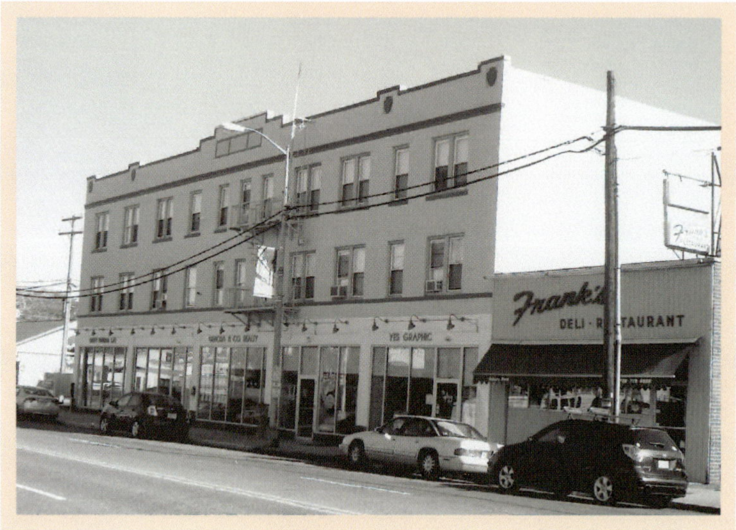

The building complex located at the eastern corner of Sixth Avenue and Main Street was built by Kate Van Cleaf in 1928. The Sixth Avenue Apartments opened for lease that very year. Dan's Market in the northernmost corner was an early long-term tenant. Louis Shoe Repair constructed the adjoining building on the far right. This 1930s view was taken before Louis had moved into the new shop, which has housed the famed Frank's Deli since 1960. (Appleby Collection.)

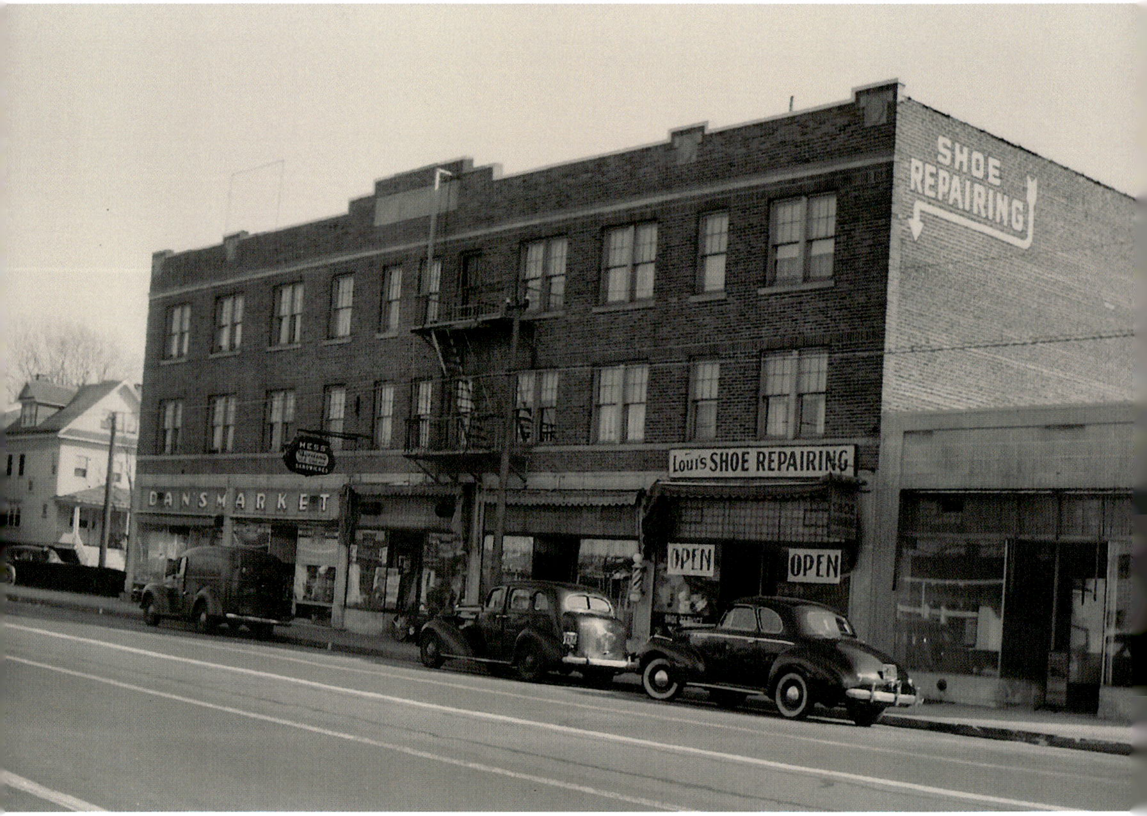

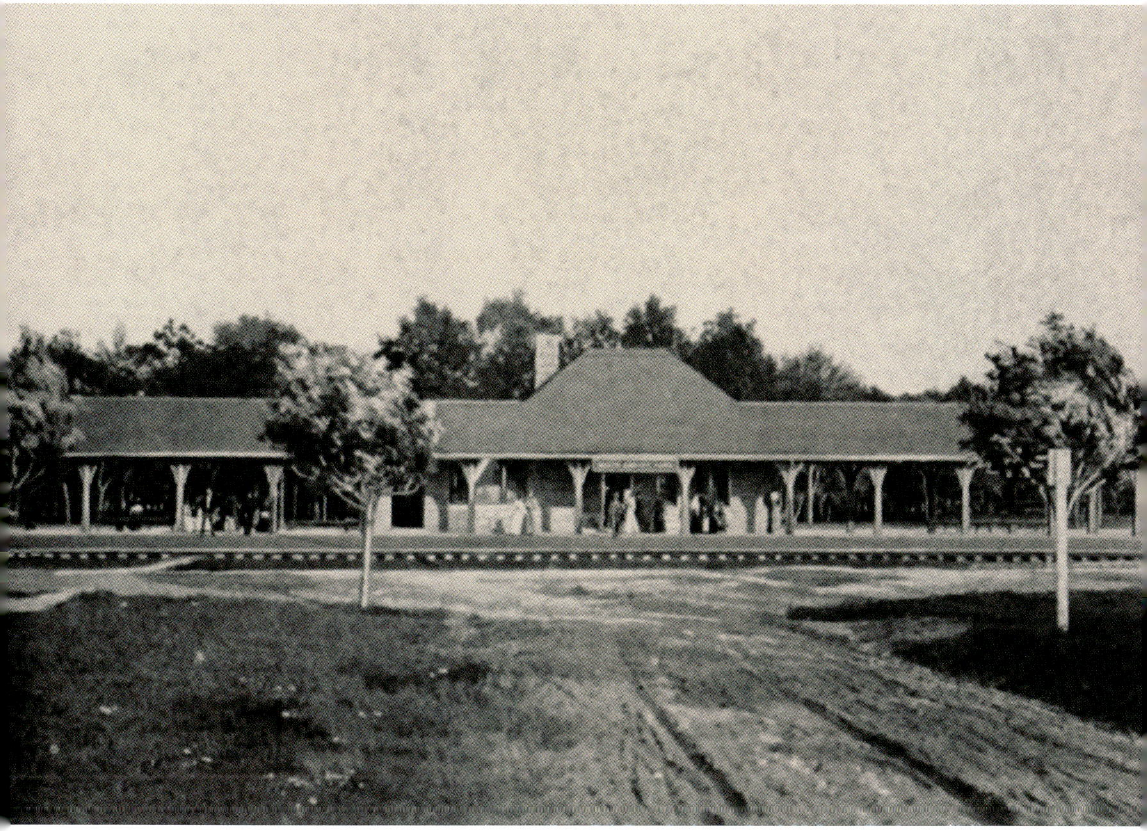

Travel to Asbury Park was so overwhelming that a secondary rail station was built in north Asbury in the late 1880s. Seen here in this 1896 view, a large covered waiting area was built shortly thereafter on the west side of the tracks. As passenger numbers dwindled, service to this station was curtailed and, by the 1980s, stopped altogether. The building is currently occupied by the Visiting Nurse Association.

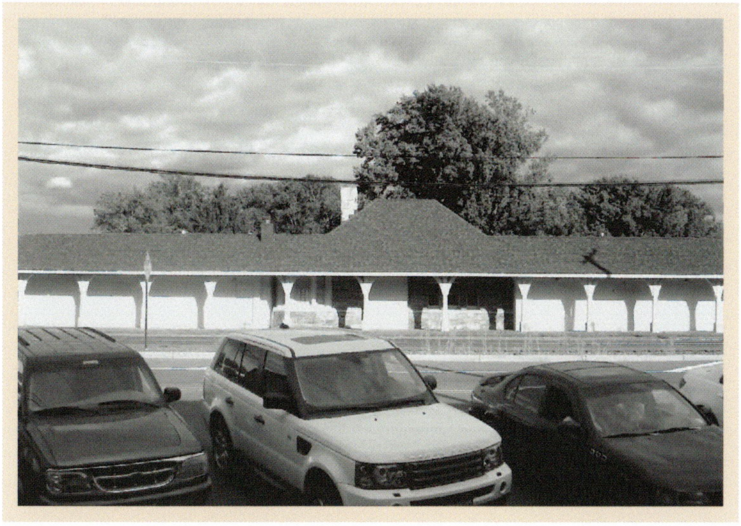

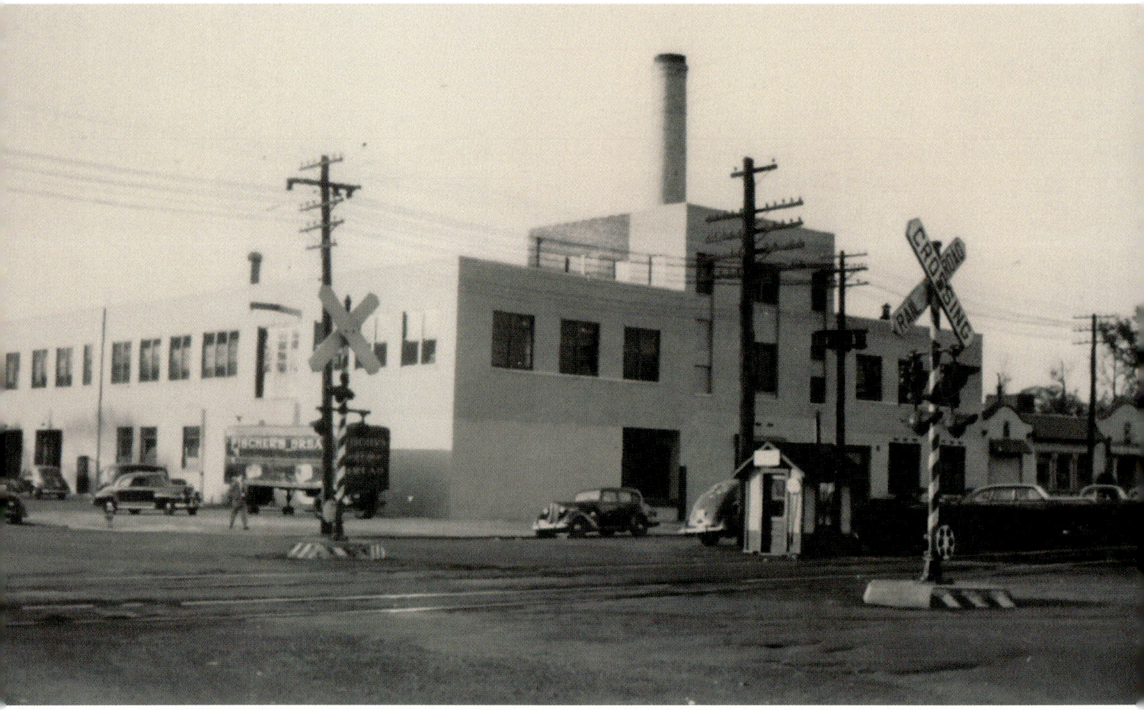

The Fischer Baking Company was founded in Newark and, in 1924, opened a branch in Asbury Park, originally located on Third Avenue. In 1929, the company built a large complex between Fourth and Fifth Avenues on Railroad Avenue (now Memorial Drive). Pictured in the 1940s after an expansion, the bakery closed its doors in 1965. In 1973, Jersey Shore Addiction Services Healthcare opened at this location. JSAS provides comprehensive outpatient substance abuse treatment and HIV counseling. (Appleby Collection.)

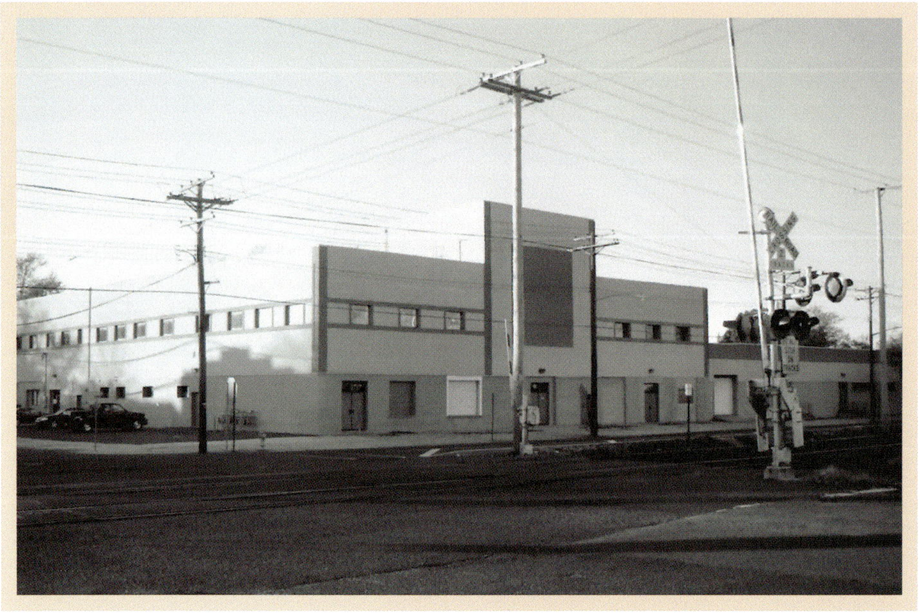

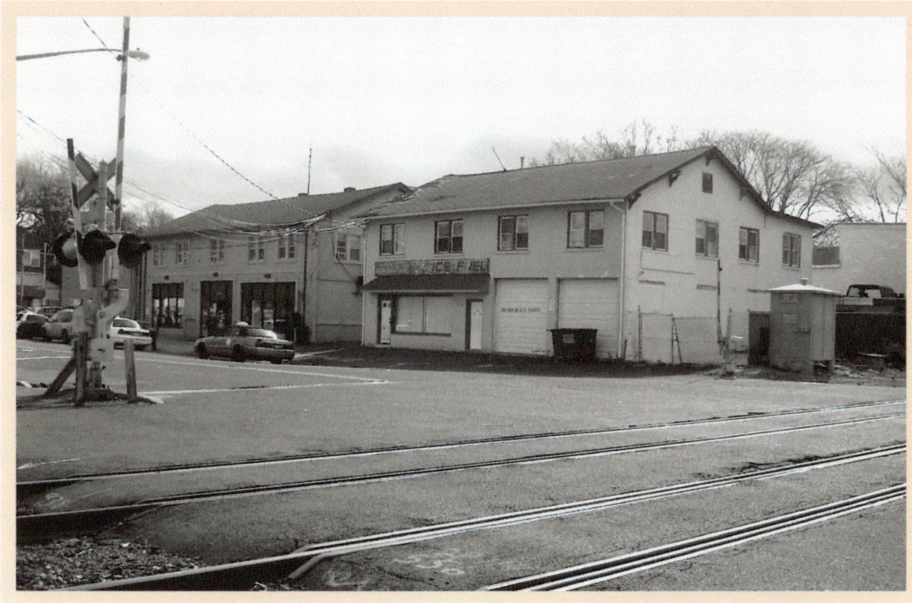

These two buildings on the 800 block of First Avenue and Memorial Drive were erected in 1923. Shown here in the early 1930s, Thompson's Garage (at left) advertised expert automotive winterization. The Olson Roofing Company, which specialized in roofing, sidewalls, and insulation, stands next to tracks with a rail spur leading to the side loading dock. Apartments and small businesses occupy the buildings at present. (Appleby Collection.)

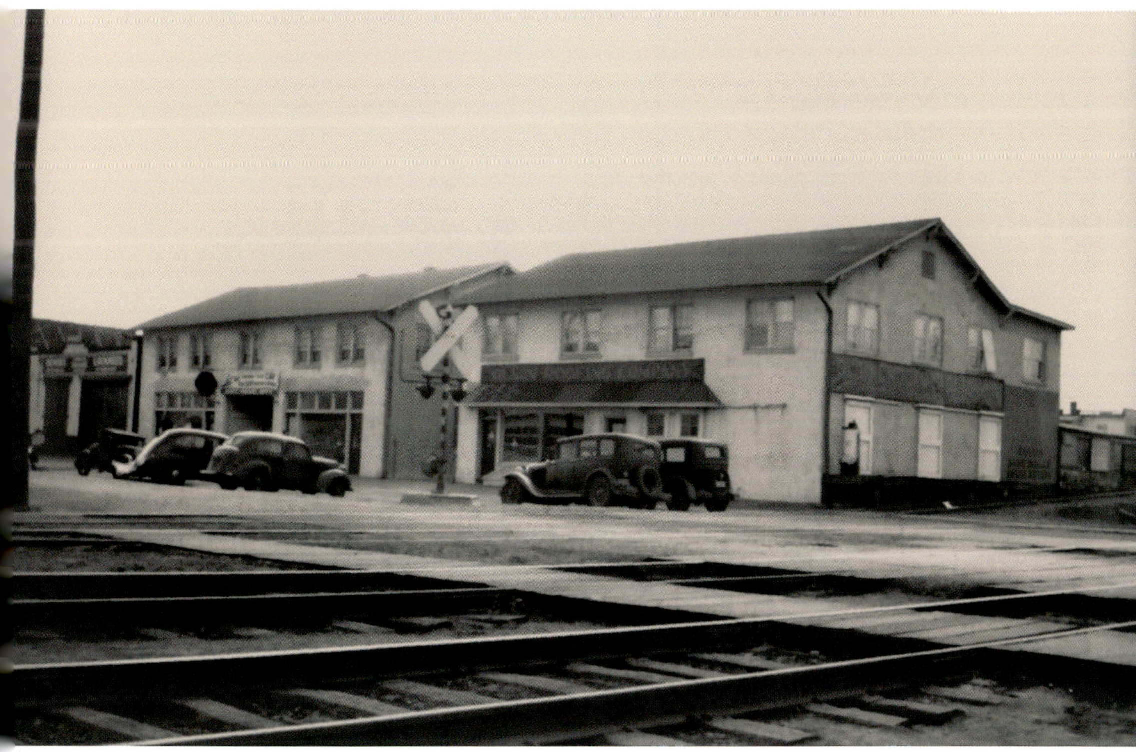

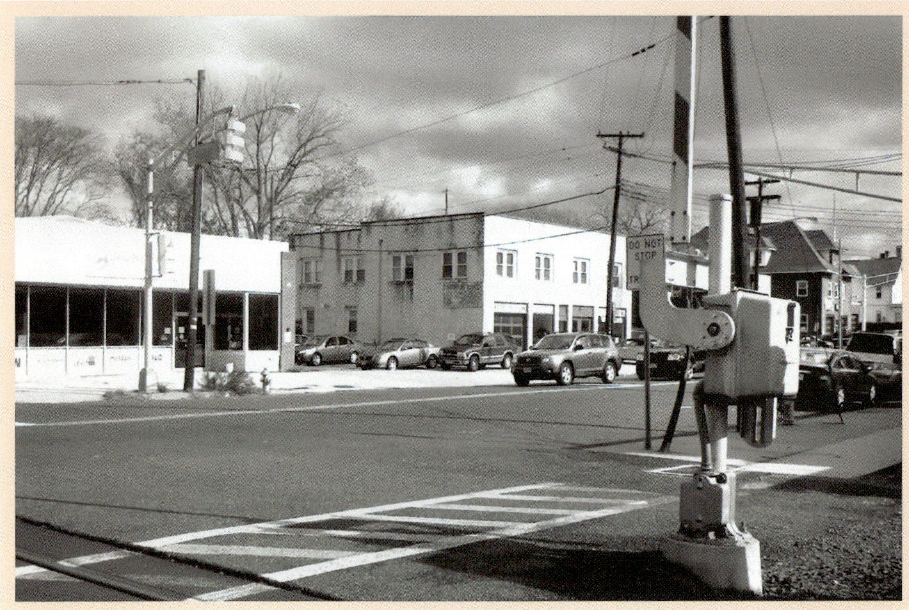

Elisha Stout started his coal yard in 1878 at the intersection of Railroad and Asbury Avenues. The buildings, pictured in this mid-1930s view, were constructed in 1932. Asbury Auto Tops still occupies the structure to the left of the coal yard office. The yard closed in the late 1940s, and the office building was razed 10 years later. In 1951, the structure that currently houses Asbury Electric Supply was built on the coal yard site. (Appleby Collection.)

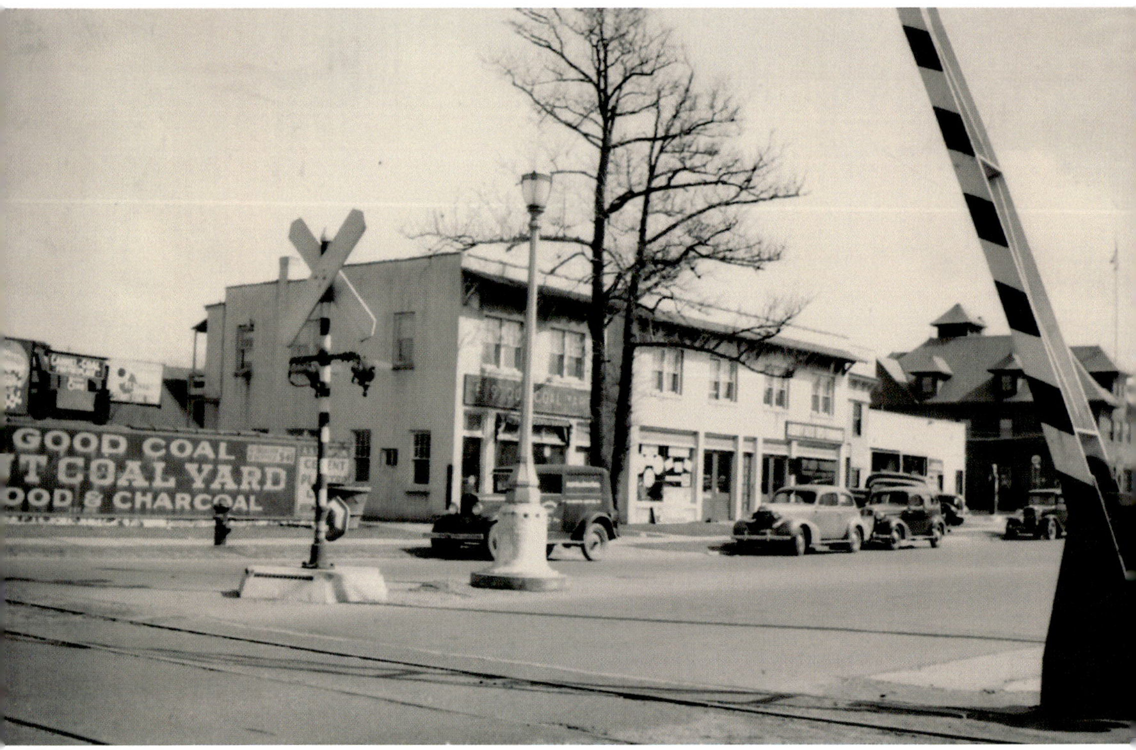

CHAPTER 2

NEPTUNE AND OCEAN GROVE

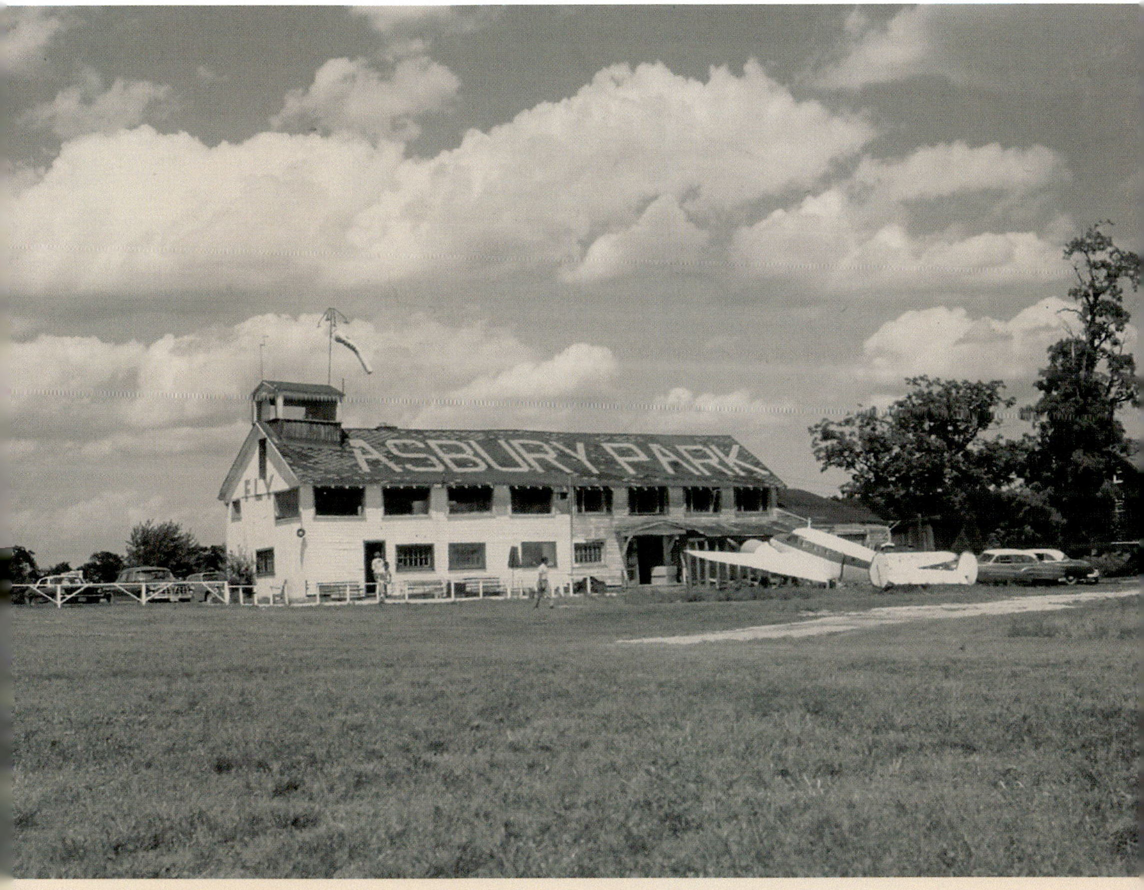

Isaac "Ike" Schlossbach, a 1909 graduate of Neptune High School, was a naval hero who accompanied Adm. Richard Byrd on his expeditions to Antarctica. After he retired in 1938, he built an airport in the vicinity of Jumping Brook Road and Route 66. This picture dates from 1965. The airport was closed in 1977. (Courtesy Emmett Francois.)

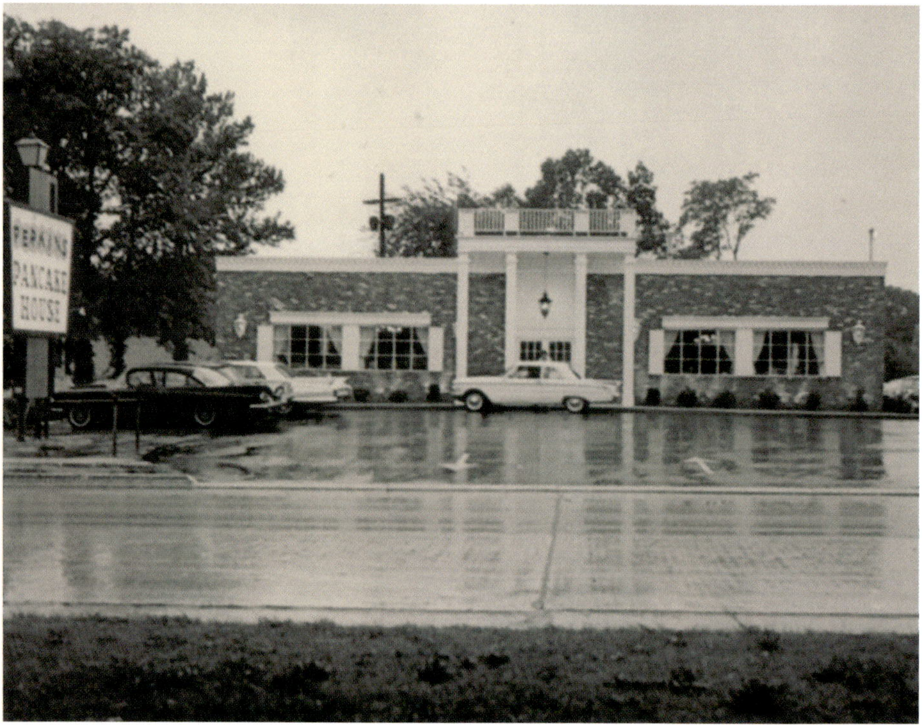

What would life be like without a rainy weekend morning out with the family for breakfast at Perkins on the Asbury Circle? The spot has hosted a number of different restaurants since the 1930s. In 1962, Ohio-based Perkins Pancakes built a new restaurant on the site. Cosmetic changes have been made to the exterior, but the overall atmosphere remains unchanged. Seen above in the mid-1960s, this is one of the oldest extant continually operated Perkins locations.

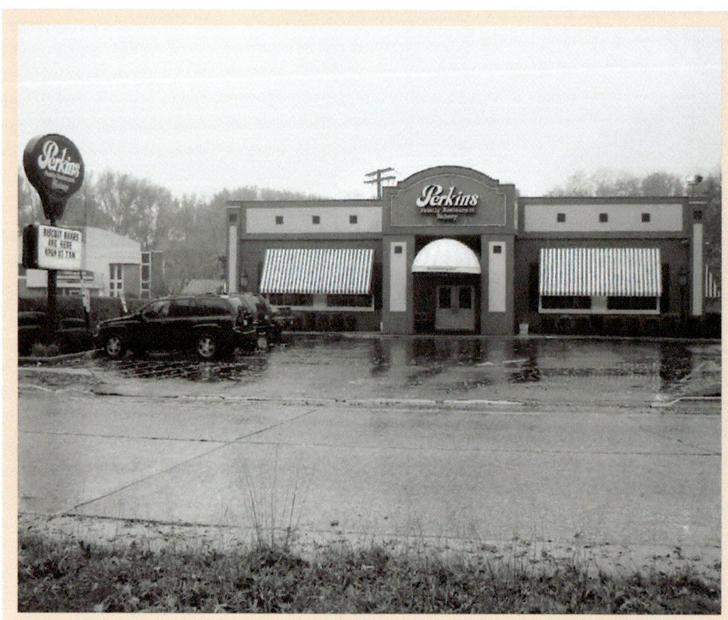

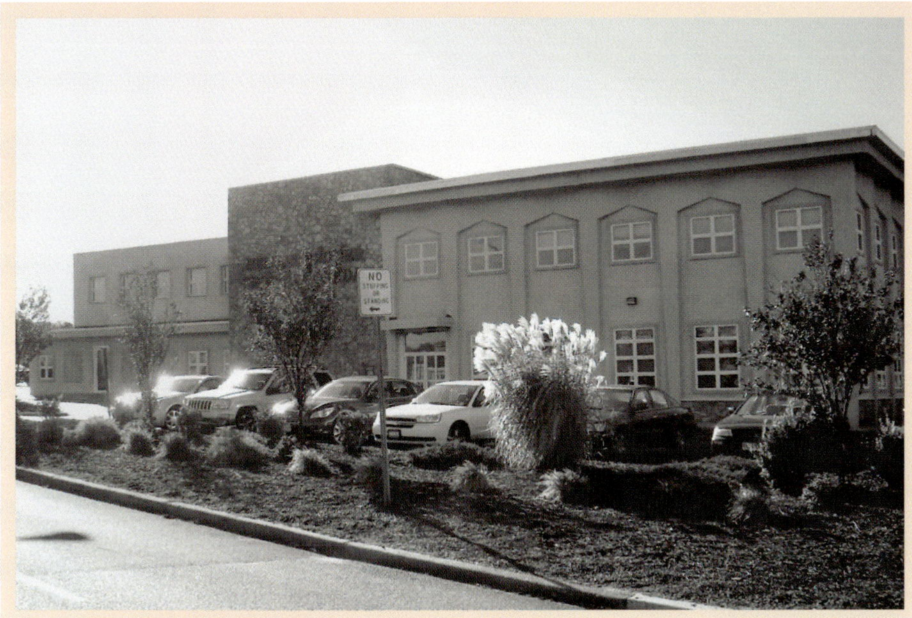

The New Jersey National Bank branch at the intersection of Neptune Boulevard and Route 66 is pictured below in 1965, shortly after it opened. The New Jersey National Bank was established in Trenton in 1889. Due to many years of growth, mergers, and acquisitions, the bank became very prevalent in the shore area by the 1950s. A law firm purchased the building in 1997 and carried out renovations to suit its needs.

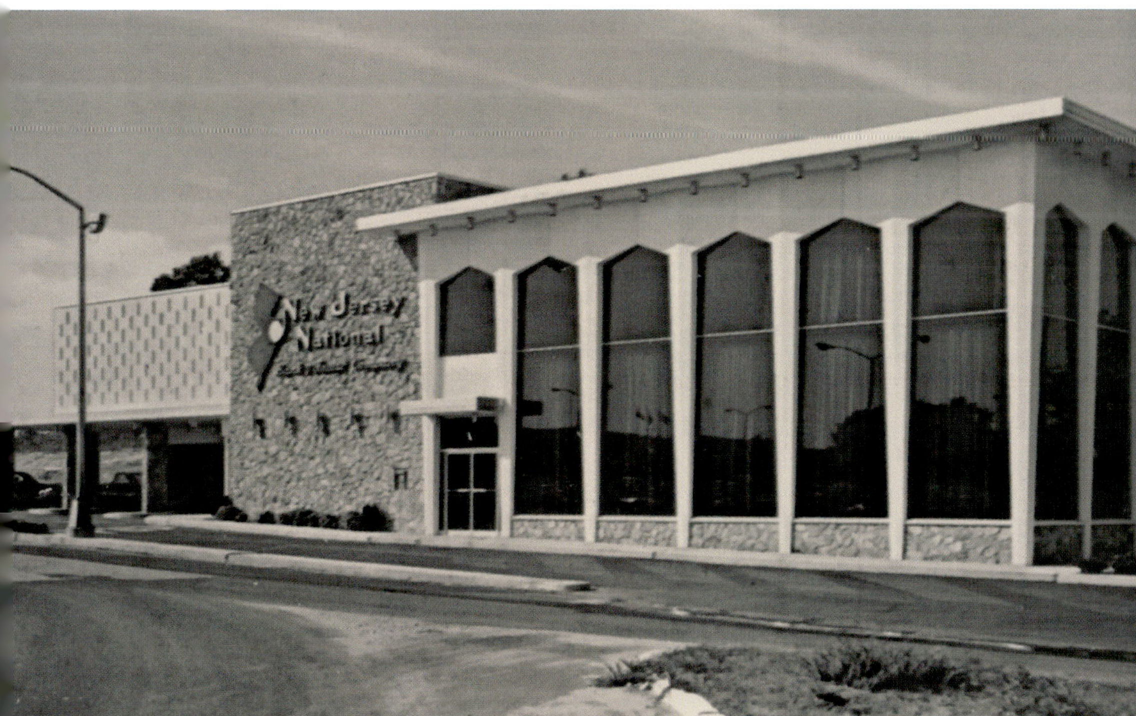

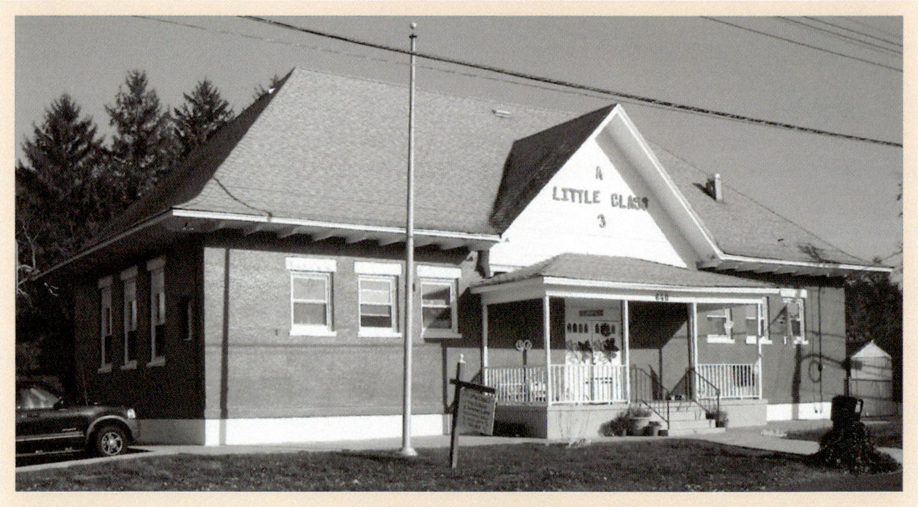

The original Summerfield School was built in 1897 on the southeast corner of Green Grove Road and West Bangs Avenue, pictured here about 1900. In 1929, the little schoolhouse was rendered obsolete when a much larger school was built a half a mile south on Green Grove Road. The original schoolhouse, which housed the Neptune Sportsmens' Club for many years, is currently a private preschool. The 1929 Summerfield building was torn down and replaced in 2006. (Neptune Archives.)

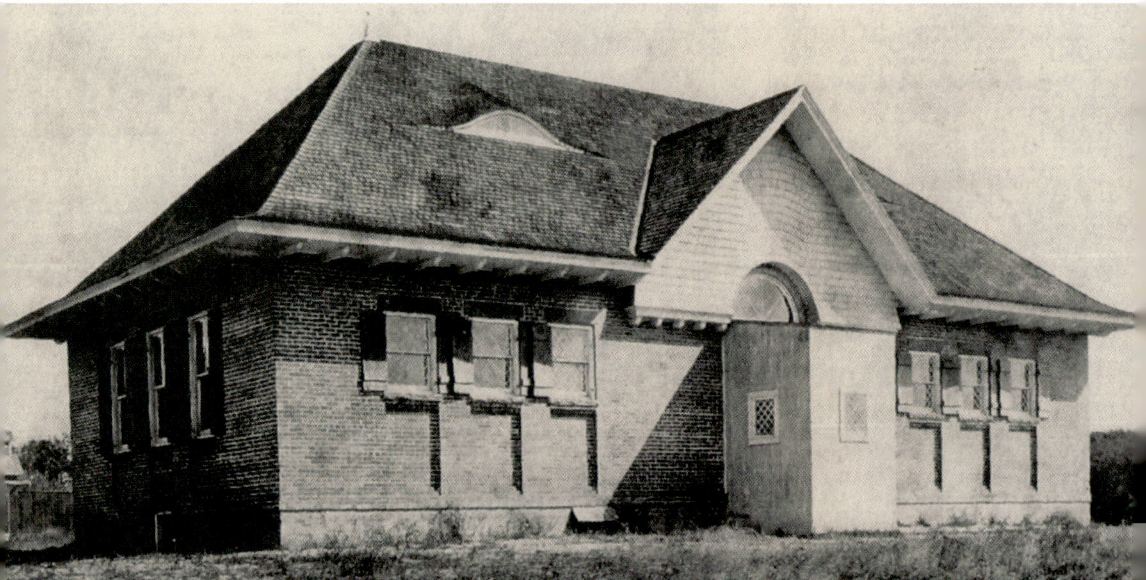

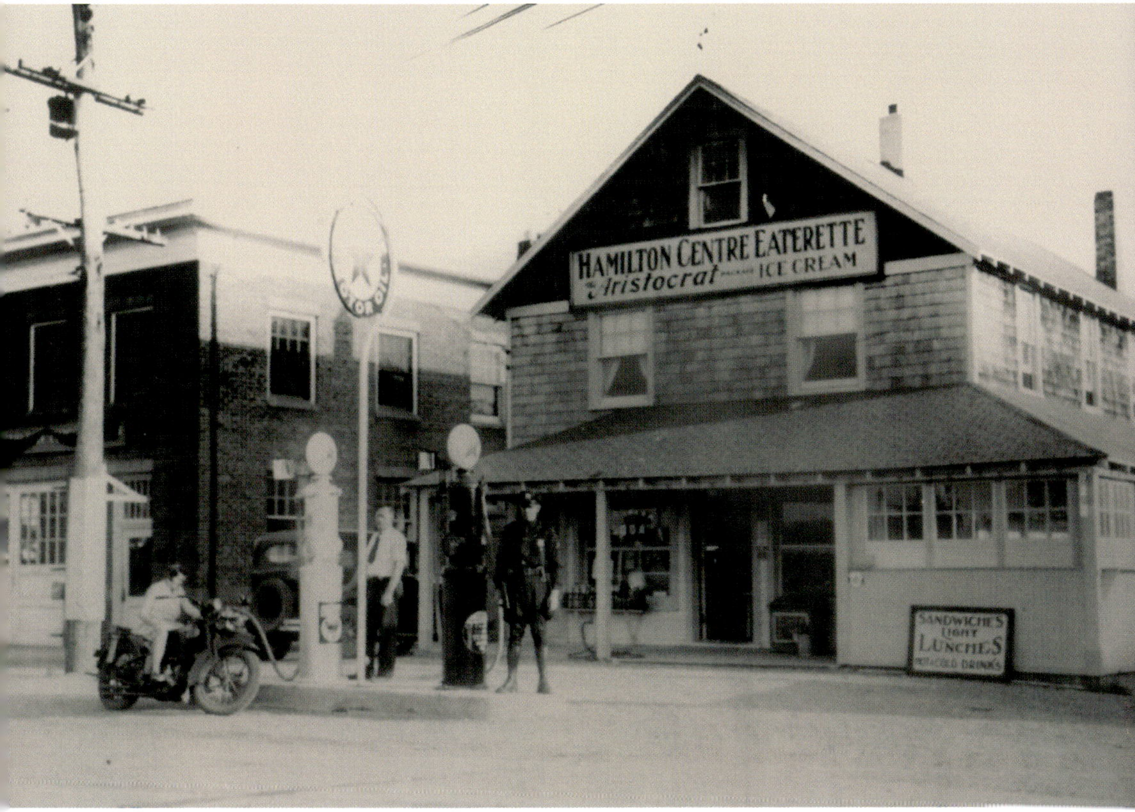

In the 1920s, Hiram Jeliff opened a grocery luncheonette on what is now Old Corlies Avenue. Jeliff lived with his family in the floors above the store. In addition to selling foodstuffs, the location also served as a Texaco vendor, pictured above about 1930. In 1943, alterations and expansions were made to the storefront. The Hamilton Deli and adjoining barbershop are still proudly serving the community. (Neptune Archives.)

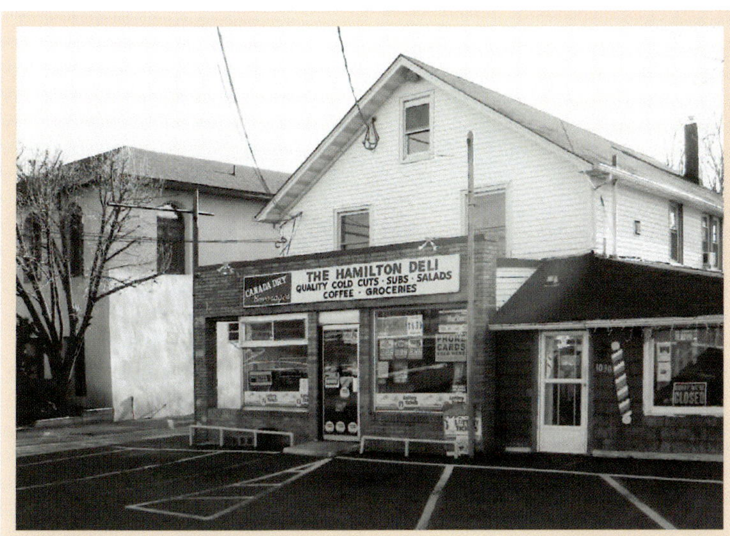

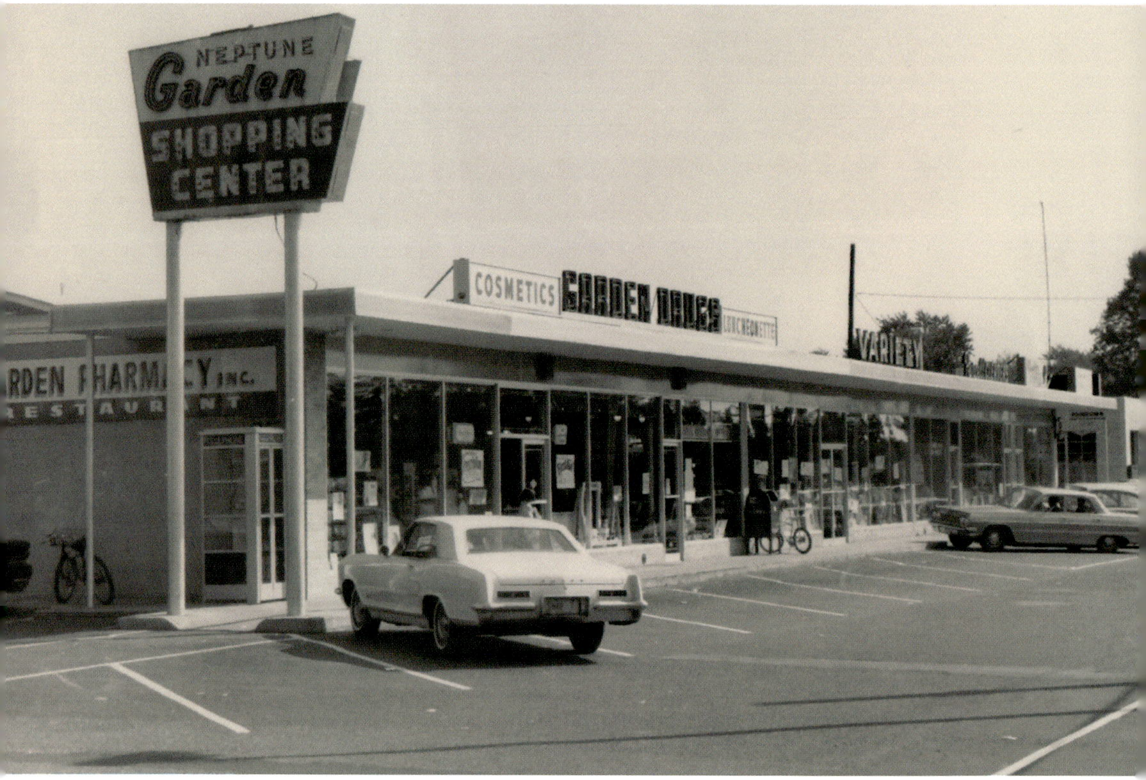

The Neptune Garden Shopping Center is pictured here in the 1960s. The shopping center was built in 1954 with Garden Pharmacy as the anchor store. The business is one of the few remaining independent pharmacy locations in the area. Purcell Cleaners has also been in tenancy since the plaza was constructed. In the late 1960s, an addition to the west was made, which originally housed a Foodtown supermarket. In 2005, a dialysis center opened at the site. (Neptune Archives.)

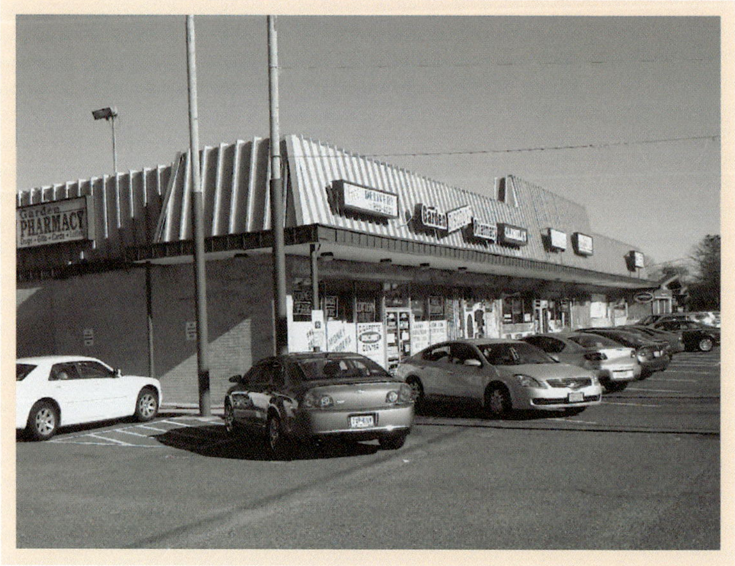

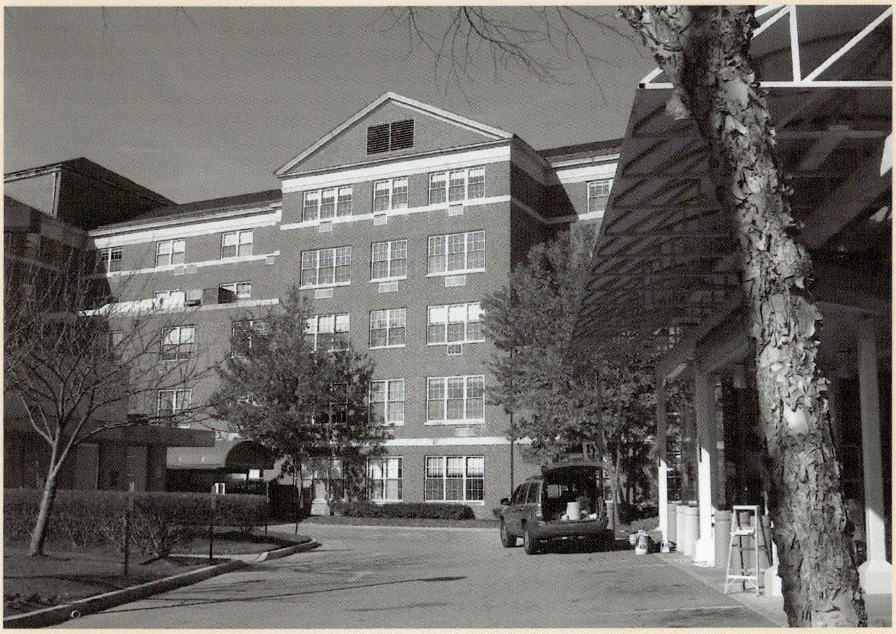

In 1932, Jersey Shore University Medical Center opened its doors as the Fitkin Memorial Hospital. Many additions have been made over the years to the original campus. This image was captured during the July 1959 construction of the east wing, which was carried out by Park Steel and Iron. In 2009, a $300-million expansion was completed, adding nearly 140 new beds, a state-of-the-art trauma center, and a 975-space parking garage. (Park Steel and Iron.)

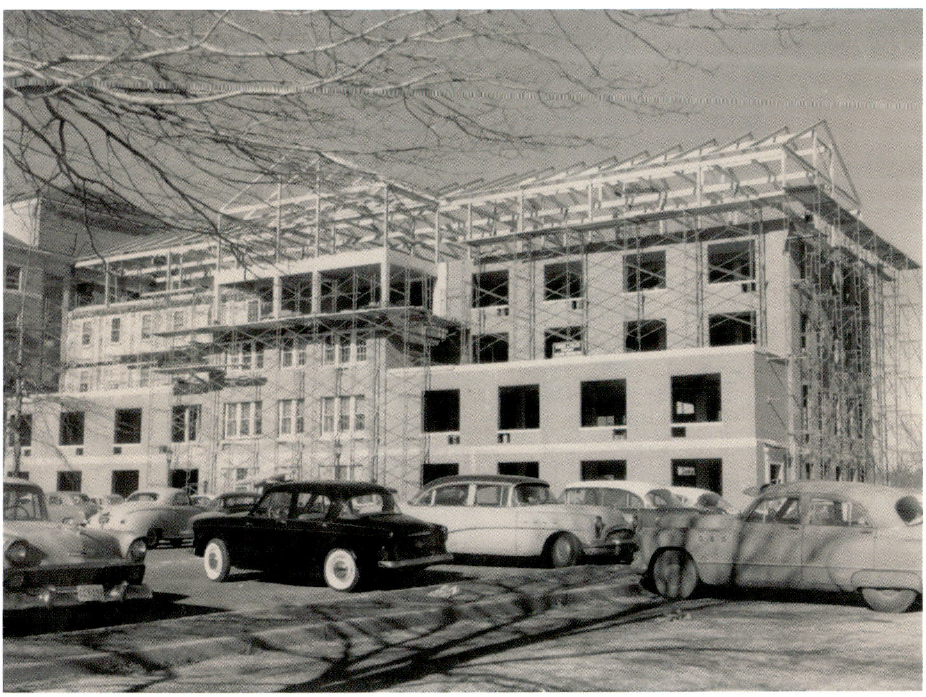

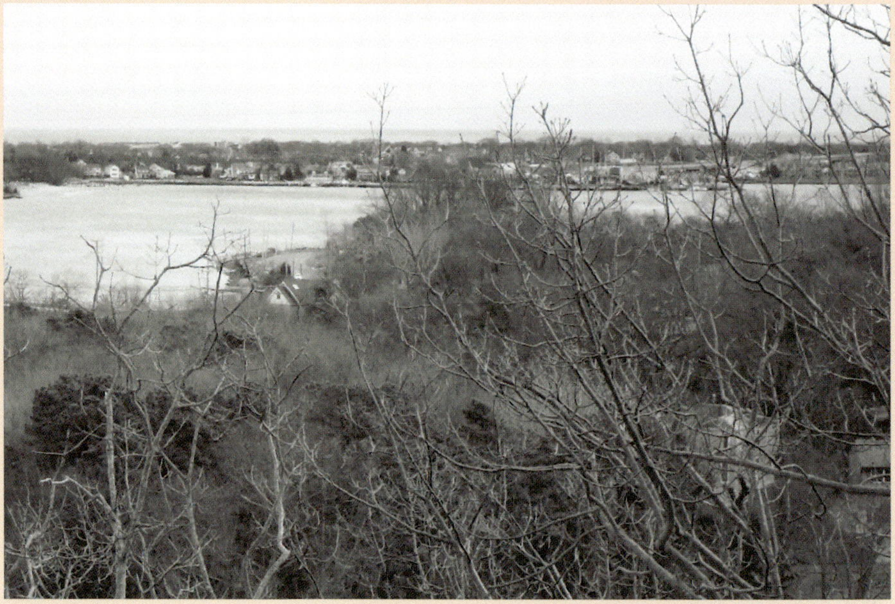

The highest point in Shark River Hills is Skytop, which rises 118 feet above sea level. It is also known as Money Hill due to rumors that have persisted for centuries claiming it is the location where notorious pirate Capt. William Kidd buried his treasure. A comparison of a 2010 view above with a 1920s scene below shows the drastic advance of the tree line. Asbury Park, Ocean Grove, Spring Lake, and the ocean can all be viewed from this spot on a clear day. (Now image courtesy James Gilligan.)

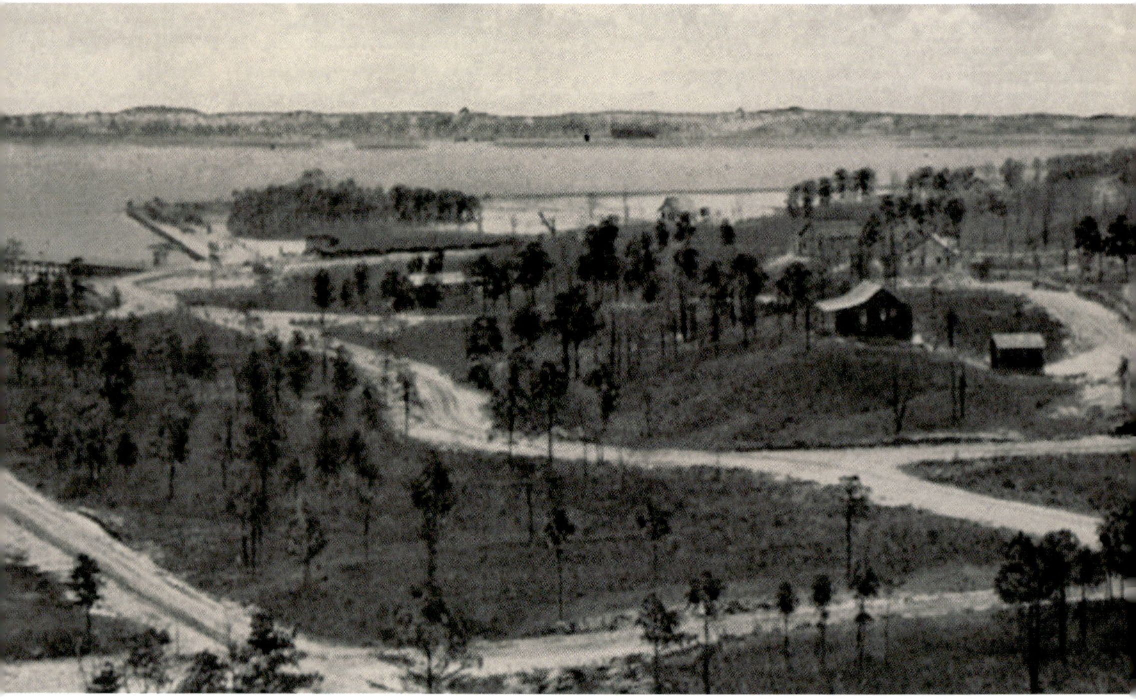

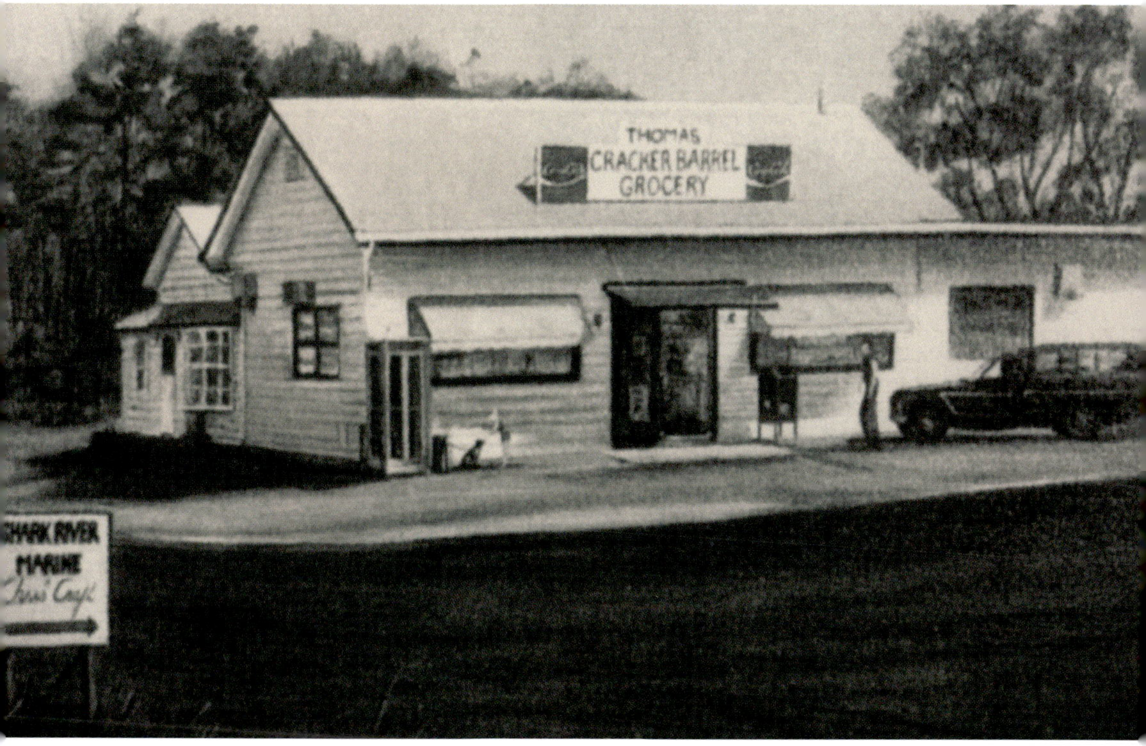

Henry Dolan opened a general store out of his home in 1925, two years after the completion of Tucker's Point Bridge, which connected Neptune City with Shark River Hills. Dolan was aware of the prime location of his venture, and it has remained a familiar destination to Hills residents to this day. The Blauvelt family purchased the property in 1951 and renamed it the Cracker Barrel. The photograph seen here is from the 1960s. (Neptune Archives.)

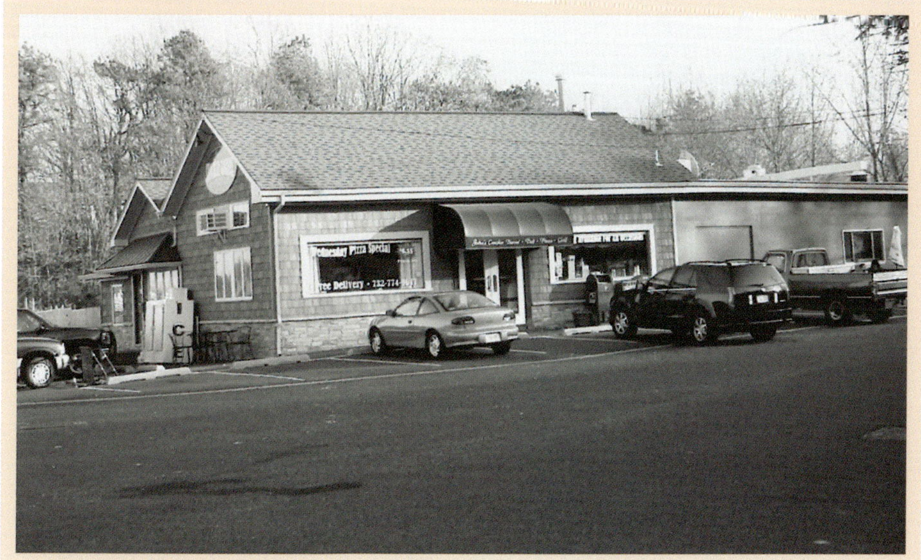

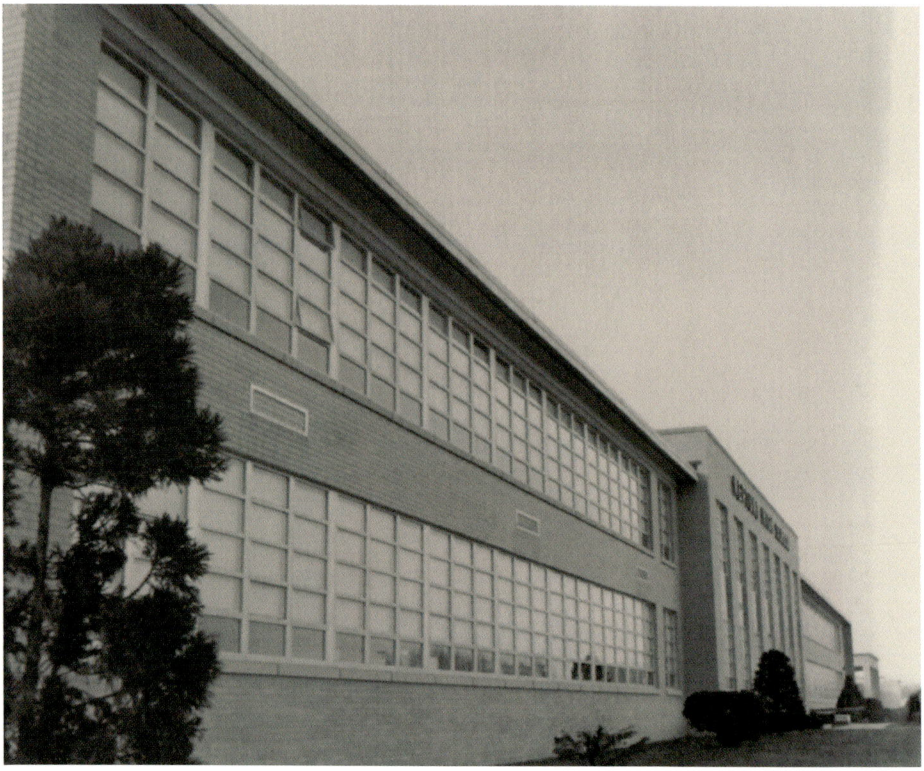

The need for a larger, modern high school that was more centrally located within Neptune prompted the township to purchase the Knight Farm property. The school was competed in 1960. In 1971, Neptune would also move its municipal offices to the south end of the property, where the township built an all-inclusive complex next to the school. This image was captured in the mid-1960s. In 2006, a 134,000-square-foot expansion was completed, more than doubling the size of the school. (Courtesy Ronan Corio.)

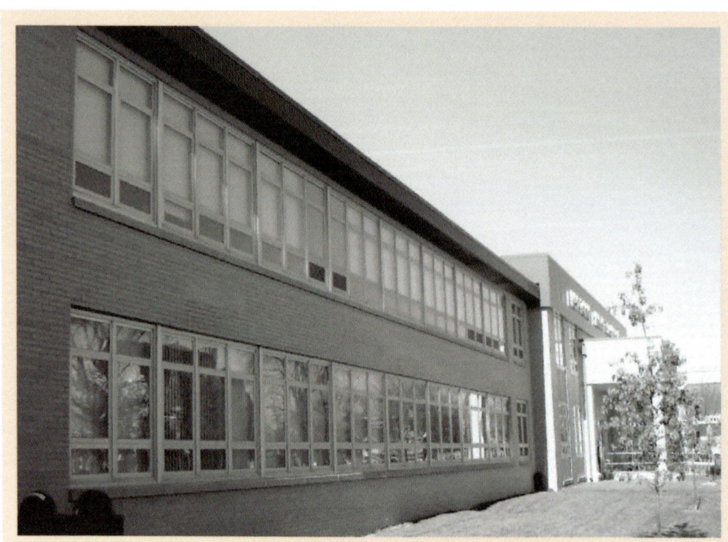

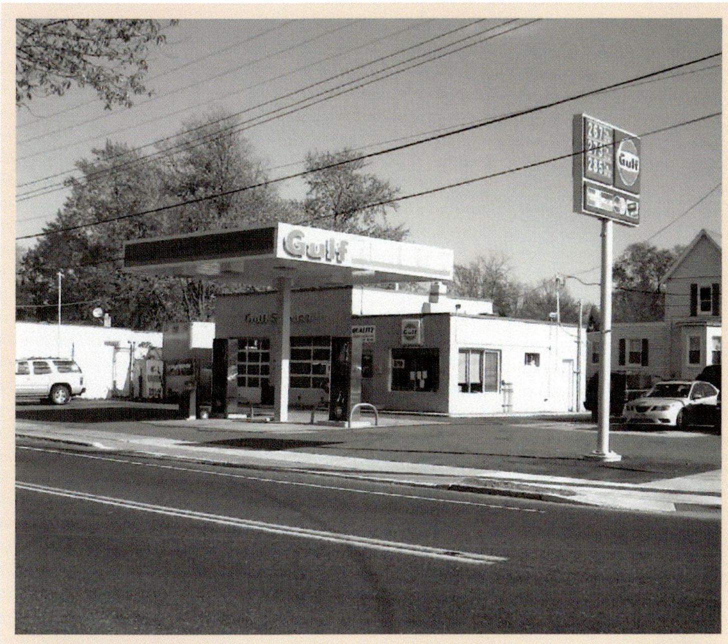

Jean Paul Getty had taken over Tidewater Oil Company in 1937, and it immediately began expanding its operations. The Flying A Service Station at the northeast corner of Route 35 and Fifth Avenue was built in the mid-1940s. In this 1965 photograph, Clem Latshaw has an auto repair service in the garage. Although it has changed hands a few times, the business is still operational, currently serving as a Gulf station. (Appleby Collection.)

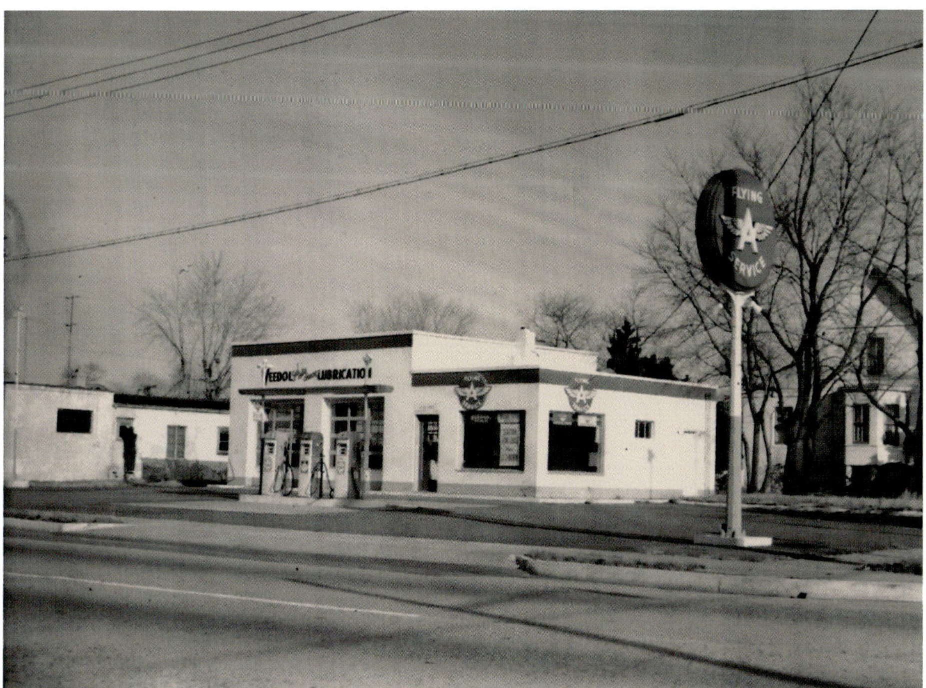

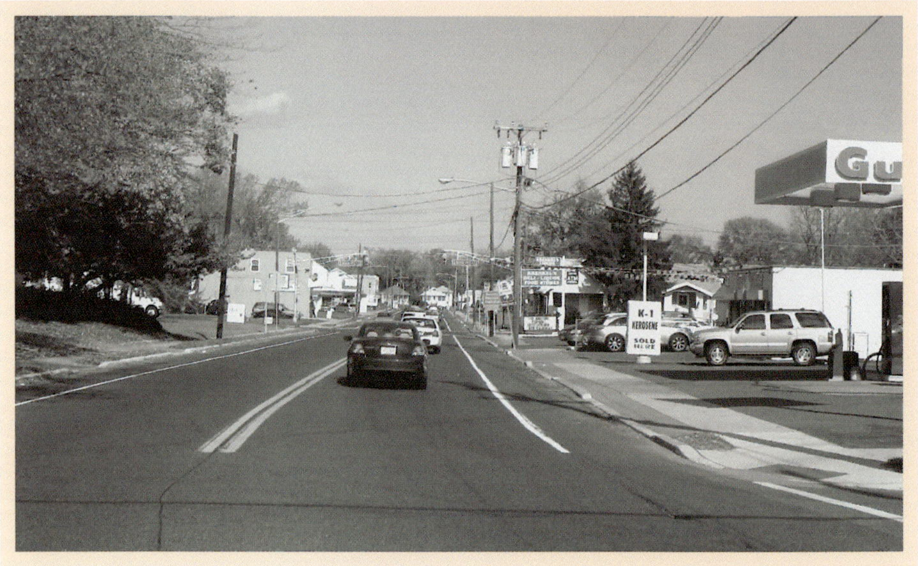

This view of Route 35 looking north from Fifth Avenue was made in December 1965. The building at the far right was constructed in the late 1940s and housed A.J. Ulrich Appliances at the time. Behind Ulrich's was the Atlantic Market, built in the early 1960s, a forerunner of today's convenience store. Today, the structures house the Neptune Smoke Shop and Krenkel's Deli and Liquors, respectively. (Appleby Collection.)

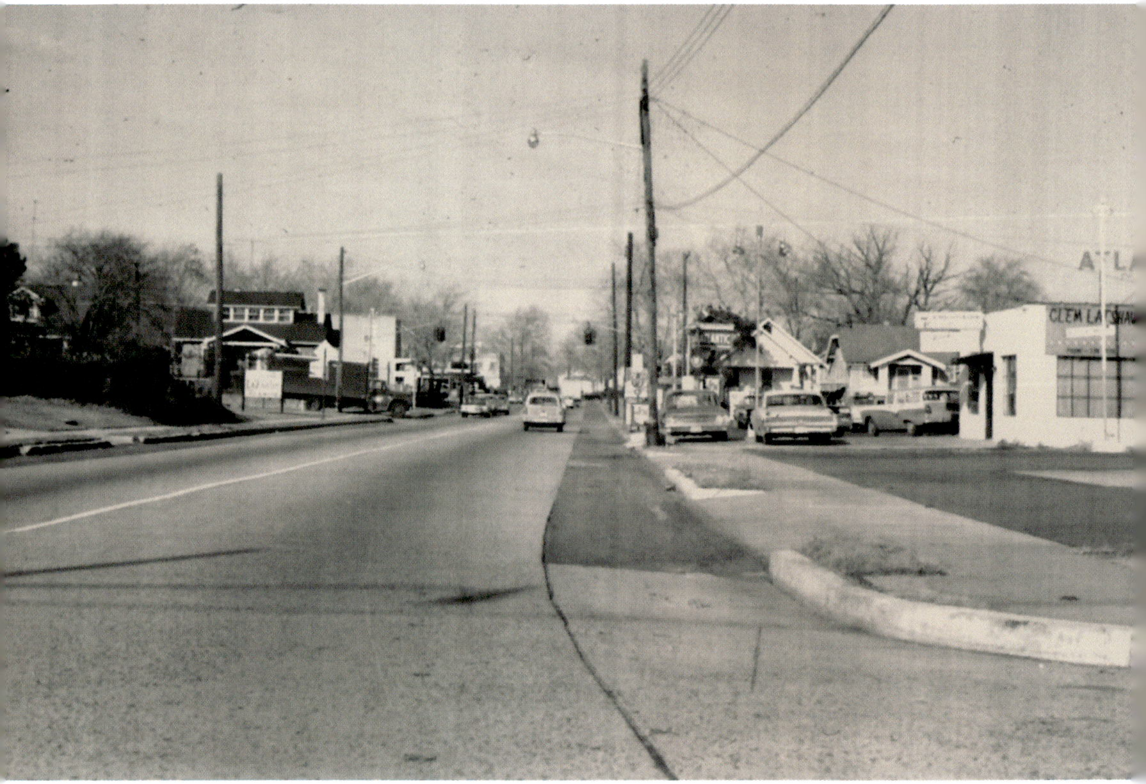

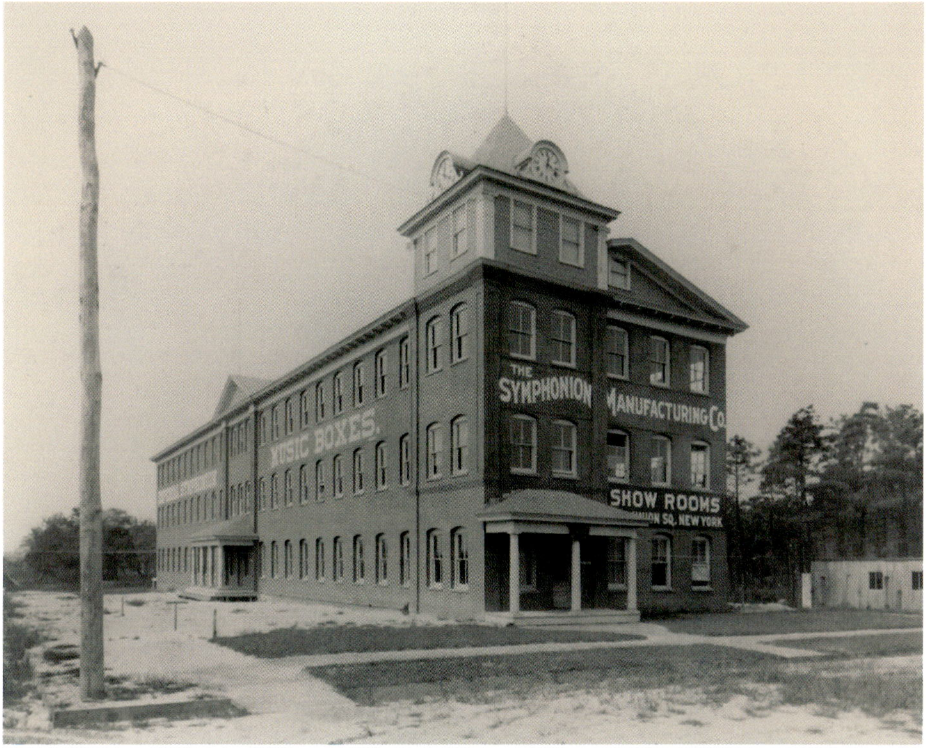

The longtime home of the S.S. Adams Company is shown here in its original incarnation in the mid-1890s. The factory was constructed in 1893 by the Symphonium Company, a German music box maker. The structure housed various manufacturing outfits after Symphonium's demise in 1904. Sorenson Adams, inventor of the dribble glass and the joy buzzer, bought the building in 1932. There are currently plans to convert the structure into condo units. (Steve and Jere Ryder Collection.)

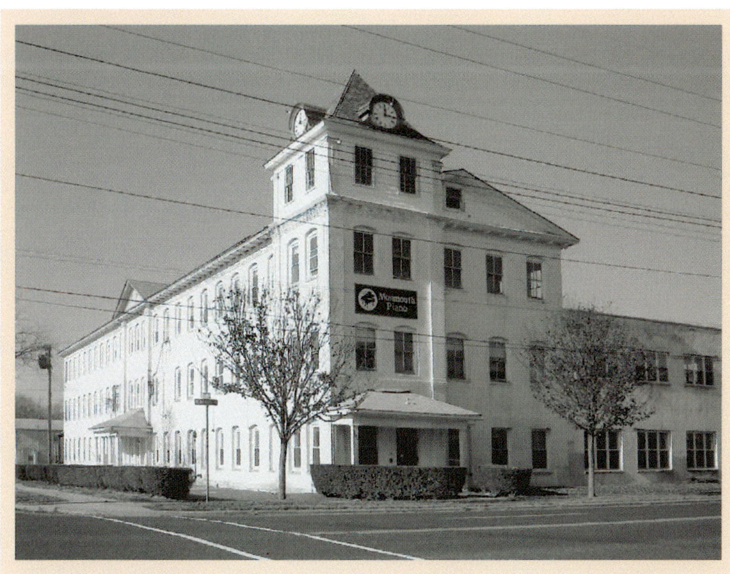

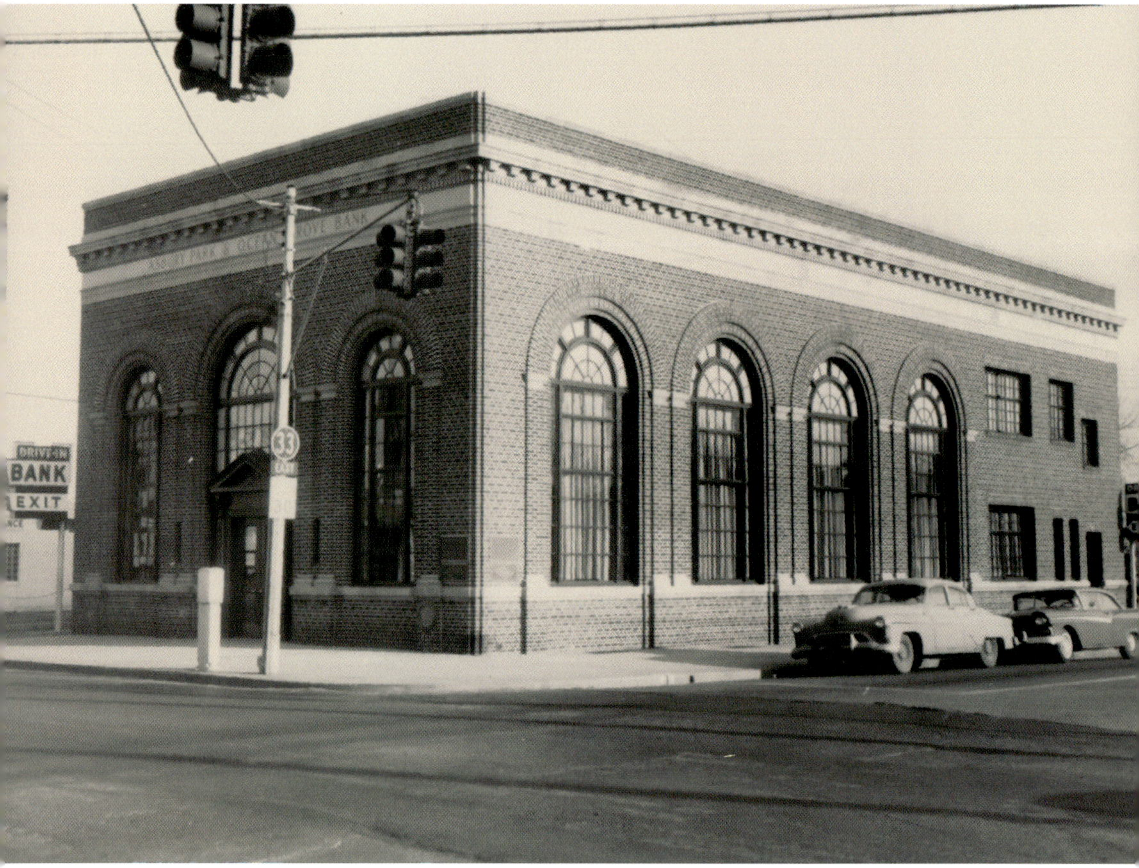

The Asbury Park and Ocean Grove Bank was established in 1889 in Asbury Park. In the 1920s, it built a branch on the southeast corner of Atkins and Corlies (Route 33) Avenues. Pictured here in the mid-1950s, the bank was one of the first area locations to offer drive-through service. The building currently houses the Capernaum French Church. (Appleby Collection.)

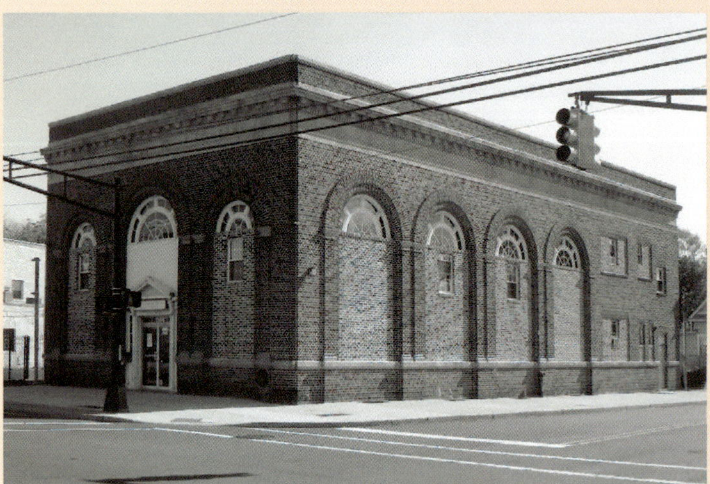

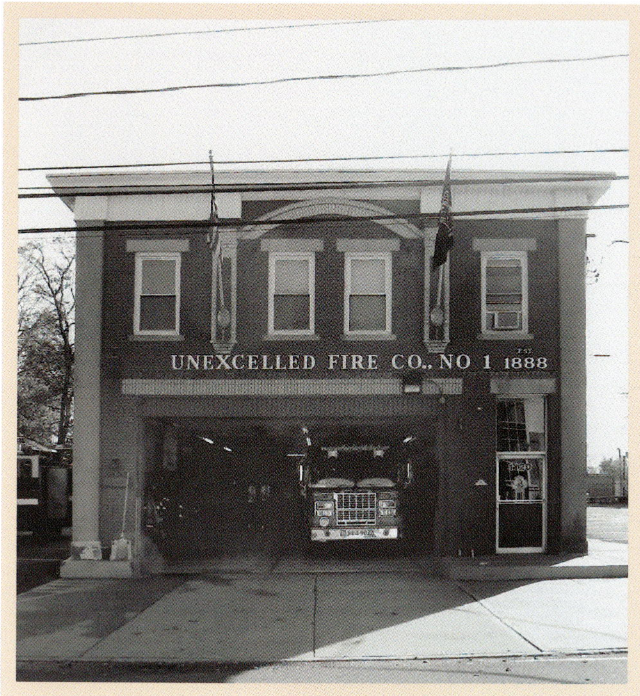

It is hard to believe that these two photographs are of the same building, but they are. The Unexcelled Fire Company was organized in 1888. In the summer of 1890, the company broke ground for a firehouse, pictured here about 1900. Extensive additions were undertaken in 1924. The original roofline was maintained in the front design of the building. (Neptune Archives.)

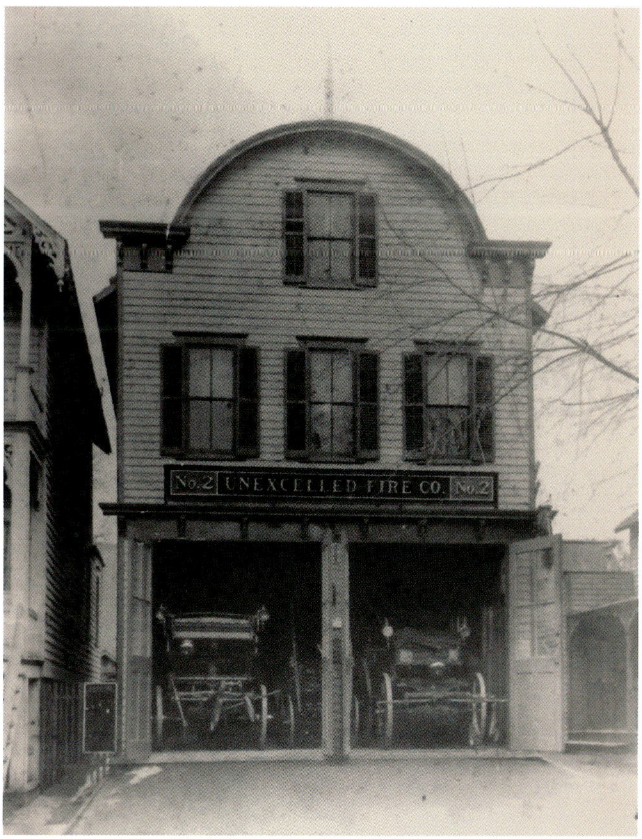

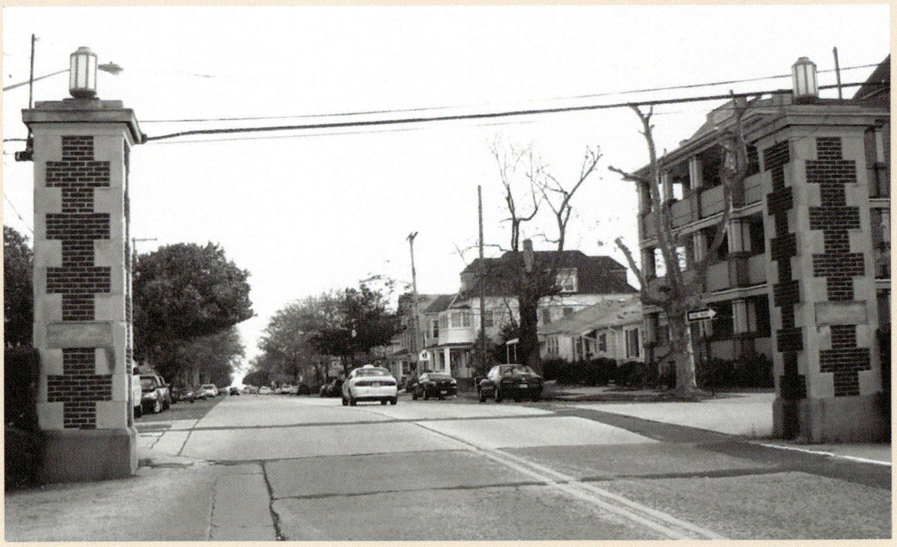

An infamous blue law prohibiting Sunday driving is documented here a few years before the courts determined that the statute was illegal in 1981. Not only was it illegal to drive in Ocean Grove, but it was also illegal to have a car parked on the street there. These gates, actually the third incarnation at the western end of Main Avenue, were constructed in 1916. The modern photograph was taken on a Sunday morning.

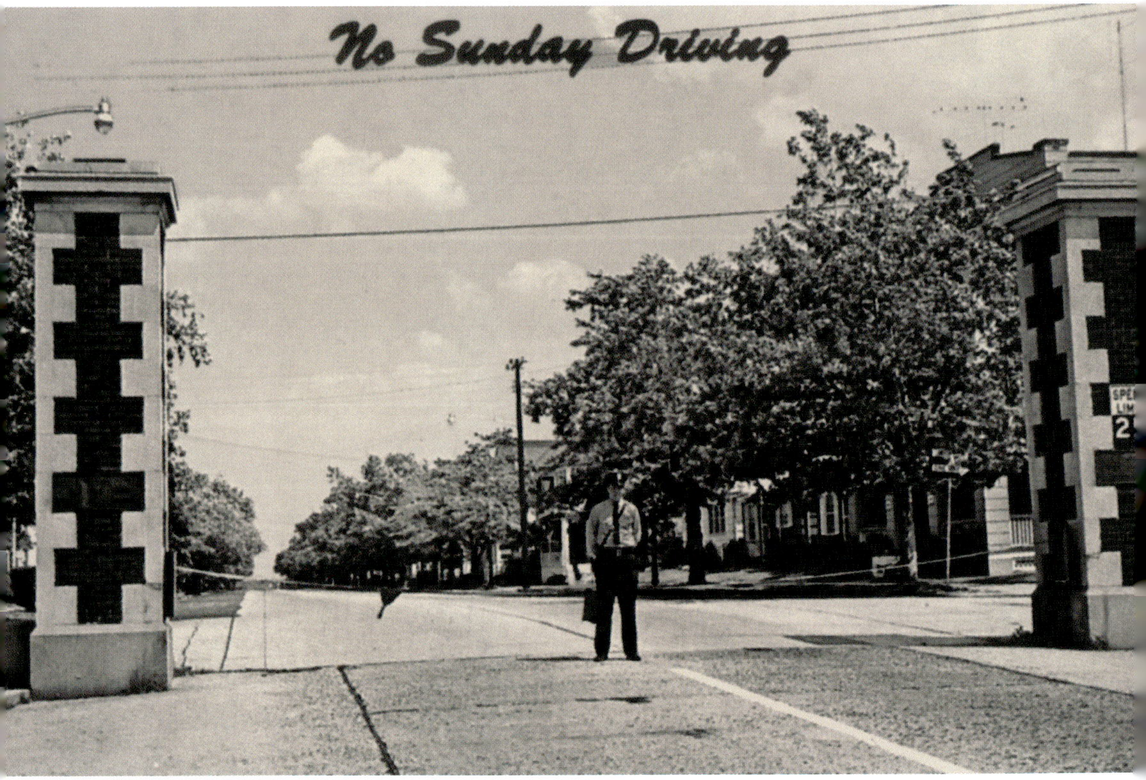

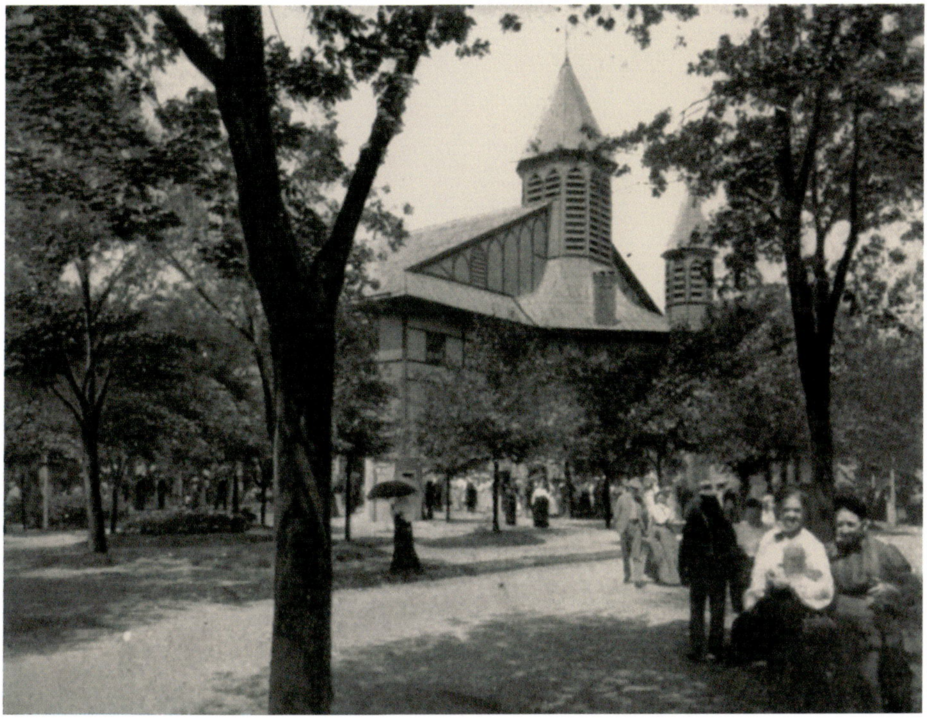

This view of the Great Auditorium in Ocean Grove was captured around 1900. Built almost entirely out of wood in 1894, the giant auditorium has remained essentially unchanged over the past century. The pipe organ, added in 1908, is one of the largest in the world. Presidents William McKinley, Theodore Roosevelt, Woodrow Wilson, and Richard Nixon have made campaign speeches here. The auditorium still hosts religious services and popular concert series.

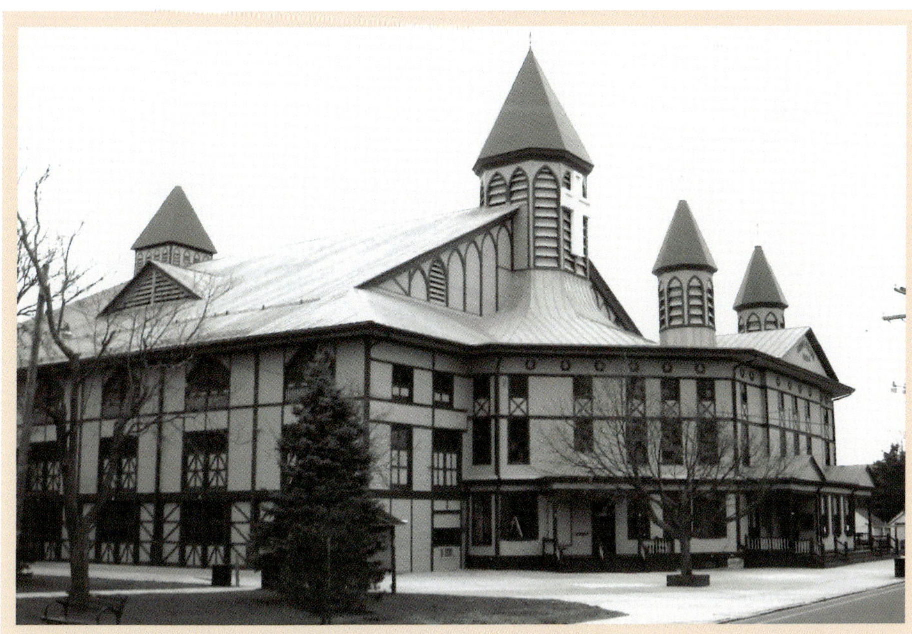

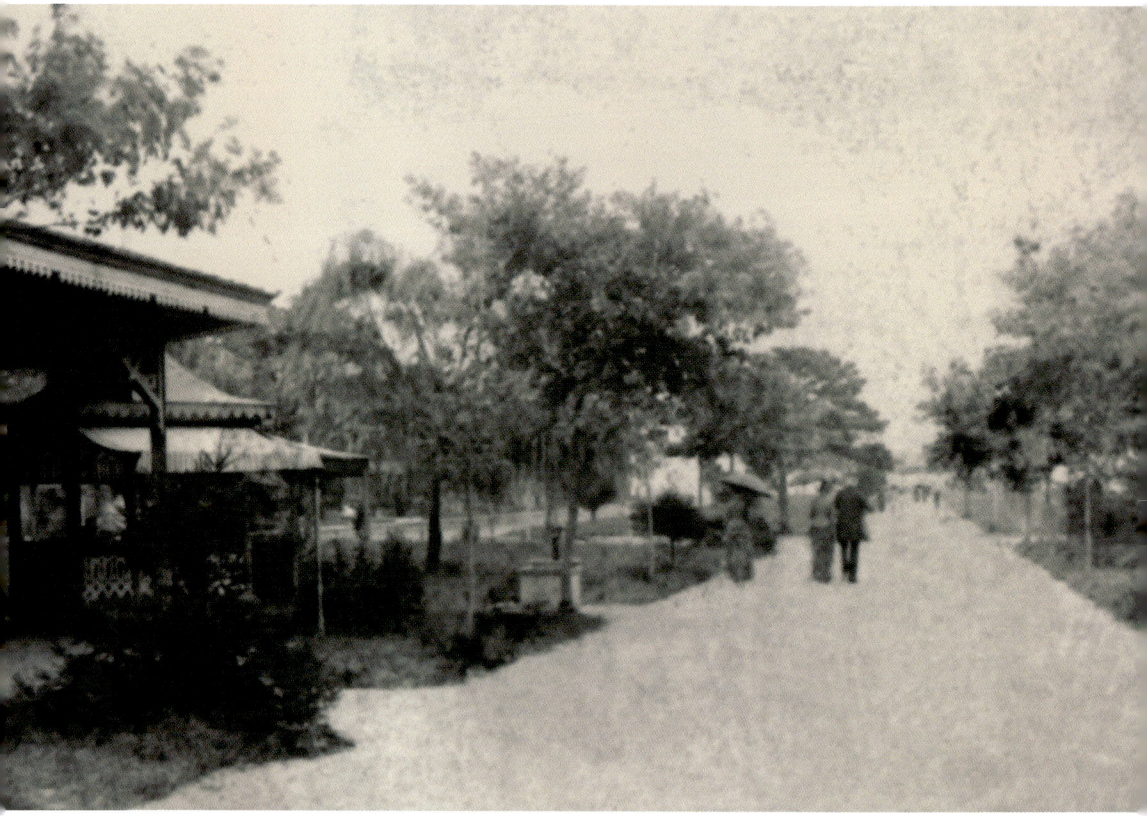

The Pach brothers shot this view facing east of Ocean Pathway in the early 1870s when Ocean Grove was in its infancy. The undeveloped flanks of the pathway would be transformed into rows of tightly crammed hotels and residences within the next 20 years, as seen on the next page. The gazebo was restored by the Ocean Grove Ladies Auxiliary in 2005.

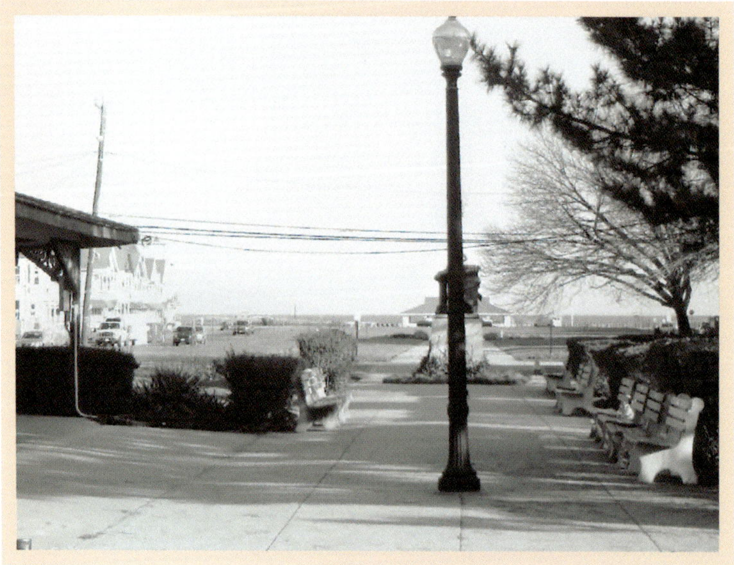

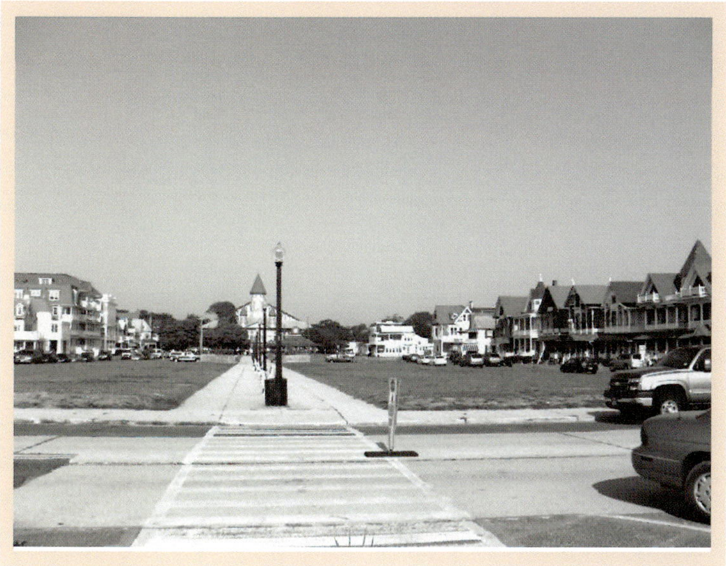

Below is a view of Ocean Pathway looking west from the pavilion in 1905. For the most part, the scenery has remained practically identical. Of the towns chronicled in this volume, Ocean Grove retains the highest level of preservation. The narrow streets with Victorian buildings serve as a major contrast to neighboring Asbury Park, which has remained a hotbed of change since both communities were founded in the early 1870s.

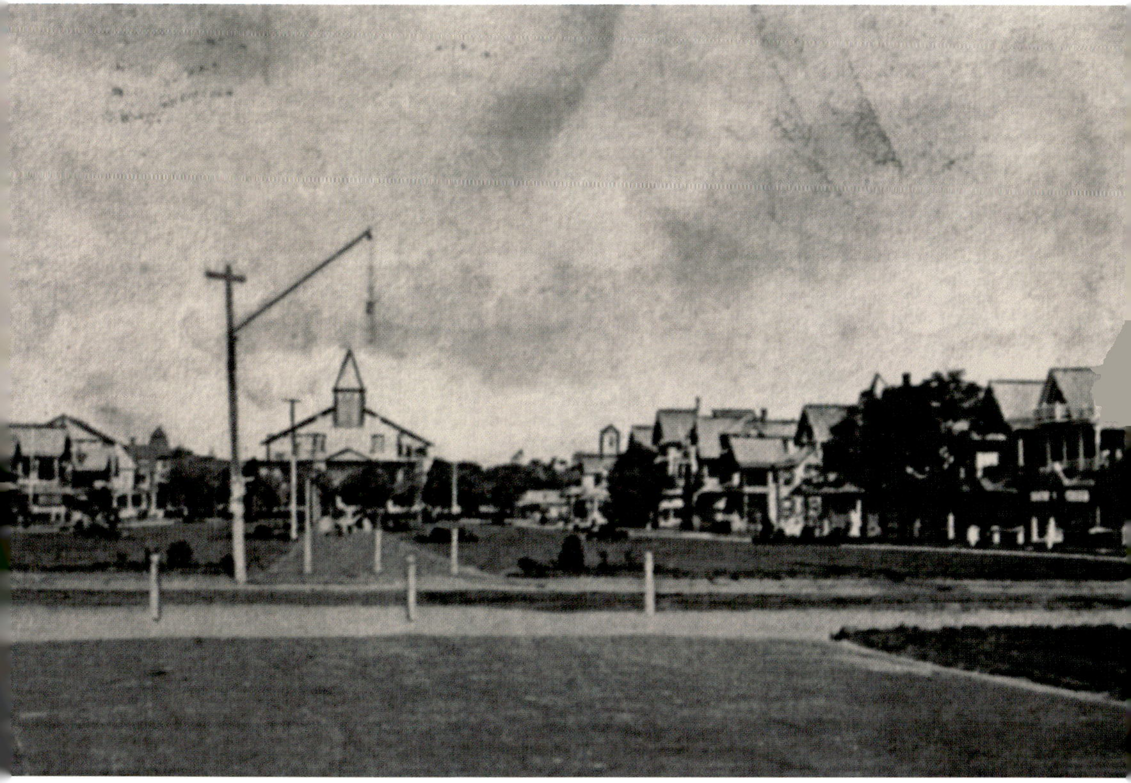

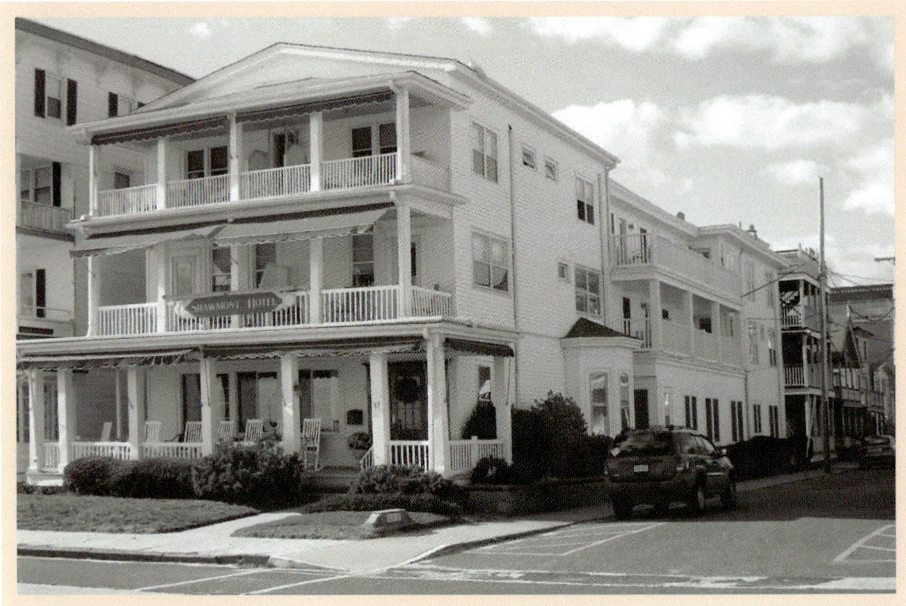

The Ocean Avenue House was built in 1871 during the very early days of Ocean Grove. This postcard view dates from around 1910. In the 1920s, Ira P. Shaw purchased the property and renamed it the Shawmont Hotel. Still in operation with only some minor cosmetic upgrades, the hotel remains as it was, offering guests the same ocean view for well over a century.

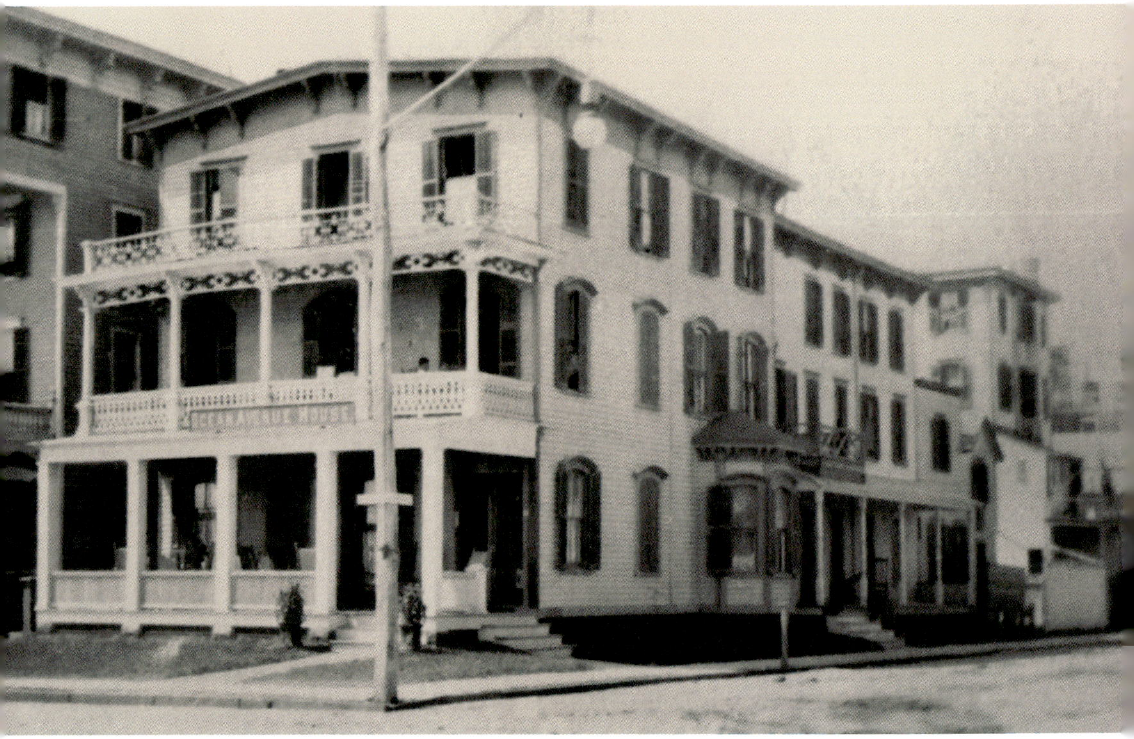

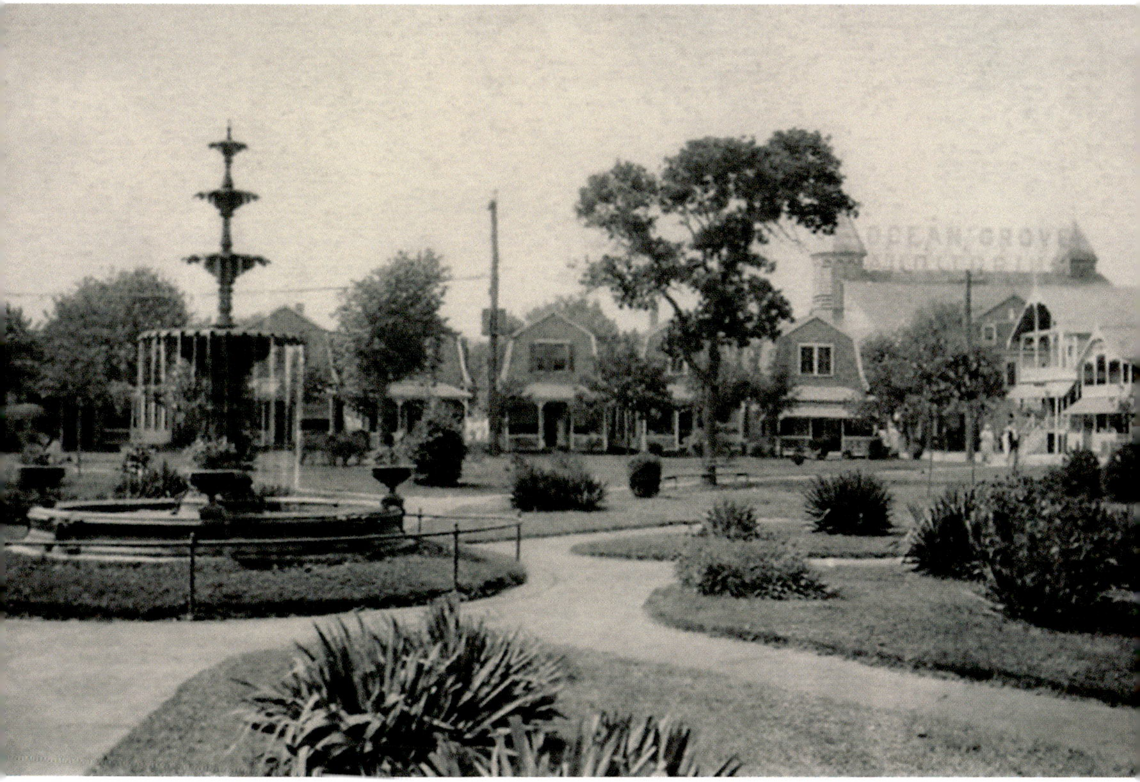

Founders' Park is pictured above in about 1915, shortly after eight-foot-tall letters were added to the roof of the Great Auditorium. The park, originally named Thompson Park, hosted the first religious service held in Ocean Grove on July 31, 1869. In 1883, a giant vase was unveiled in the park, and within a number of years, it was converted into a fountain, which was restored during the 1960s. The letters were removed from the auditorium roof in 1986.

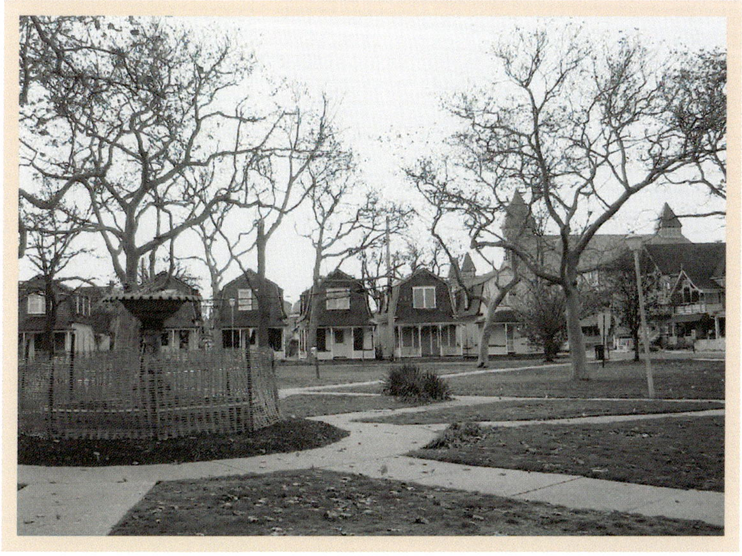

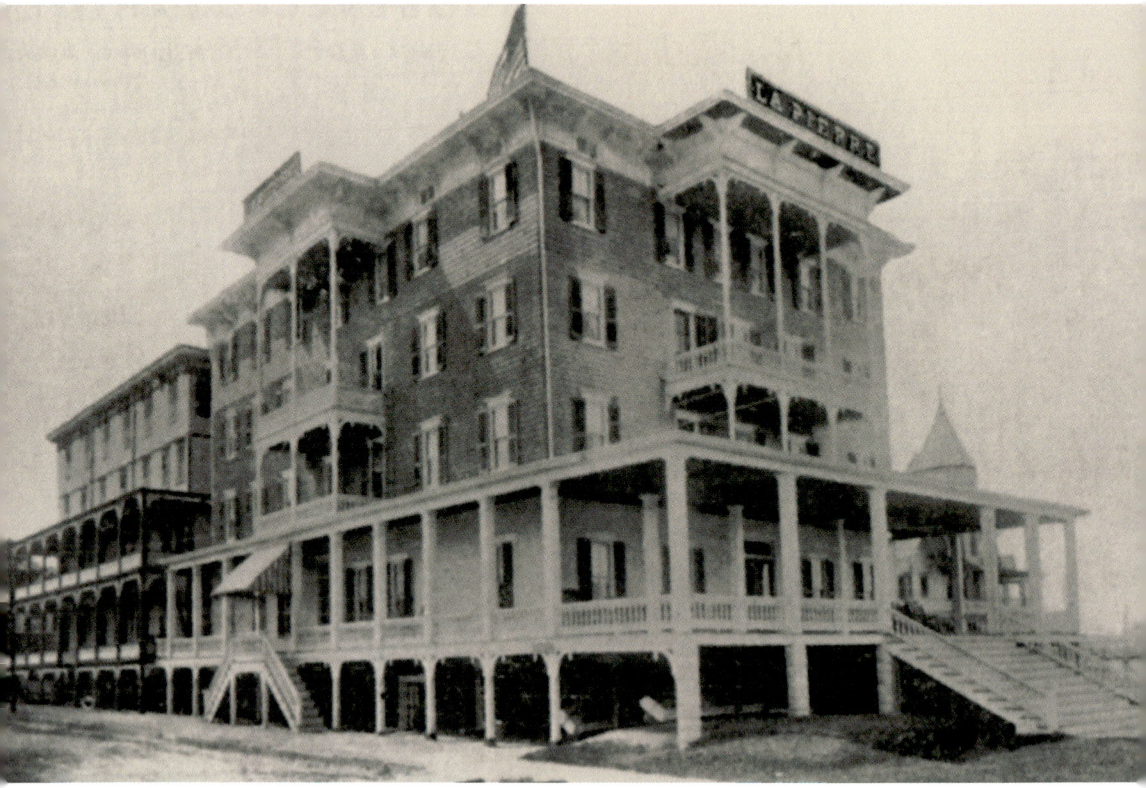

The La Pierre Hotel is pictured on a postcard from about 1900. Built in 1881, the hotel was purchased in 1907 by Robert Watt, who built an addition to the west in 1915, doubling the occupancy of the hotel. In 1989, it was converted into condominium units. In contrast to the many exterior changes made to the La Pierre, the Marlborough House, also built in 1881 and seen at left, remains incredibly intact. It was also converted into condominium units in 1997.

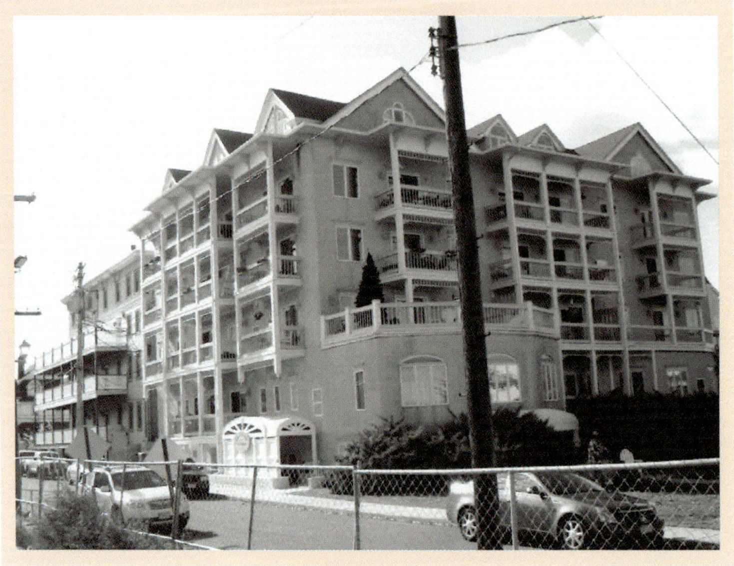

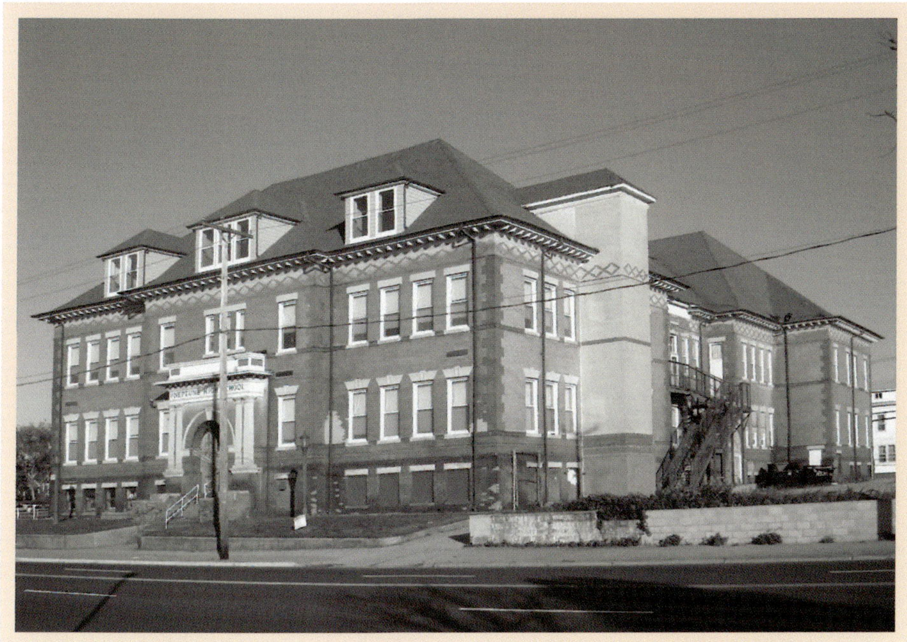

The original Neptune High School on South Main Street in Ocean Grove, pictured here around 1905, was completed in 1898. This building was vacated and remained so for many years after the new high school opened in 1960. Restorations were initiated in the late 1990s. The three dormers in the roof had been removed in the 1940s, but they were restored in 2007. The building currently houses a variety of small businesses and performing arts ventures.

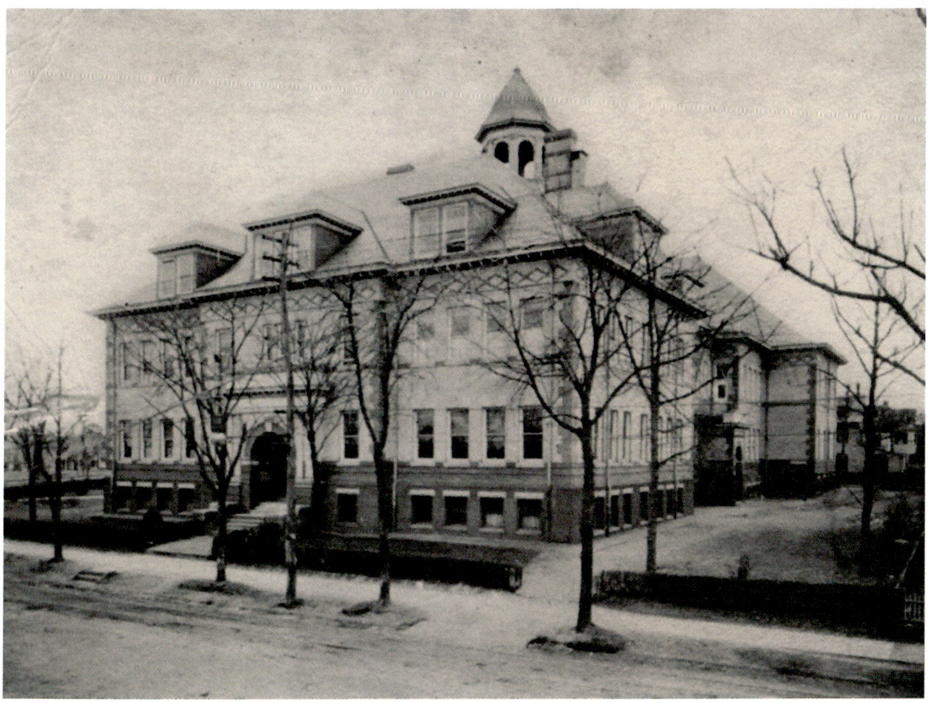

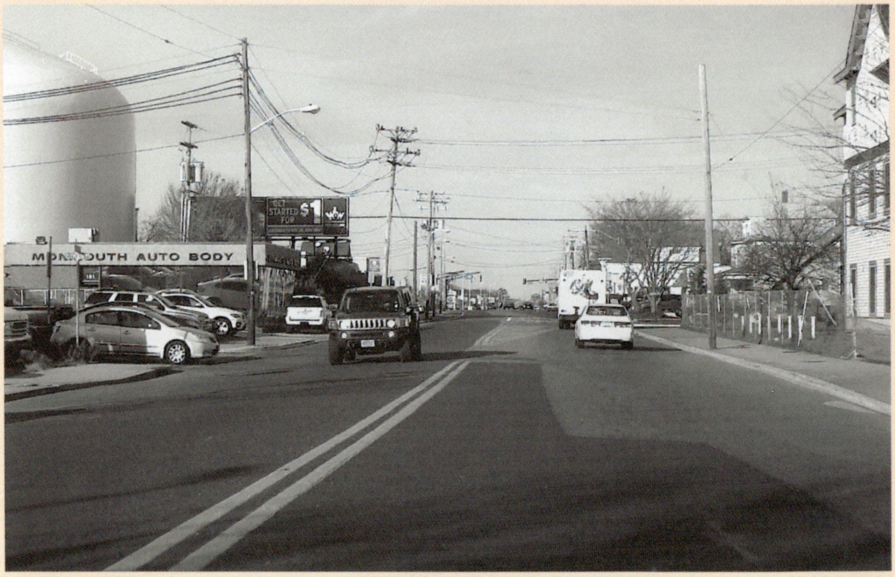

The stretch of Main Street at the Neptune/Bradley Beach border remains fairly intact compared to this snapshot taken in the early 1960s—right down to the billboard placements. Monmouth Autobody moved into the building at left in 1963. Originally constructed in 1952, it was then the home of Harry Rosenfeld's car dealership. The home pictured on the right was built in 1900. (Neptune Archives.)

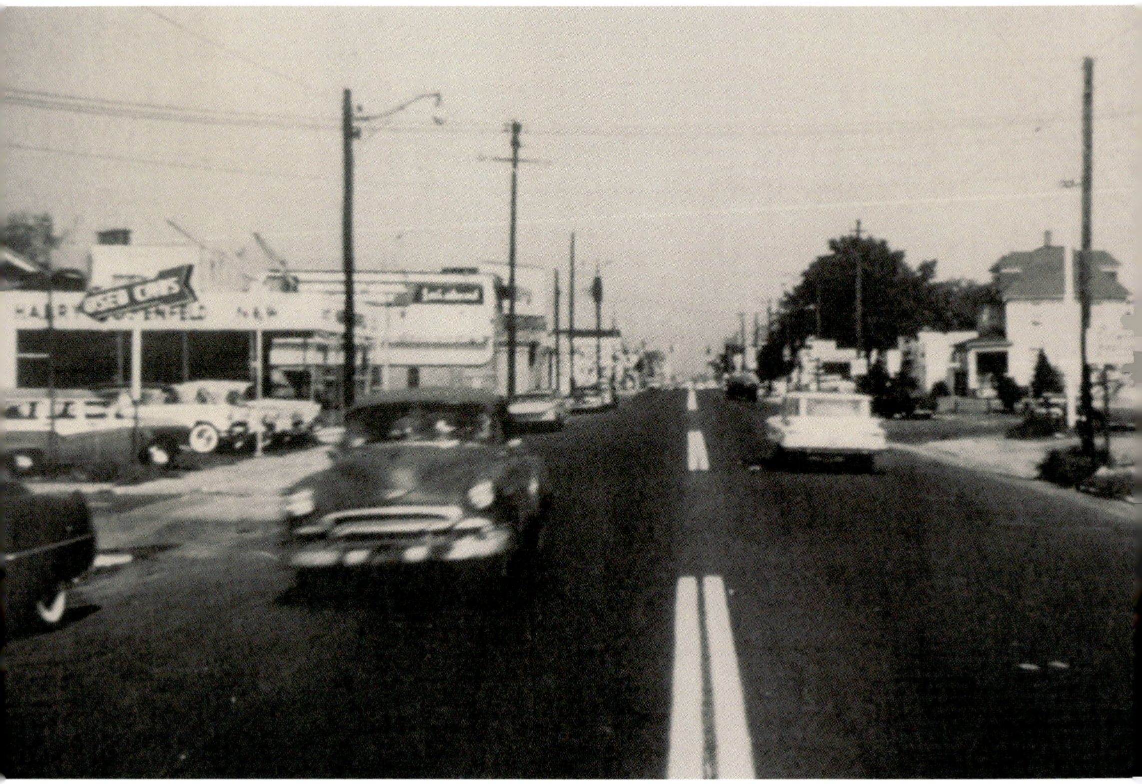

CHAPTER 3

Bradley Beach, Avon, and Neptune City

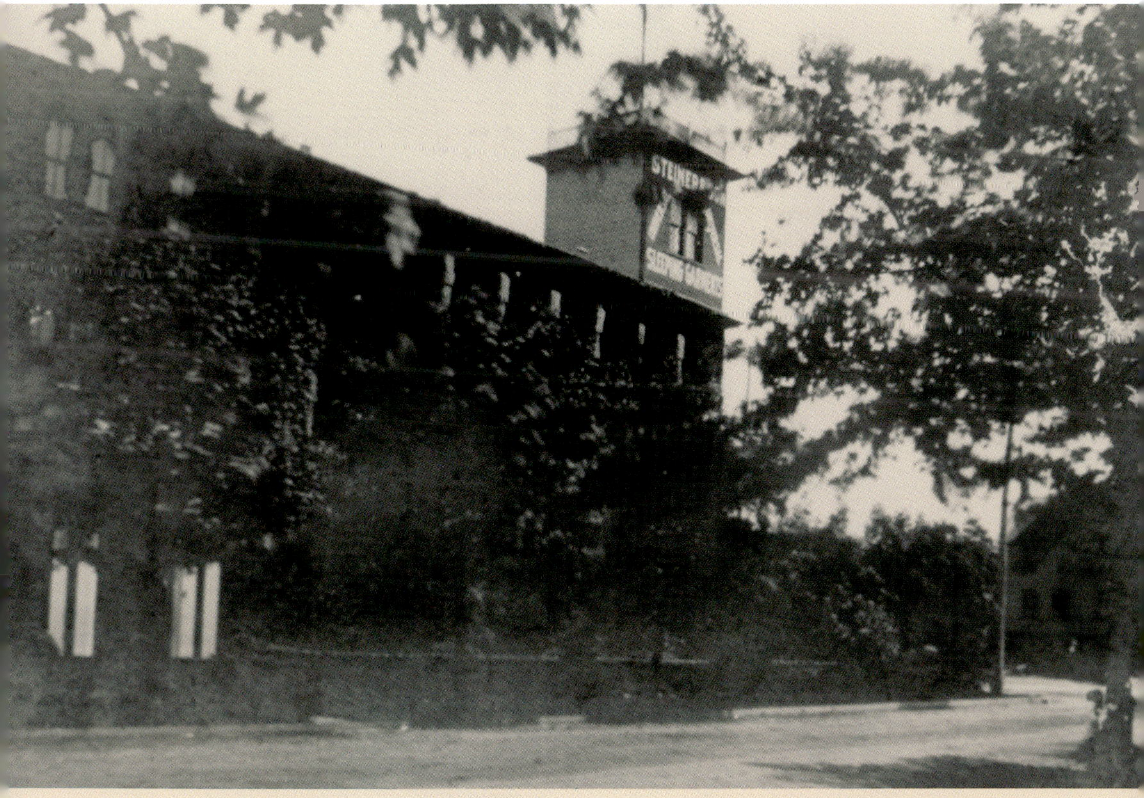

Emanuel Steiner ran a successful nightshirt company in Peekskill, New York. In 1891, he relocated his operations to the northwest corner of Fourth and Railroad Avenues in Neptune City. Pictured in 1905, Steiner and Son was ahead of its time, offering medical attention, benefits, sick time, and disability pay to its 500 employees. The building was demolished in 1999.

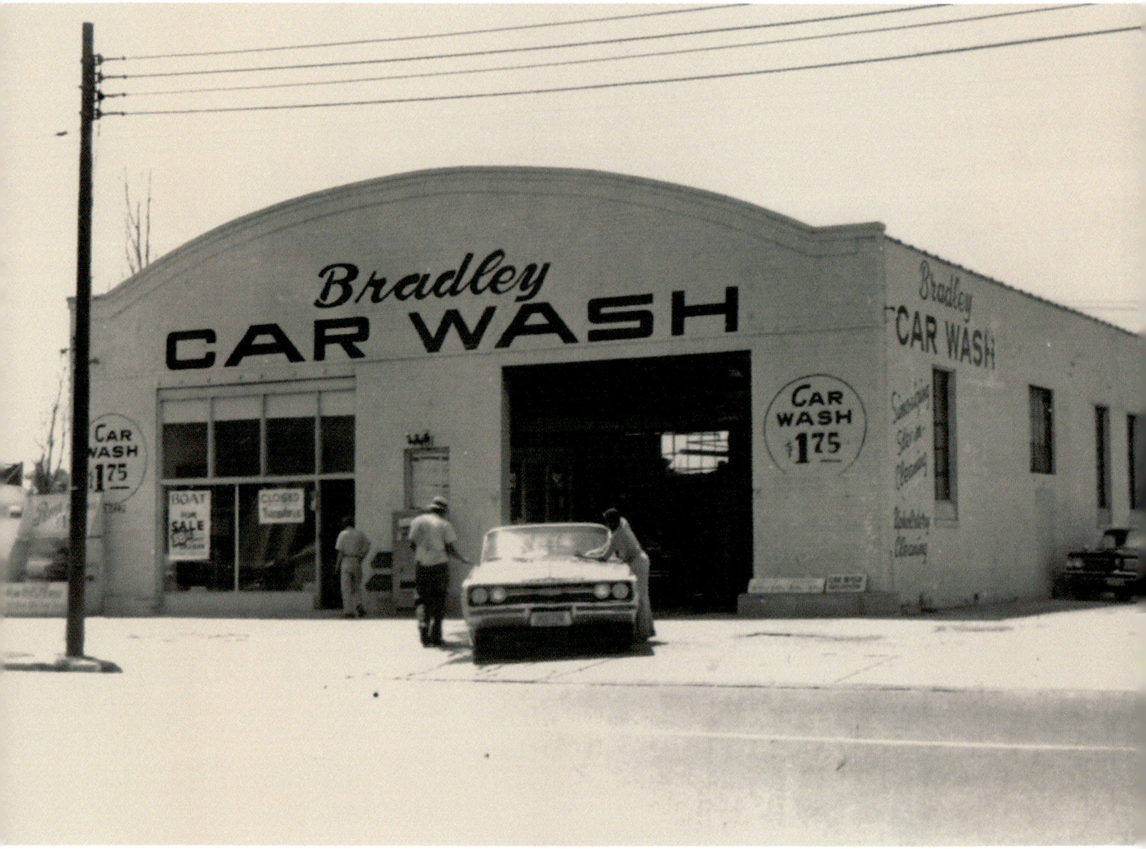

The Bradley Car Wash was built in the early 1930s. Beginning life as a garage, it was utilized primarily as a car wash by the 1940s. Pictured here on June 29, 1968, its house specialties were detailing, simonizing, and upholstery cleaning. The business changed hands over the years, and in 1972, it was purchased from the Wagner family by Charles L'Hommedieu and Carol Vreeland, who renamed it the Rain Tunnel Car Wash. It was sold again in 2007. (Appleby Collection.)

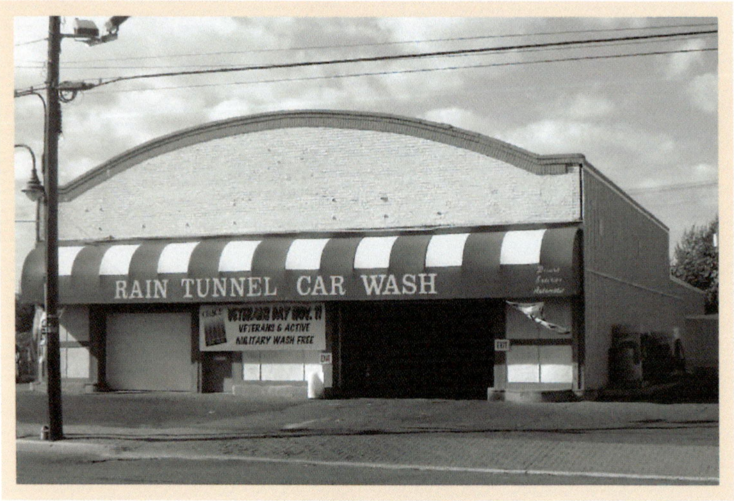

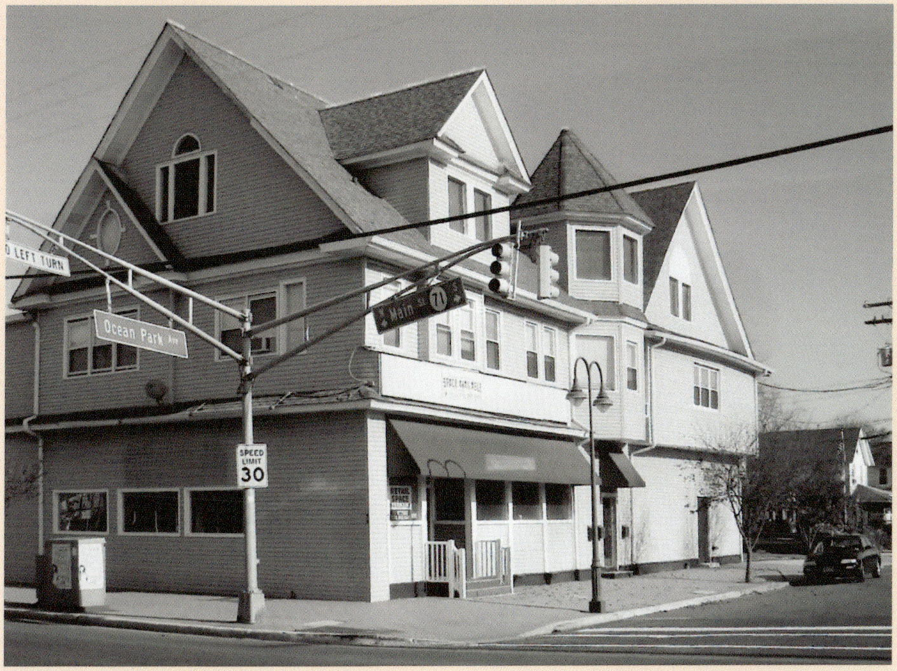

William J. Paynter built his general store on the corner of Ocean Park Avenue and Main Street in the early 1890s on land donated to him by James Bradley. From 1894 to 1918, it also served as the town's post office. Paynter, owner of the first car in town, was obsessed with innovation. His store was the first outfit in Bradley Beach that had electricity and telephone service. The photograph below dates from about 1913. (Bradley Beach Historical Society.)

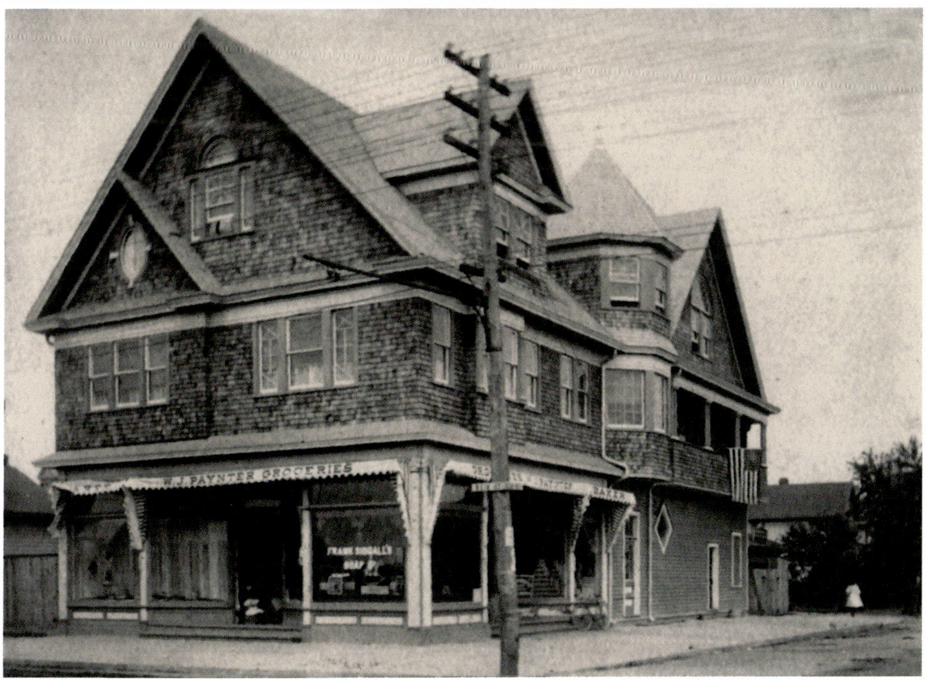

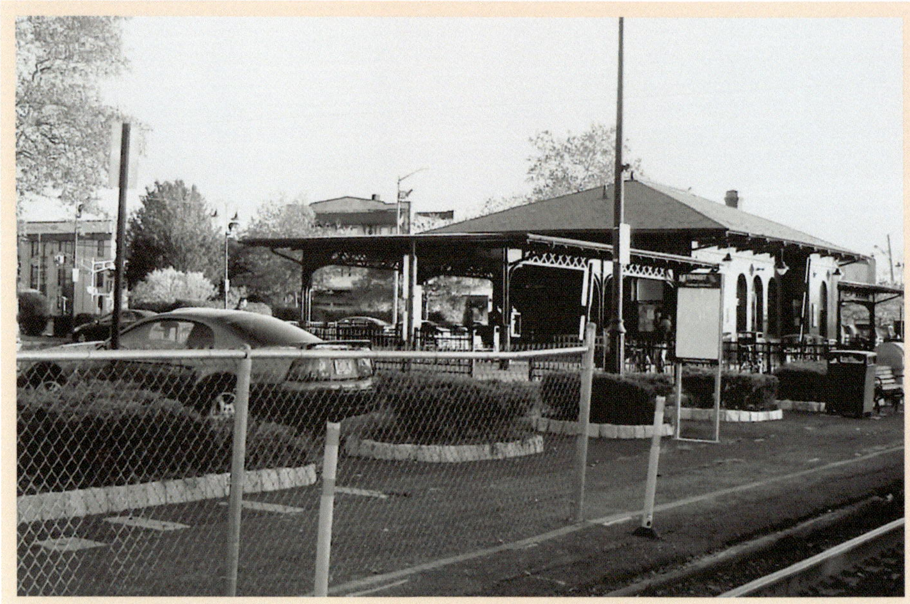

The Bradley Beach train station is pictured in 1913, a year after its construction. Train service was extended to Bradley Beach in the 1880s by the New York and Long Branch Railroad. The building, designed by Joseph Osgood, was added to the National Register of Historic Places in 1984. Restorations were performed during the early 2000s. Although there are no longer rail ticketing agents within the building, it does host a small breakfast/brunch-hour eatery. (Bradley Beach Historical Society.)

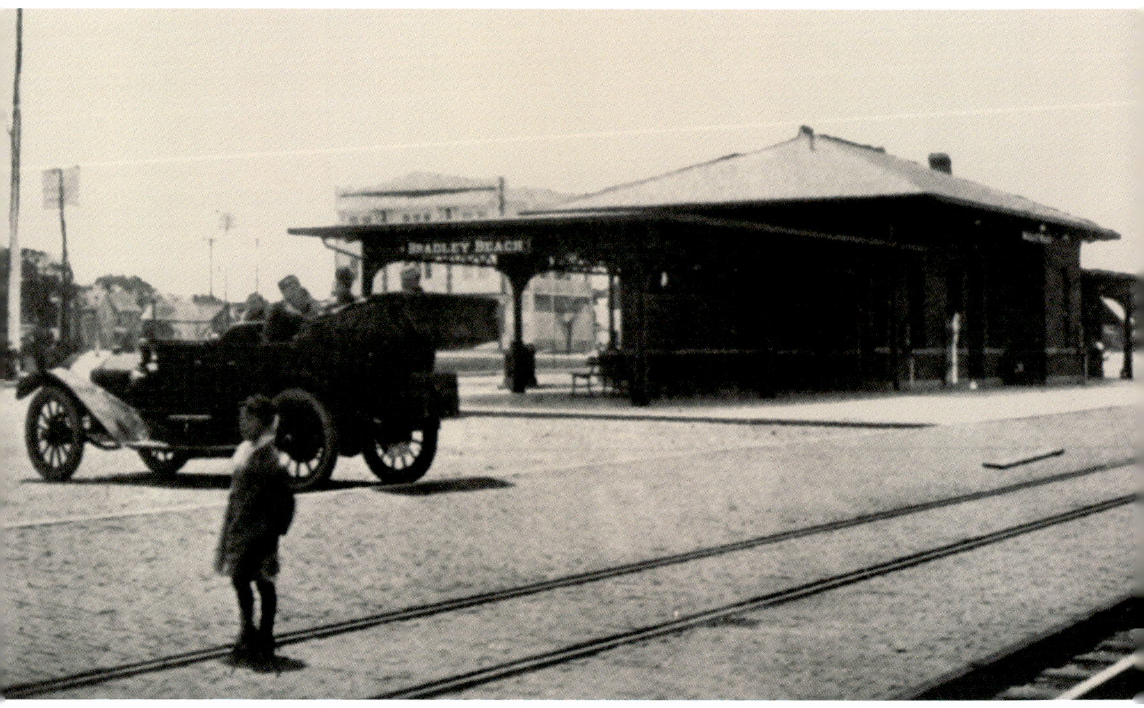

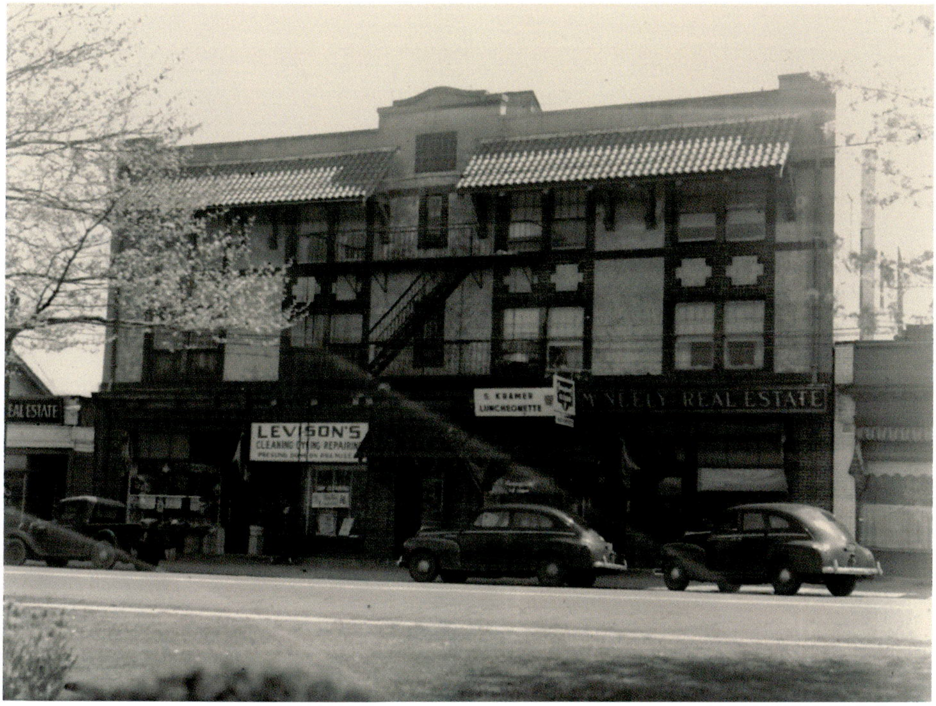

This 1890s building was the original home of the First National Bank. In 1918, the bank constructed a new location on the southeast corner of Brinley Avenue and Main Street. This edifice next served as the home of the Richard McNeely Real Estate Agency. In 1994, the McNeely Agency moved into the structure featured on page 79. This January 1953 view of the former bank building shows the Kramer Luncheonette and Levison's Cleaners, also tenants at the time. (Appleby Collection.)

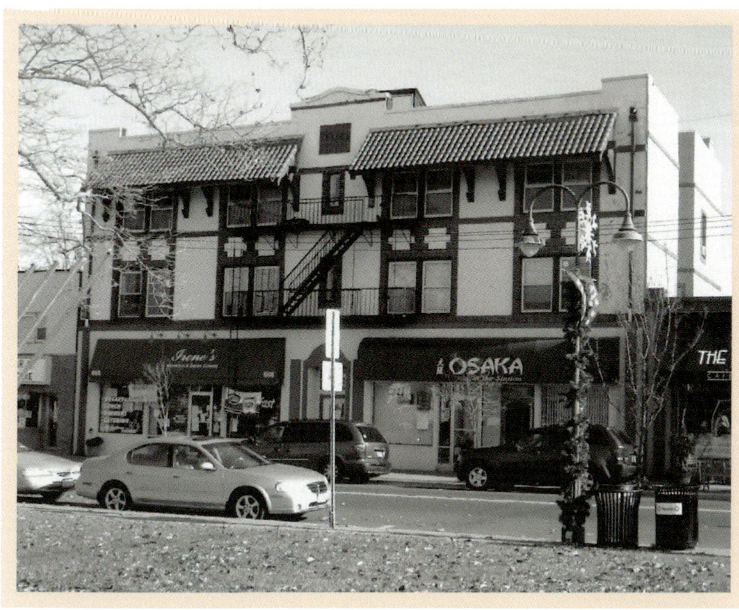

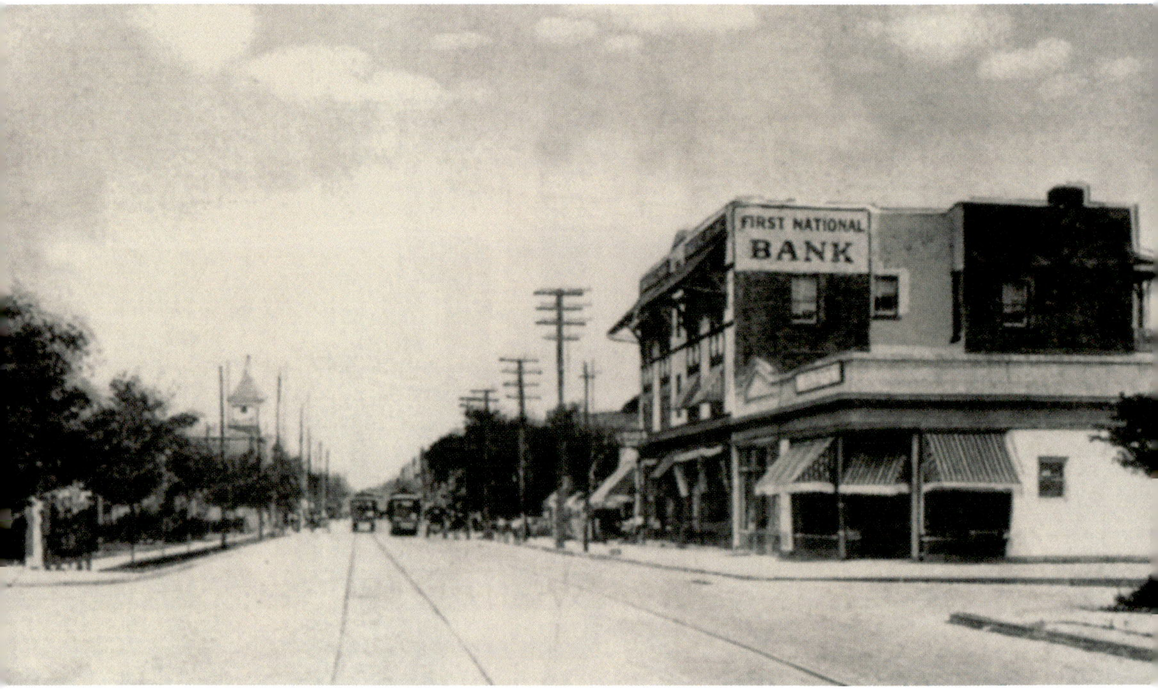

The heart of Main Street in Bradley Beach was complete by about 1910, when this postcard image was made. The building to the far left has been a bakery since the 1930s, when it became Master Bakers, although the back portion facing Brinley Avenue has been converted into shops and restaurants. Born in Austria, baker Anchel Mirrer would walk from his home at 312 Brinley Avenue before dawn every morning to begin the day's work.

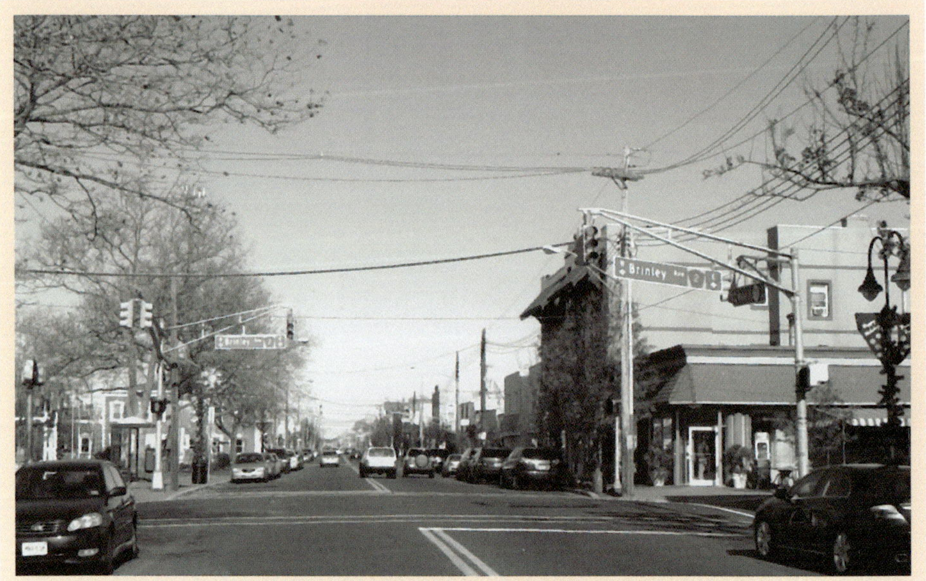

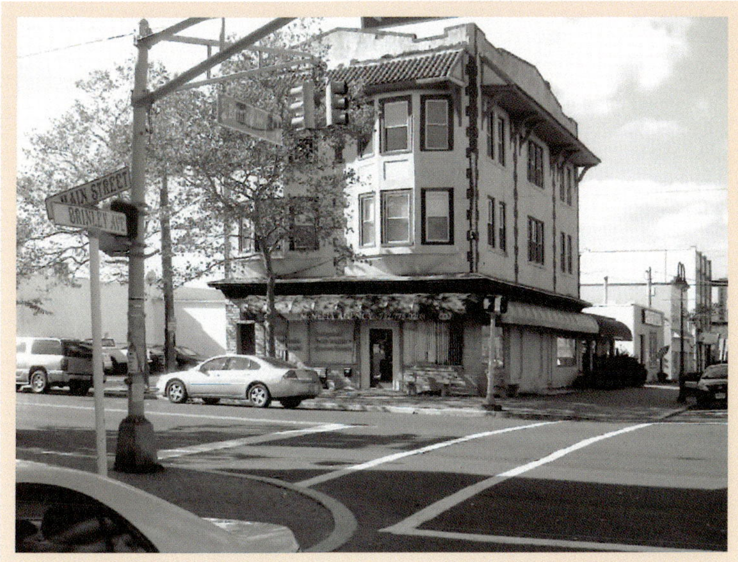

The turn-of-century building pictured here has long played host to real estate offices. This early 1920s view shows that the first floor was divided between a real estate office on the right and the New York Restaurant on the left. By the time the earlier photograph was taken, the buildings that currently house the Jersey Shore Fitness gym and the Aten Solar Panel Company had been built, as seen in the far right. The Steiner and Son water tower is seen on the left. (Appleby Collection.)

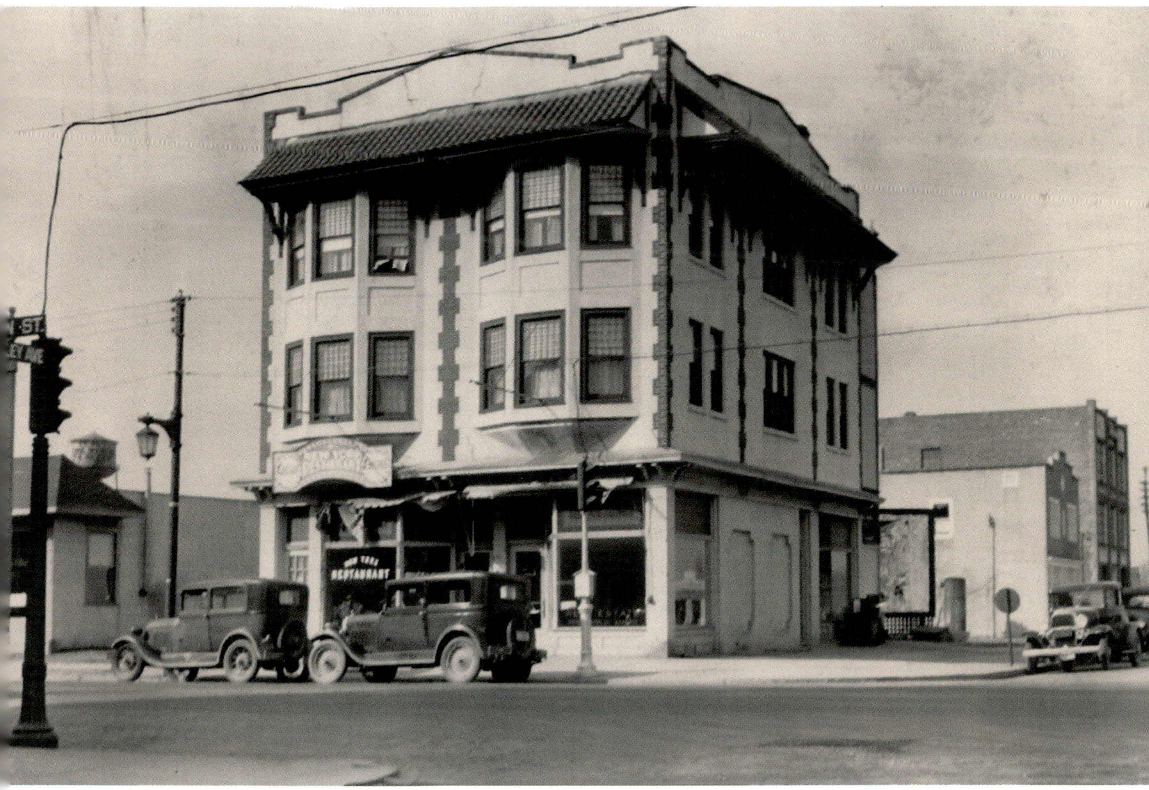

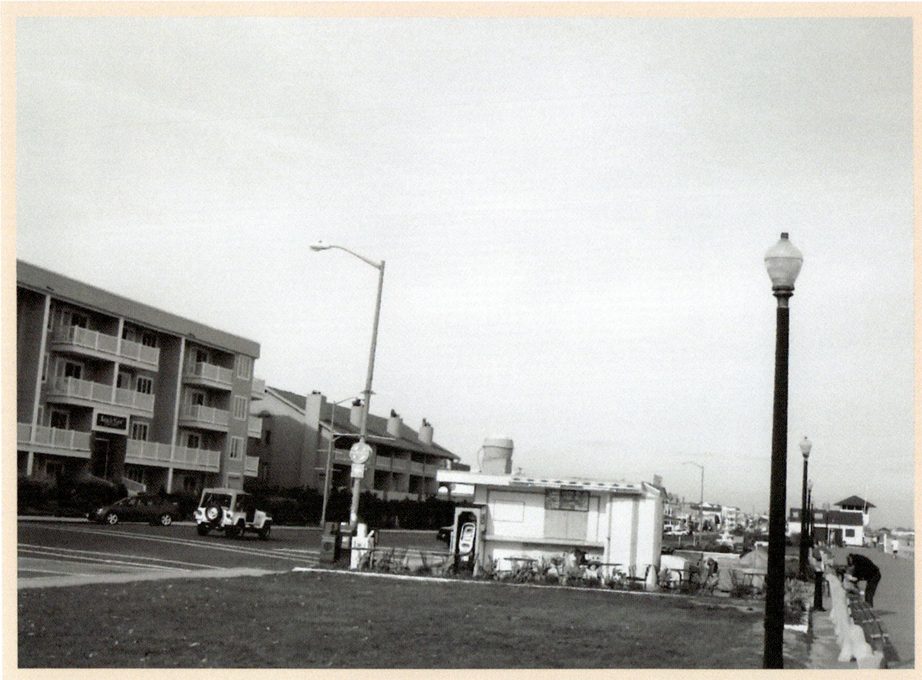

Kite-flying activities are documented below on the Brinley Avenue boardwalk lawn on an autumn day in the early 1970s. After the powerful nor'easter of 1992, which left the Bradley boardwalk in ruins, a brick promenade was constructed echoing the original oceanside pathway laid into the sand a century before. The borough laid the brick walk a good deal west of the original boardwalk location to maximize beach space. The beach badge booth (now the Jetty Grill) was built in the mid-1940s.

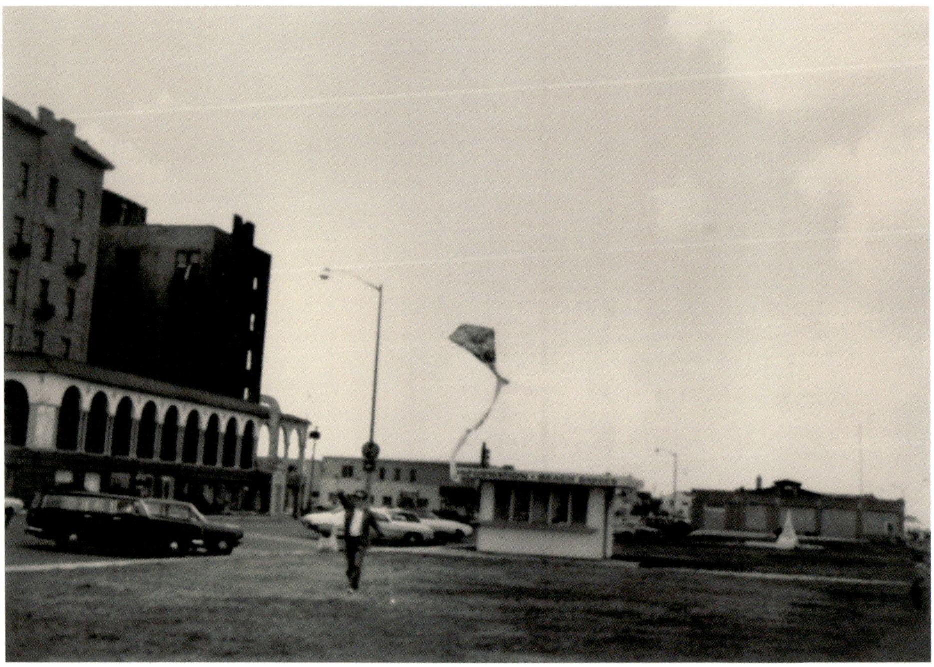

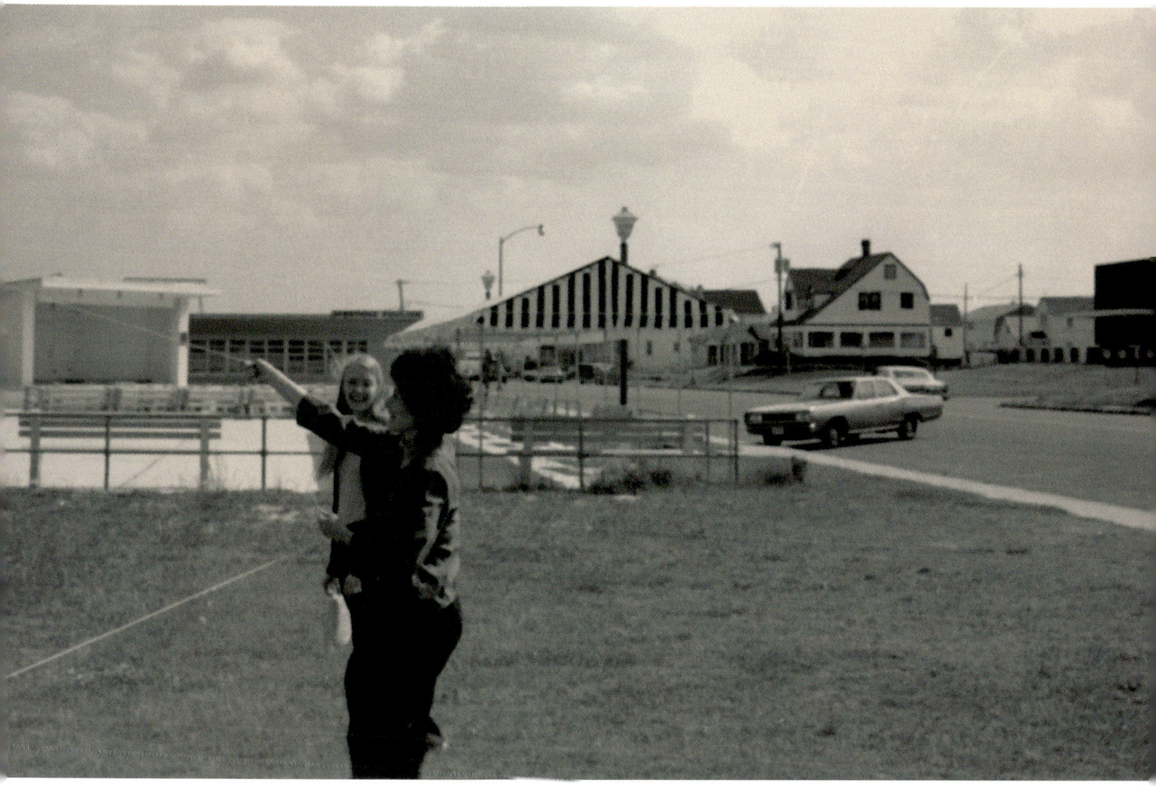

This photograph was taken at the same time and location as the previous one, but it faces south. The scene is almost completely unrecognizable save for the Magen David Temple at the far right, which further demonstrates the aftermath of the 1992 nor'easter. The band shell building was constructed in about 1971. Keeping with the Victorian-themed reconstruction efforts, it was replaced during the overhaul with a gazebo, visually based on the one that existed there 90 years before.

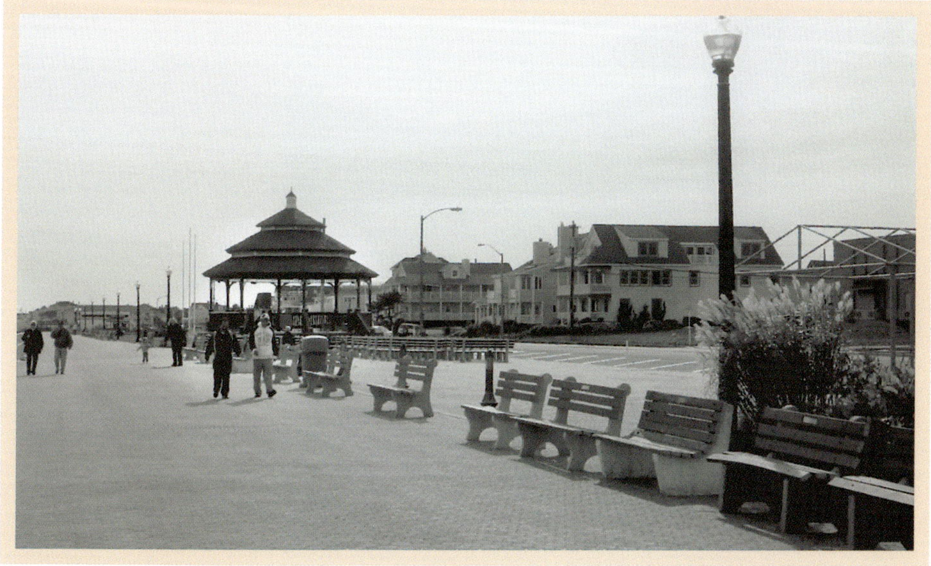

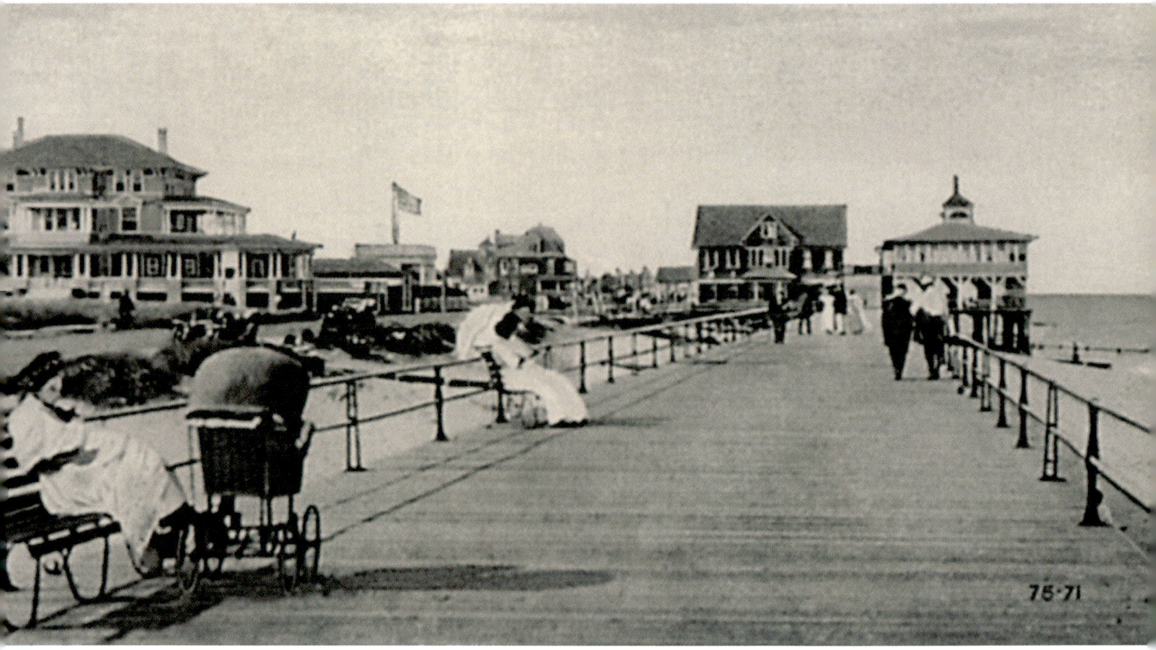

This Avon-by-the-Sea boardwalk view from around 1910 focuses on the first two major structures built by Edward Batchelor. Batchelor was a cigar magnate in Philadelphia when he purchased the majority of the land that is now Avon in 1879. In 1883, he built the Berwick Lodge (renamed the Columns in the 1950s) seen at left and the Avon Pavilion complex. Avon moved its boardwalk slightly west to maximize the beach area in the late 1930s, much like Bradley Beach did 60 years later.

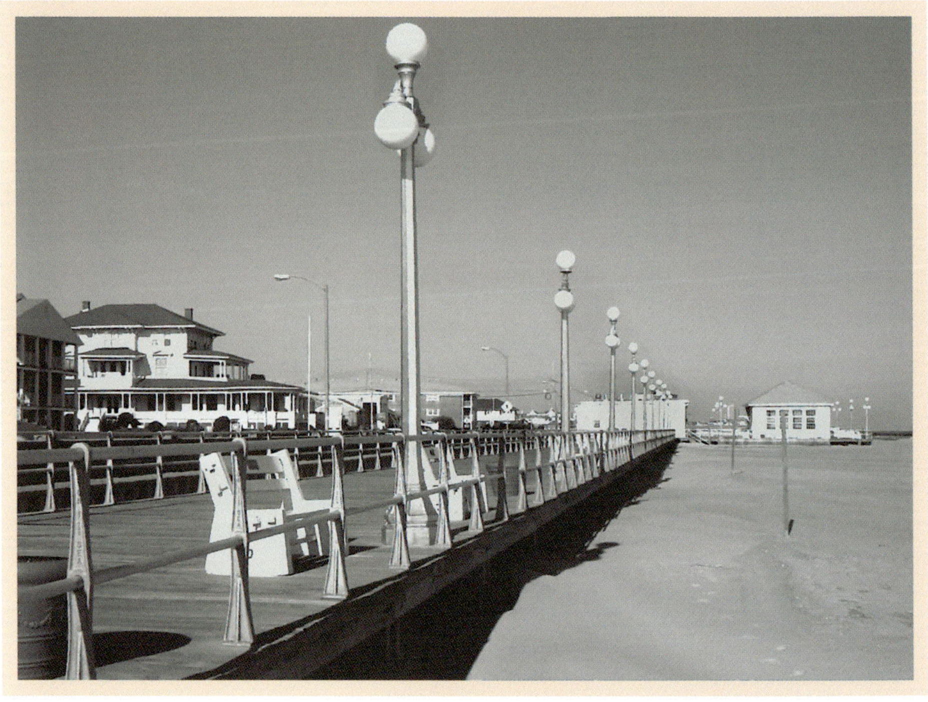

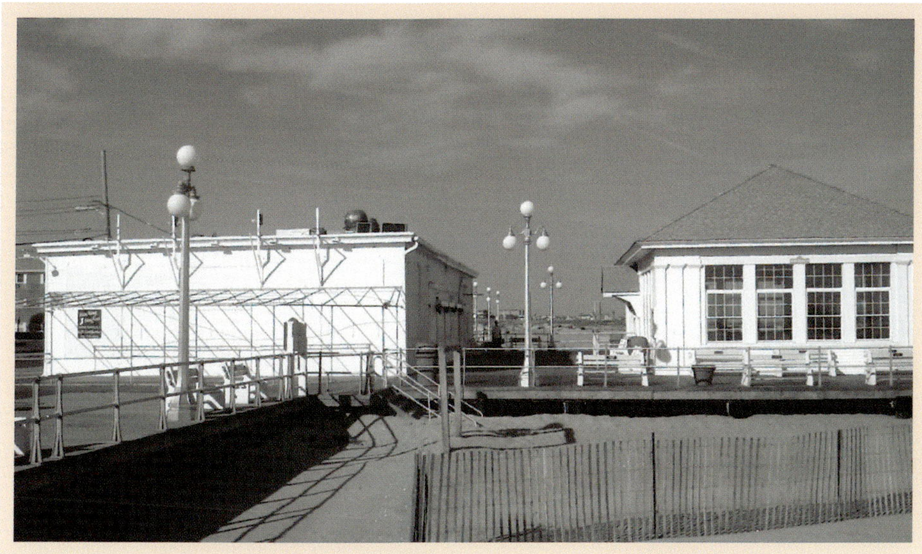

The Avon Pavilion was considerably revamped during the early 1920s. The second story of the concession casino was removed. The promenade portion, as originally designed, was also split-level. An open-air seating area was located on the boardwalk, and the level above served as an enclosed community room connected by a footbridge to the second story of the casino. The upper-floor enclosure was lowered to boardwalk level. Pictured here in the mid-1920s, this is the basic configuration that exists today.

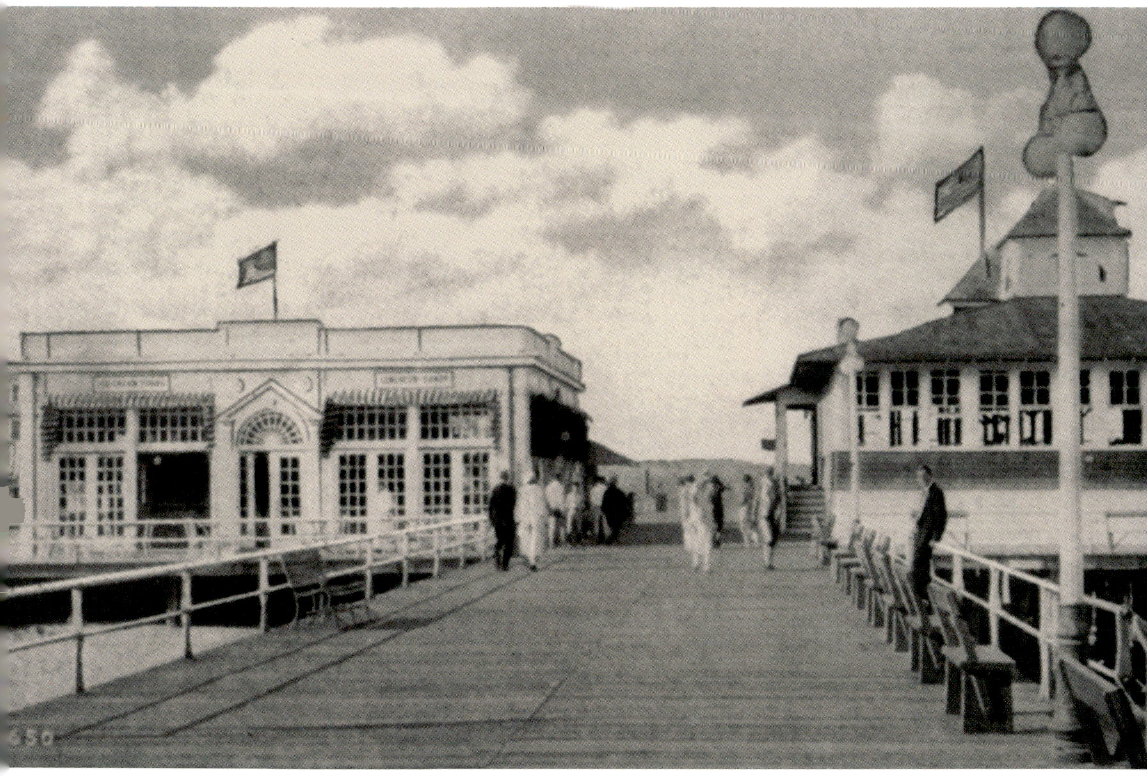

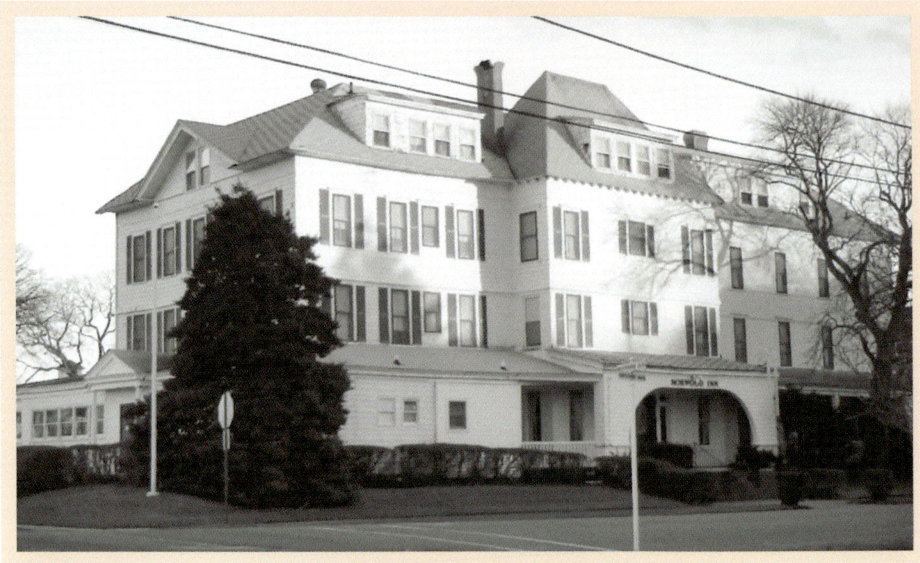

The Norwood Inn was built as the Marlborough in 1888 by Albert Turner, who had intentions of establishing a large health resort in Avon. In the late 1930s, the building was renamed the Norwood. The edifice underwent serious renovations during the 1950s, including the removal of the decks on the second and third stories and enclosure of the wraparound porch. The inn still operates regularly during the summer months.

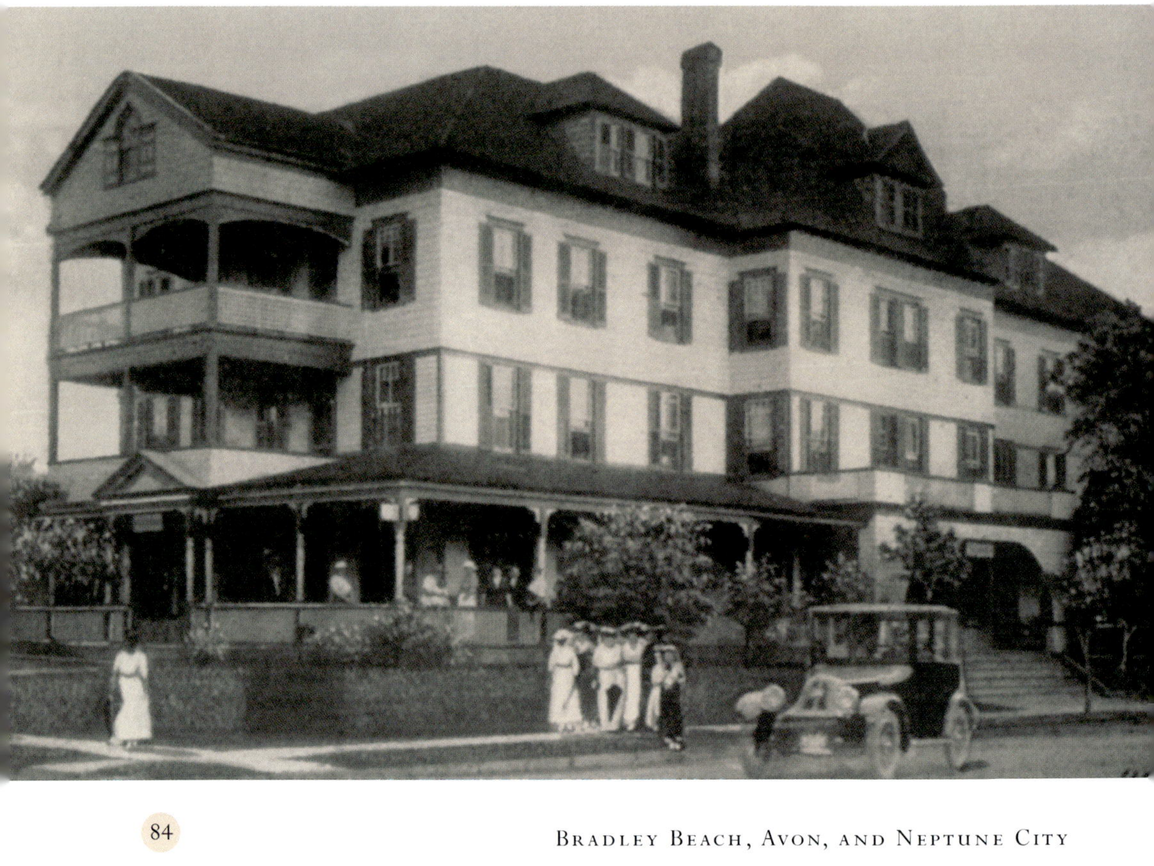

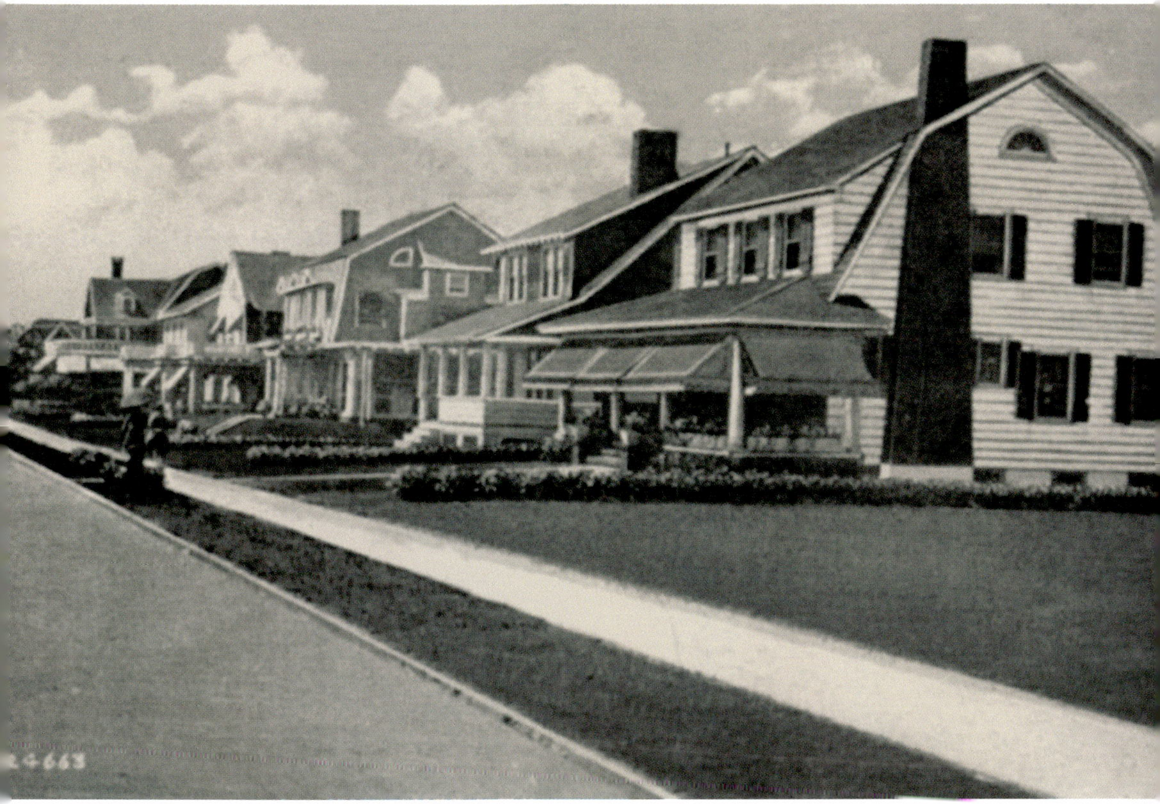

The northeast side of the 100 block of Lincoln Avenue is pictured in the late 1930s. Most of the houses along this stretch were built during the 1920s and 1930s. This was the golden period of suburban growth for Avon-by-the-Sea. The homes have been altered and improved upon, but for the most part, they are recognizable today. Avon has on the whole retained a formidable level of preservation.

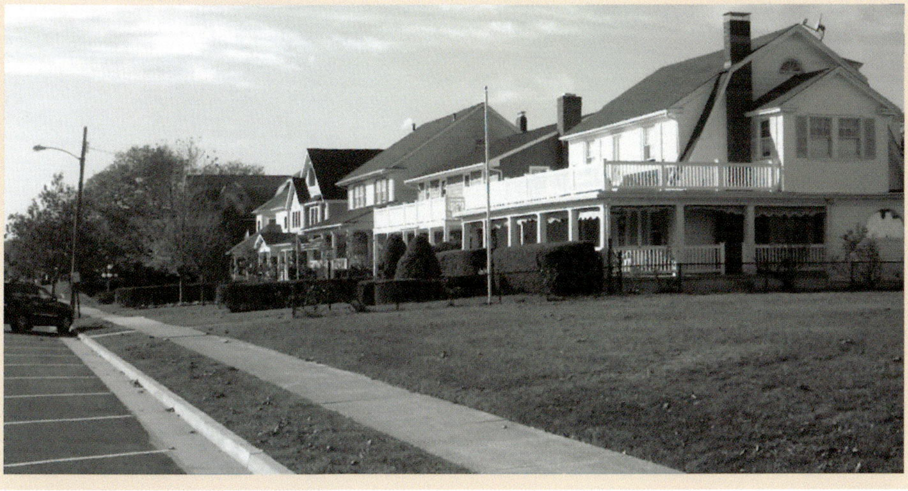

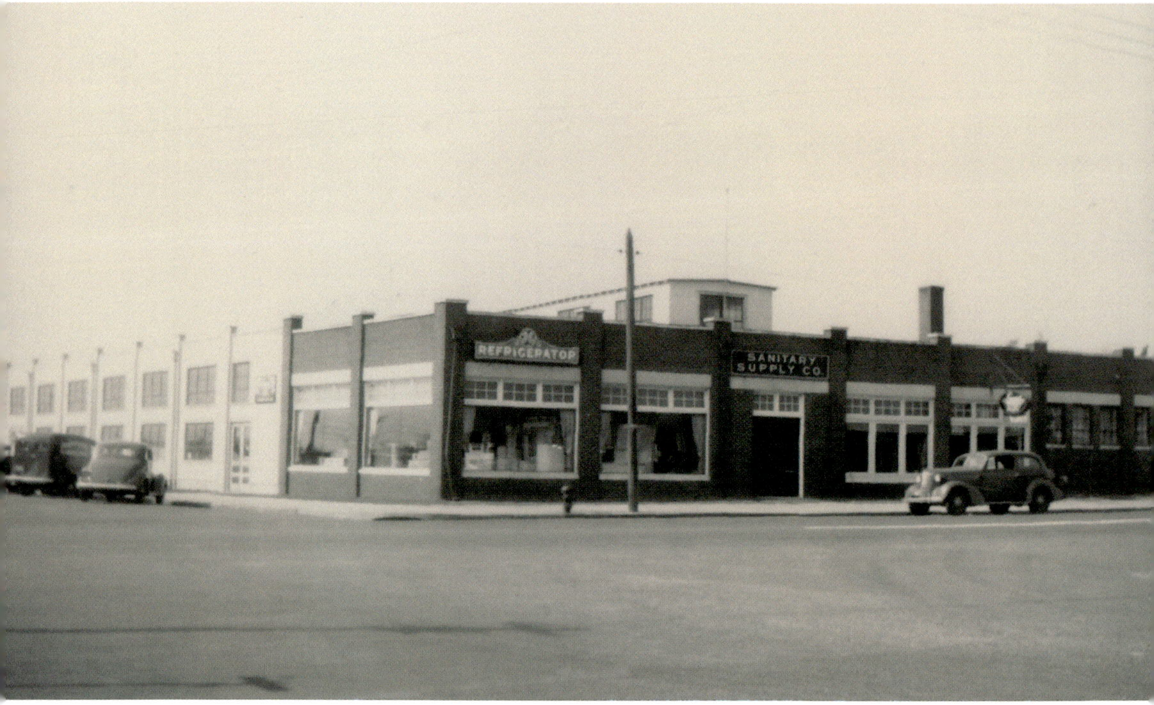

The Sanitary Supply Company, an appliance retailer, built this wedge-shaped structure on the western side of the intersection of Garfield Avenue and Main Street in the late 1920s. Pictured here in the early 1940s, the firm offered the latest in household appliances and plumbing supplies. Eventually, L&H Plumbing and Heating took over, which, in turn was bought out by Virginia-based plumbing wholesale giant Ferguson in 1998. (Appleby Collection.)

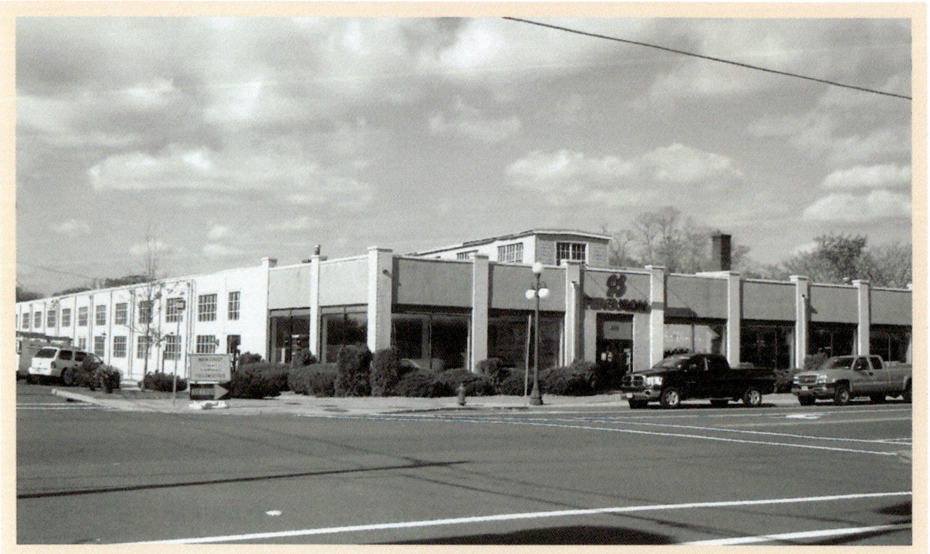

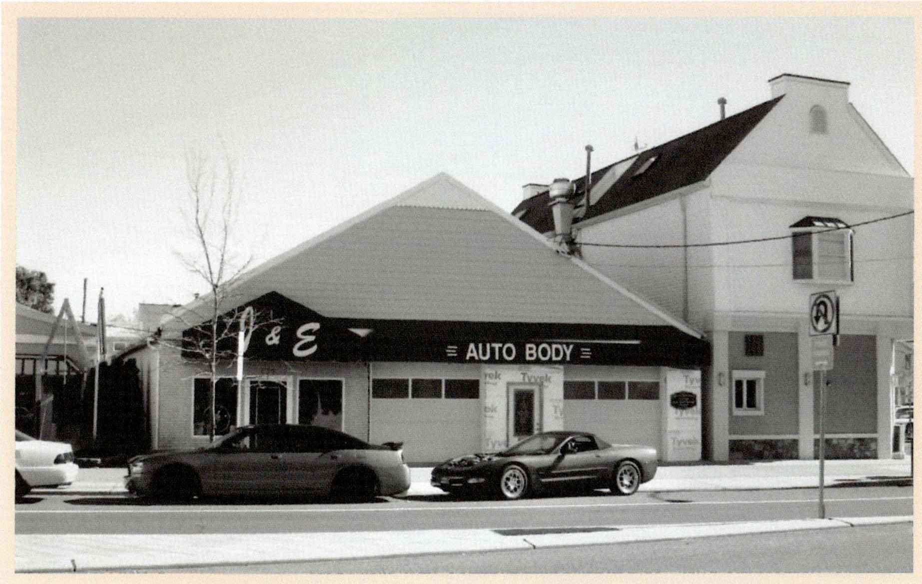

Pictured here is a 1940s view of Curt's Garage and the American Express office on the right at the northeastern corner of Garfield Avenue and Main Street. These buildings were constructed in the 1910s. Although they have been extensively remodeled, reroofed, and refaced, they remain somewhat recognizable. The center structure still operates as a garage and auto body shop, and the American Express office building long served as a restaurant. (Appleby Collection.)

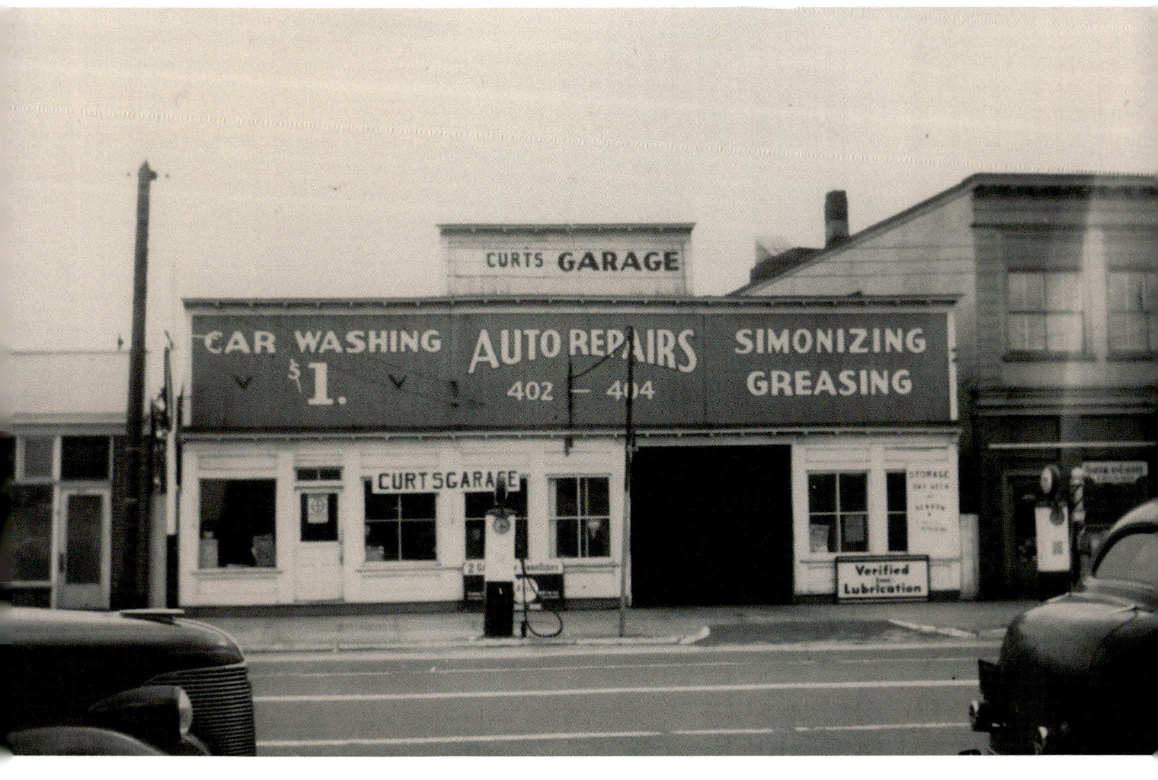

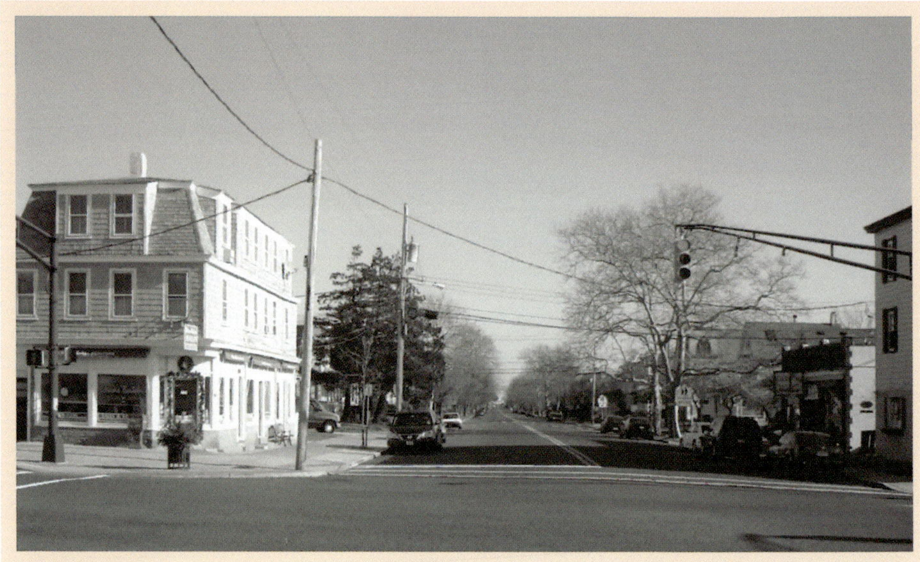

C.D. Snyder opened a real estate office in Avon-by-the-Sea in 1897. The rising interest in the shore area brought him immediate success. Within 10 years, he had moved his office to the three-story Victorian building at the northeast corner of Main Street and Sylvania Avenue, seen here around 1910. Another perennial realtor location, the building houses the Turton Agency today. (Courtesy Jane Gannon.)

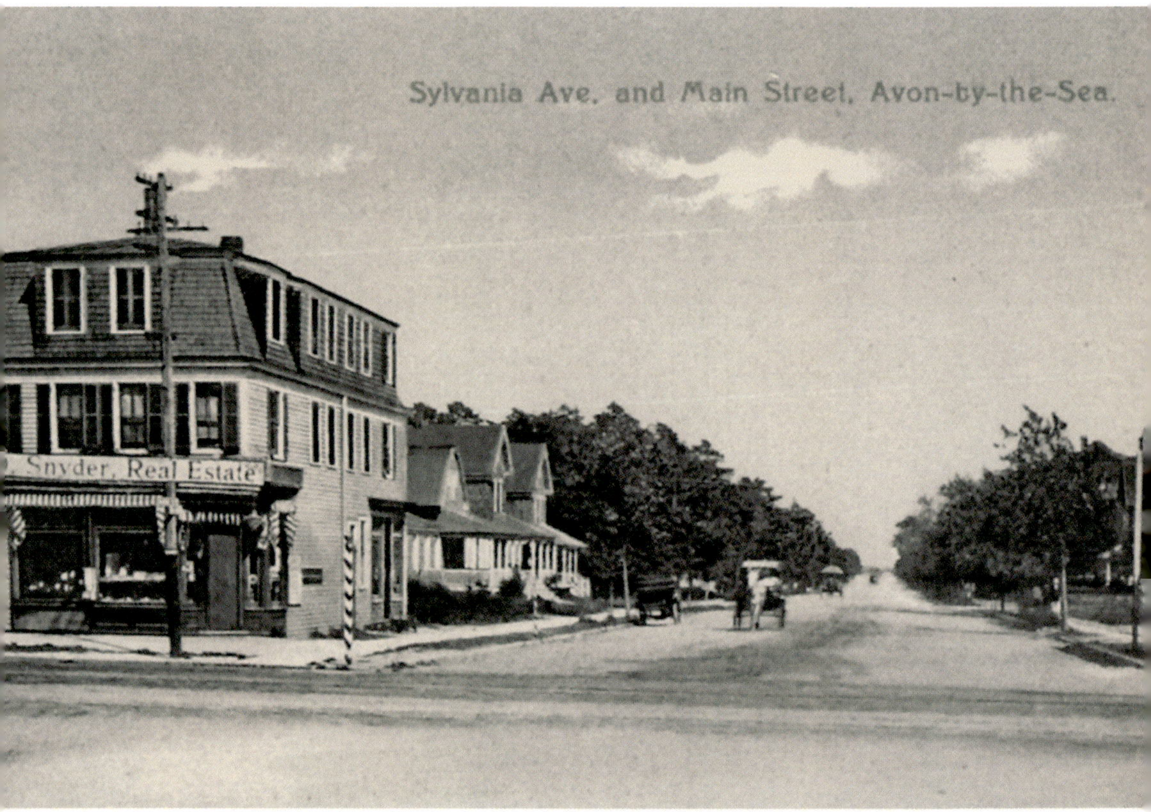

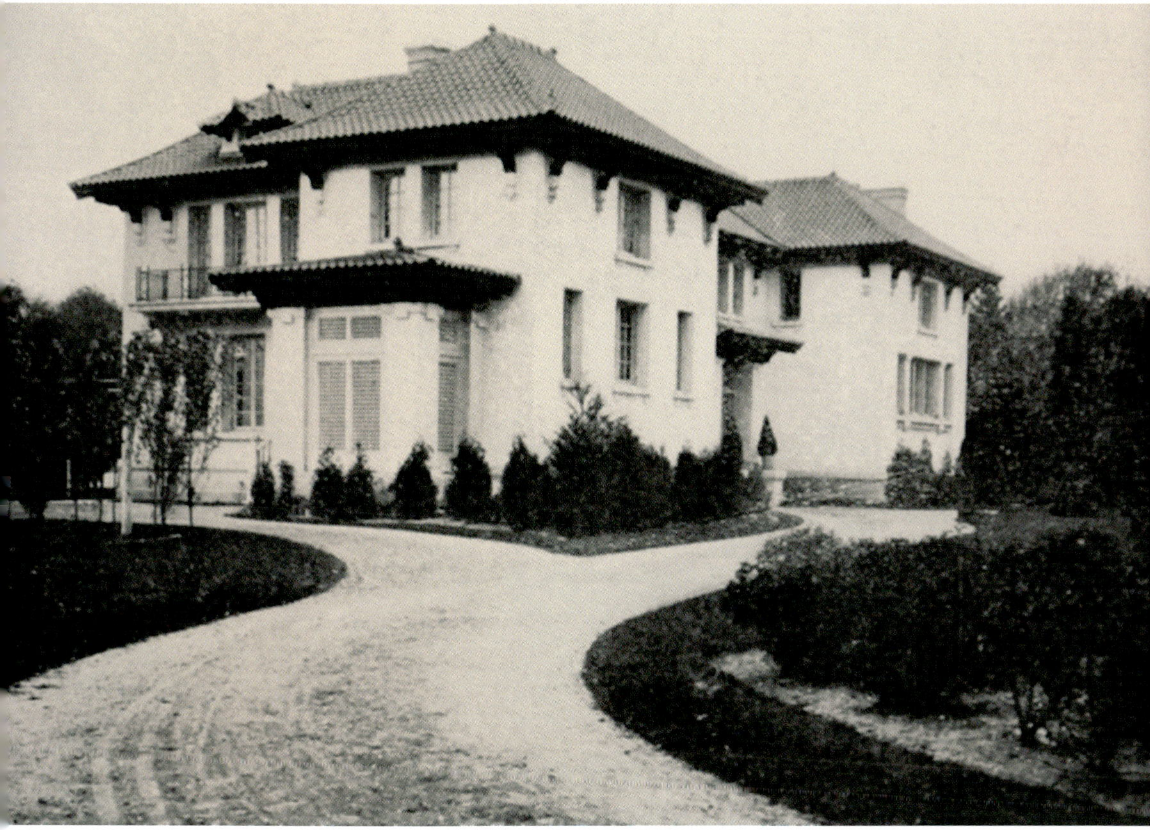

In 1904, Arthur Durant Sneden, head architect for the New York City Board of Education, built a magnificent summer home overlooking Shark River in Neptune City. Sneden built the house of LaFarge stucco on brick, with elaborately tiled and reinforced concrete floors. Falling on hard times, Sneden sold the home in the 1920s to John Kaltenbach, who operated it as a hotel. In the 1940s, it was the location of the Frances Convalescent Home. It is currently a private residence.

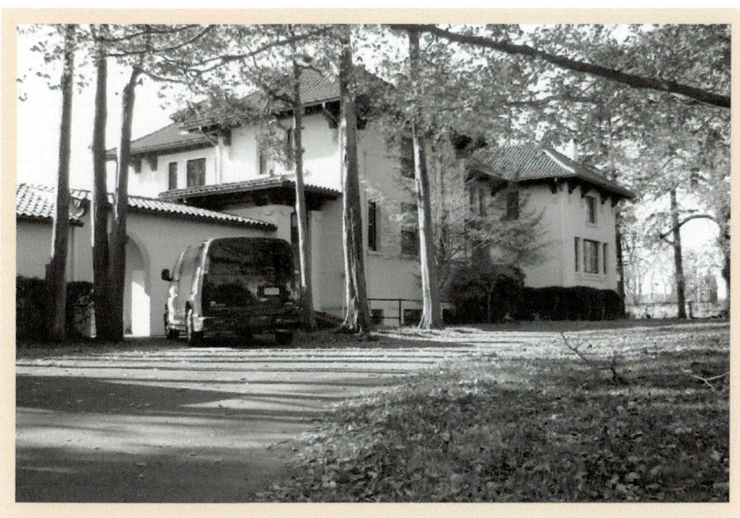

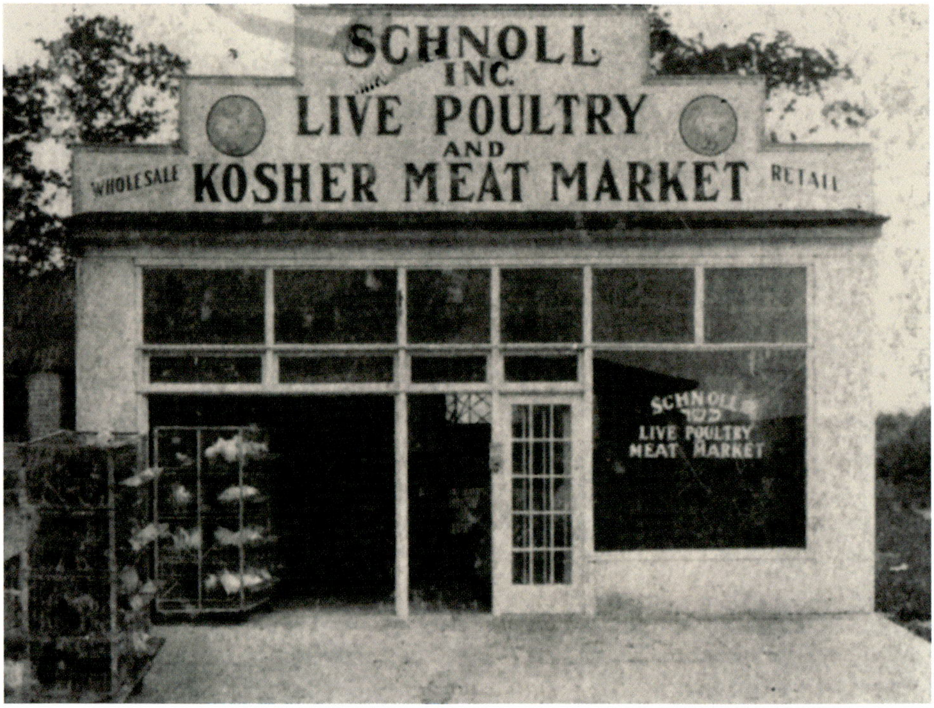

In 1920, Frank Schnoll opened a kosher poultry and meat market in Neptune City on Steiner Avenue across from the Steiner factory. Schnoll offered special wholesale services to area hotels and restaurants. He sold the shop and retired from the business in 1943. In a bittersweet twist, Frank and Ethel, husband and wife for 63 years, both passed away within minutes of each other on July 2, 1963. The building is currently a homebuilder office. (Monmouth University Library Archives.)

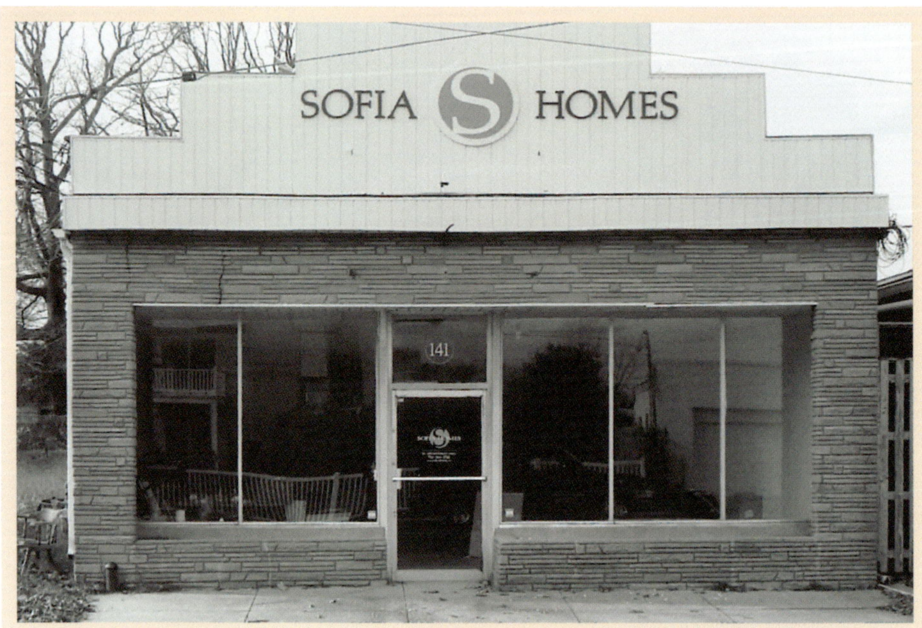

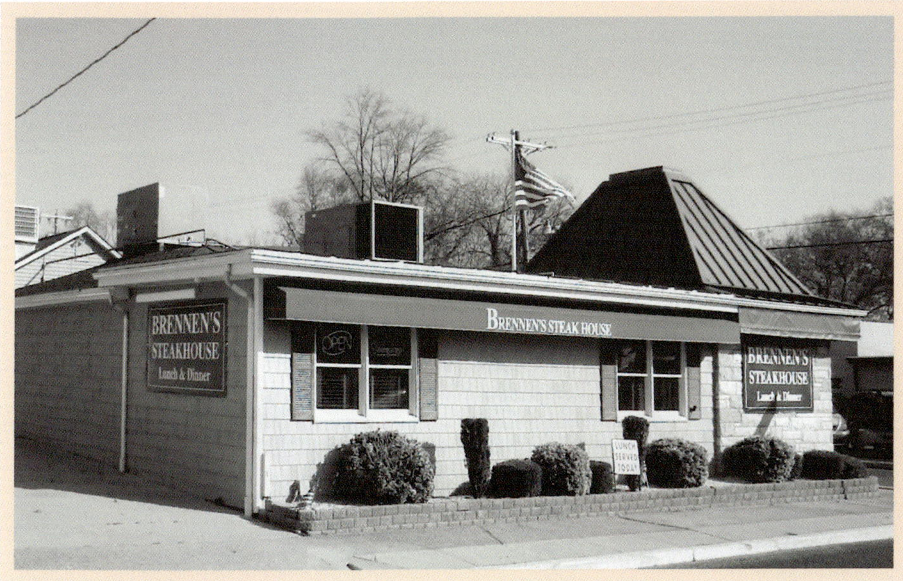

Lindy's Italian Restaurant on Sylvania Avenue is pictured here in the late 1950s. Built in 1929, it was known until 1950 as the Beverly Tea Room. At this juncture, Olindo "Lindy" Siciliano purchased the property and turned it into an Italian restaurant. The "Lindy Salad," consisting of lettuce, garlic, Provolone cheese, red onions, and lemon juice, became wildly popular and was often copied for decades in the area. After the restaurant changed names and ownership several times following Lindy's closure in 1978, Brennen's opened in 2003.

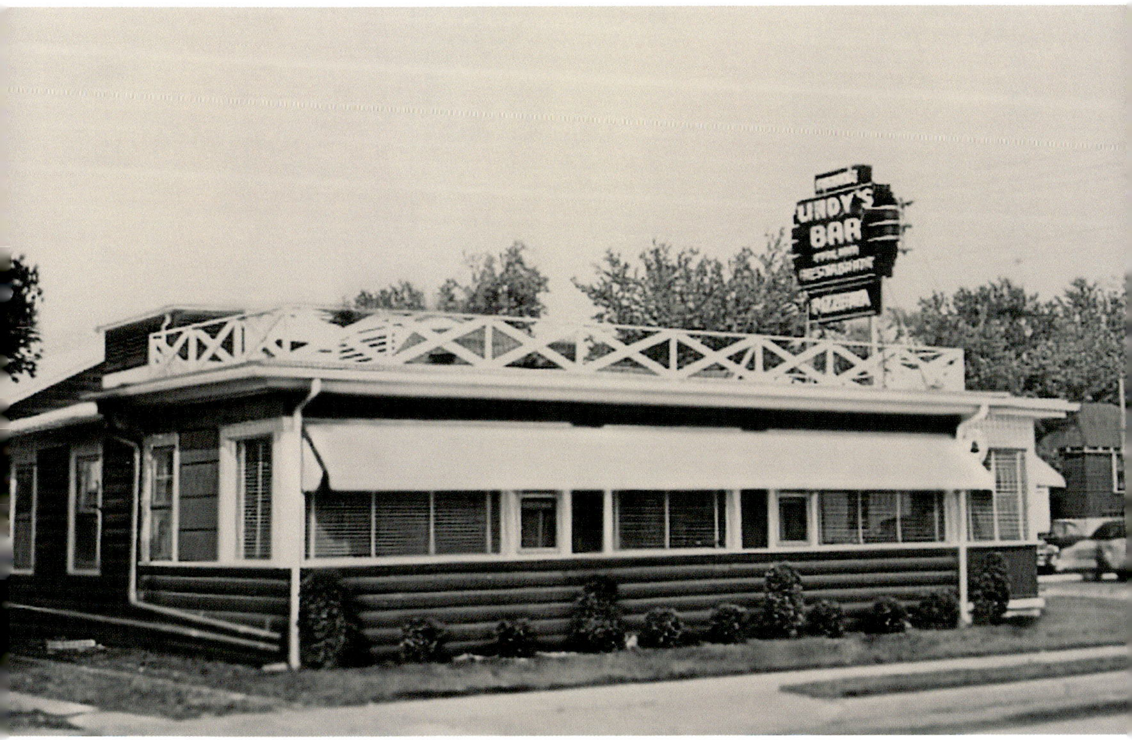

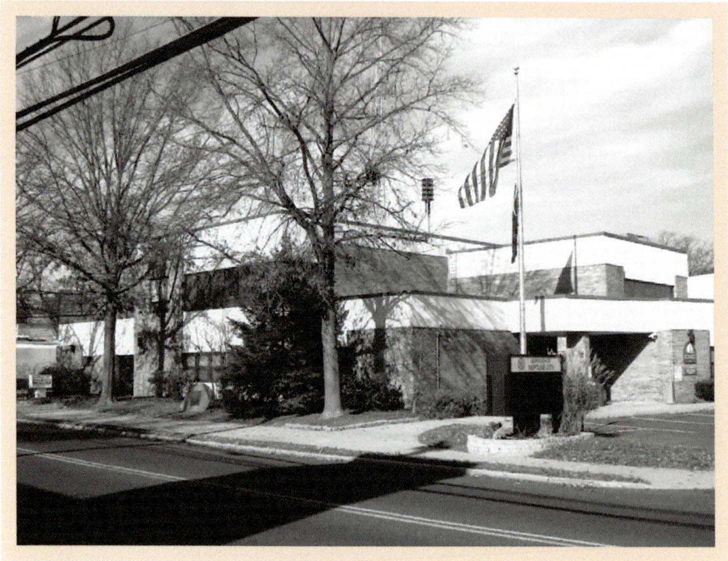

Neptune City built a new municipal complex on West Sylvania Avenue in 1973. The complex included a courthouse, police department, public works, library, firehouse, and various municipal offices. Construction began in late 1972 and was carried out by the A.P. Busch Company. Photographed here in 1975, the apparent exterior changes during the 35-year interval are primarily limited to the tree growth.

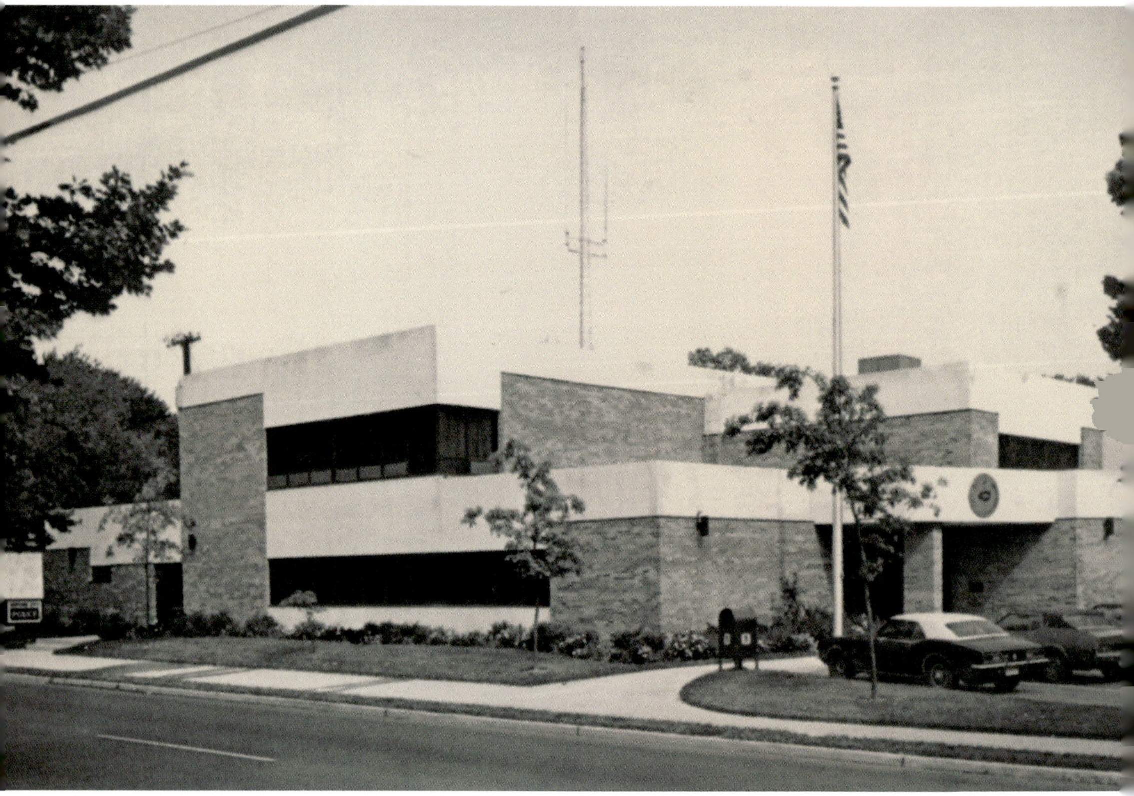

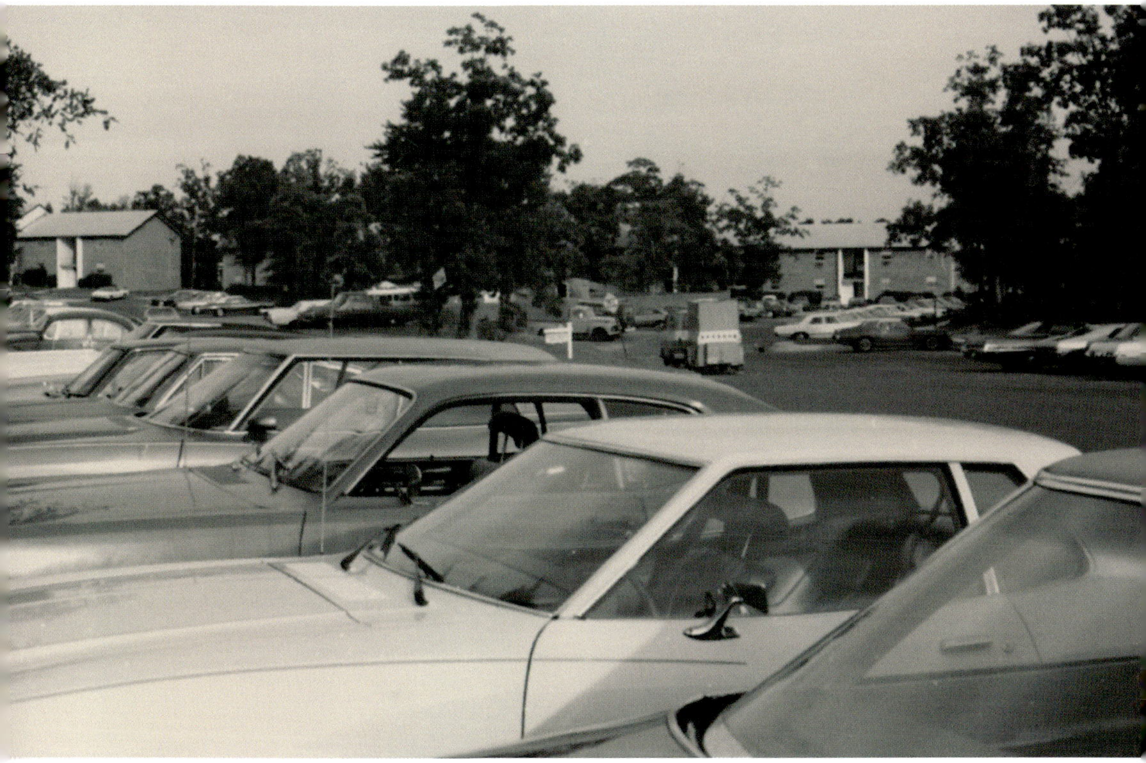

The Brighton Arms Apartments, a 428-unit complex, was carved out of the woods that encompassed the western tip of Neptune City between West Sylvania Avenue and Shark River from 1966 to 1968. The complex was designed with two swimming pools and tennis courts. Other than the vintage automobiles, little difference can be discerned between this photograph taken of Brighton Arms I in 1973 and a 2010 view.

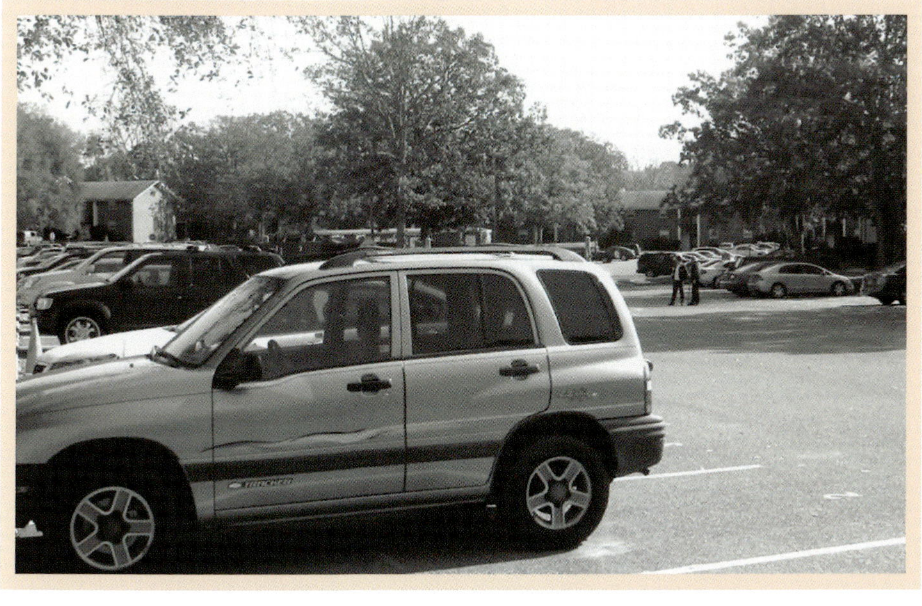

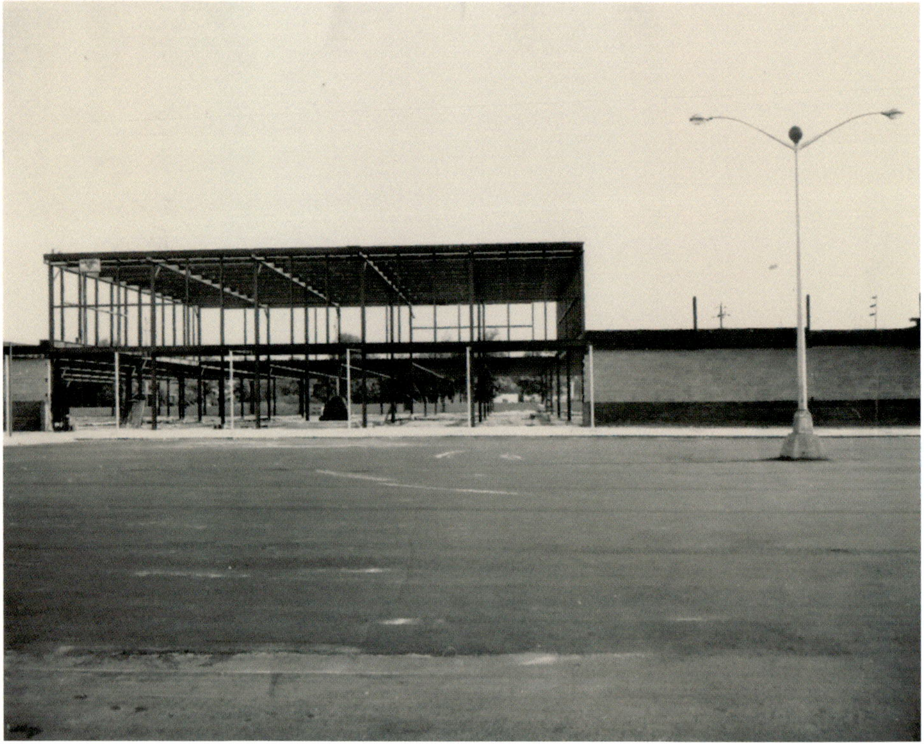

This photograph is of the Two Guys building under construction during March 1959. Two Guys was a discount store chain headquartered in Harrison, New Jersey. At its peak, there were over 100 stores nationwide. Financial troubles forced the parent company to liquidate its assets, and it closed all of the locations in 1982. The building currently houses offices for TFH, a Neptune City-based publisher of pet-related literature and makers of the Nylabone line of dog chew toys. (Park Steel and Iron.)

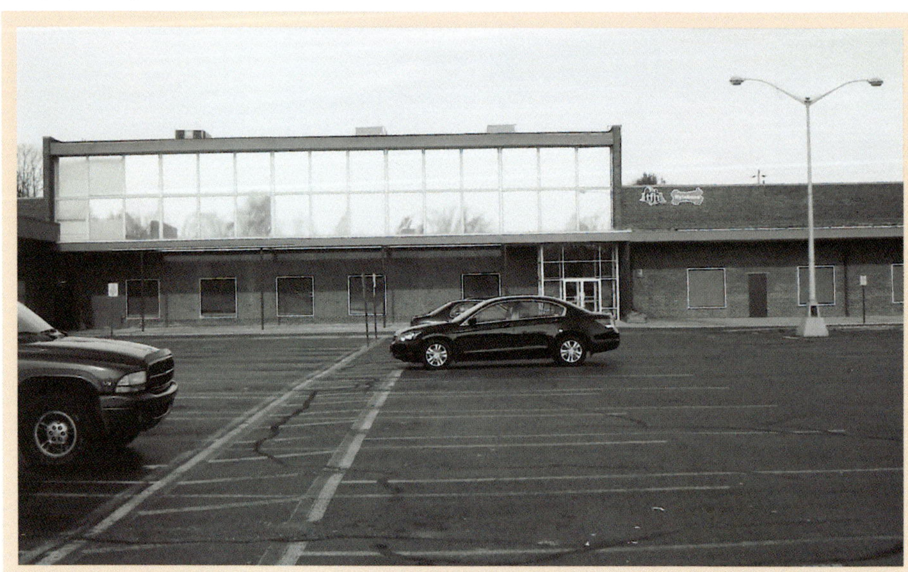

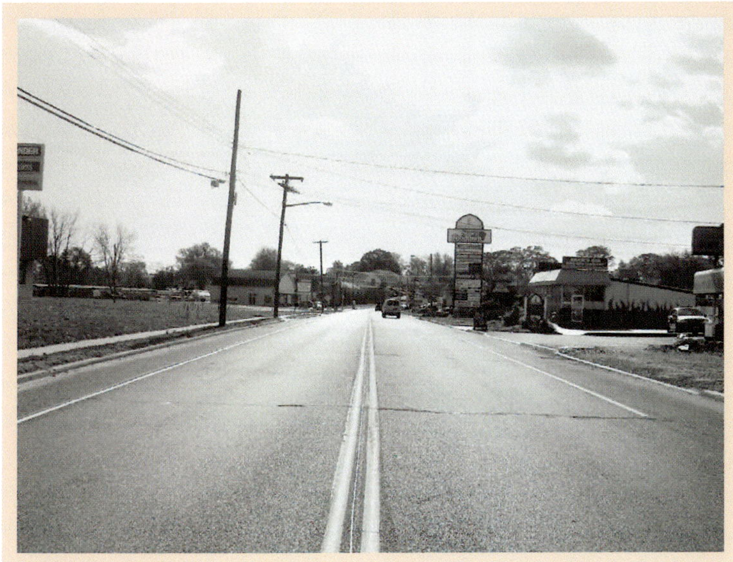

Below is the Neptune City Shopping Center as viewed on New Year's Eve in 1965. Construction of the center began in 1957. The first anchor supermarket was A&P. The distinctive shape of the Carvel ice cream shop is easily made out, despite the numerous different eateries that have occupied this space over the past few decades. Grant's Department Store (later Jason's Furniture) and the Baker's Dozen donut shop also occupied the plaza at the time. (Appleby Collection.)

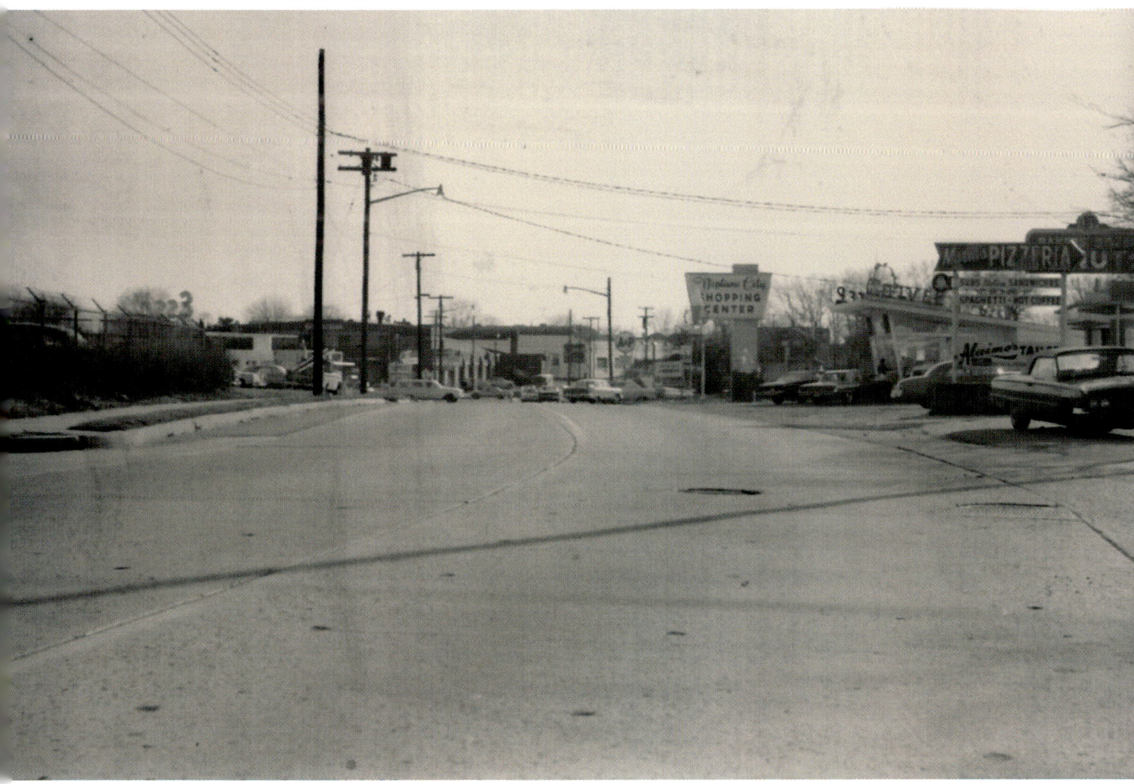